W9-AQQ-363

Praise for *Weighing Anchors*

"When network anchors murder the language—which they do night after night—thank goodness there's Merv Block to perform the autopsy.

"No one has a better ear or sharper pencil than Merv Block. He's a one-man quality control department for the broadcast news business. His wise and witty dissections of TV's highest-paid poobahs and their verbal blunders are both hilarious and appalling. After reading his collection of spot-on critiques, you'll never watch TV news the same way again."
   —Robert Feder, media critic, *Time Out Chicago*

"For anyone interested in TV news, *Weighing Anchors* is a great read. In his unique and entertaining style, Mervin Block not-so-gently points out broadcasting's high crimes and misdemeanors—from the spectacular to the mundane, offering example after example of what NOT to do to keep your credibility in TV news. This is a fun and delightful book from the very best teacher of the craft of news writing in America."
   —Valerie Geller, consultant, author, *Beyond Powerful Radio*

"Mervin Block is to writing what gasoline is to driving. Indispensable. If you want to be smart or even look smart, buy this book!"
   —Kitty Kelley, author of *The Family* and *His Way*

"Merv Block writes with precision and pushes every journalist to do the same. If you feel uneasy while reading this, it may be the unsettling feeling that you, too, have committed every one of the sins he exposes in this book."
   —Al Tompkins, author, teacher, senior faculty, Poynter Institute

"It's a *compelling* read, especially if you put network anchors like Diane Sawyer, Brian Williams, and Scott Pelley, plus CNN's Anderson Cooper, on pedestals."
   —Mona Scott, writer of NewsBlues.com's daily Grammar Yammer

"This is a treatise for truth, justifiable headlines, and plainspokenness that network (and cable) journalism should return to."
   —Steve Grant, KY3-TV anchor, Springfield, MO

WEIGHING ANCHORS

Also by Mervin Block

Writing Broadcast News Shorter, Sharper, Stronger: A Professional Handbook, 3rd ed. (2010)

Broadcast Newswriting: The RTDNA Reference Guide, co-published by the Radio Television Digital News Association, 2nd ed. (2011)

Rewriting Network News: WordWatching Tips from 345 TV and Radio Scripts (2010)

Writing News for TV and Radio: The New Way to Learn Broadcast Newswriting (with Joe Durso Jr.), paperback. (2010)

WHEN NETWORK NEWSCASTERS DON'T KNOW WRITE FROM WRONG

WEIGHING ANCHORS

A Veteran TV Newswriter Critiques the Networks' Top Anchors

MERVIN BLOCK

Marion Street Press

Portland, Oregon

Acknowledgment

My deepest thanks to my editor, Julia B. Hall. She weighed in often—and earned an A+.

Published by Marion Street Press
4207 SE Woodstock Blvd # 168
Portland, OR 97206-6267
USA
http://www.marionstreetpress.com/

Orders and review copies: (800) 888-4741

Anchor images courtesy of Wiki Commons.

Printed in the United States of America
ISBN 978-1-936863-39-6

Library of Congress Cataloging-in-Publication Data pending

CONTENTS

PREFACE

The evening stars come out at 6:30 p.m. Eastern Time, but they don't always shine. When they go on the blink, the stars—Scott Pelley, Diane Sawyer, Brian Williams—lose some of their glow.

About 20 million Americans were said to be watching the stars' newscasts in mid-July 2012. The largest audience—an estimated 7.74 million—watched Brian Williams, anchor of *NBC's Nightly News*. He has been the ratings winner of the evening star wars for eons. And he's said to be the highest paid. *TV Guide* reported NBC pays him $13 million a year.

The second largest audience, about 7.32 million, was watching Diane Sawyer, anchor of ABC's *World News*. And the third largest audience, about 5.72 million, watched Scott Pelley, anchor of CBS's *Evening News*. *TV Guide* said Sawyer is paid $12 million a year, Pelley $5 million.

Evening star-watchers don't need to risk eyestrain peering through telescopes, but they do need to risk mental balance by sitting through a slew of unappetizing commercials for various maladies—indigestion, overactive bladder and a bellyful more. But the evening stars themselves need remedies for their own maladies. Their main malady causes them to overlook many scripted mistakes. Unfortunately, mistakes make for bad news.

Sure, we all make mistakes, don't you? Okay, that *you* should be *we*. But, at least, I don't broadcast my mistakes; the evening stars make their mistakes in front of millions of people. And their mistakes matter: words misused, language confused, facts abused. Even so, these anchors aren't about to be cast overboard.

How were the mistakes that are reprinted in this book collected? I watch the news several nights each week. And I listen. I hear a lot by listening. And I heard enough to write an article. So I began writing about what the anchors were saying. Article after article. For 10 years. I posted the articles on my website, mervinblock.com. But this collection of my articles—enhanced here by new material and a comprehensive index—enables a reader to get a clear, compact, convenient view of the problems that bedevil network newscasts.

Most scripts at the Big Three networks are free of mistakes, but network scripts shouldn't have so many defects. So why write about faulty scripts, which are in the minority? No city editor worth her salt would run a story reporting that 310 million Americans slept soundly last night. But she would report on the one person who didn't sleep soundly—someone shot dead in bed. So it is with scripts. The focus here is on network scripts for several reasons: we expect a network to do good work; when it doesn't, it's worth a story. And a recounting of networks' mistakes tells us something about the networks. Besides, wouldn't you rather see the mistakes made by the mighty in midtown Manhattan than mistakes by mere mortals in Mudville?

The articles here are grouped by anchor and network. In some articles, more material has been added—and dated. At the bottom of each article is the date of the article's posting.

A book titled *The Evening Stars*, published in 1983, told the history of network anchors, covering 17 in all. It's a good book, though its index has no entries for writing, editing or journalism. Those topics are what this book is all about; it focuses on today's evening stars: Pelley, Sawyer and Williams. And also looks at the work of three CNN anchors: Wolf Blitzer, Anderson Cooper and Don Lemon. And a former CNN anchor, Paula Zahn. Also, a look at the work of several other anchors and correspondents (as networks call reporters), including ABC's David Muir, and CBS's Steve Kroft, Dan Rather and Lesley Stahl.

The evening stars face a challenge even before they go on the air: reading all the scripts to themselves before reading them to us. Among the stars' responsibilities: recognizing write from wrong.

Not only should the anchors spot mistakes before going on the air, but they should also correct them. As the last set of eyes to examine scripts before a newscast, anchors serve as backstops to correct any faulty English, faulty writing, faulty journalism, faulty fact-finding.

Two of the Big Three networks have given their evening anchors an additional title: managing editor. So Scott Pelley of CBS and Brian Williams of NBC have two titles: anchor and editor—*managing* editor.

A look at the scripts the three evening stars have broadcast tells us that no matter how much editing they do, they don't do enough. (At the end of some newscasts, editors' names flash by, but they're generally video editors. Though copy editors—where they still exist—do get credits, some deserve blames.)

The stars probably didn't write all the excerpts reprinted here; most were written, probably, by the writer(s) on each newscast's staff. Even so, the anchors are responsible for every word they speak on the air. And just as newspaper publishers are held accountable for every word they print, broadcast managing editors, too, are responsible for every word spoken on their newscasts, even the words of their correspondents.

Widespread interest in the evening stars' comings, goings and doings extends to their misdoings. You'll see some of them soon when you read excerpts from their newscasts.

As you might have suspected, the title of this book is indeed a script-tease.

ABC News

How News Causes Blues

Diane Sawyer: When Words Fail Her

Diane Sawyer has a problem: her scripts.

As anchor of ABC's *World News*, she reads about six minutes' worth of scripts every weeknight. Let's review a few:

"Good evening. Something terrifying took the South by surprise last night. No warning, 25 tornadoes striking in less than 24 hours, roaring through four states in the darkness." (Jan. 23, 2012) *No warning*? The chief meteorologist for the ABC affiliate in Birmingham, Alabama, blogged that Sawyer was wrong, that the storm had been forecast days in advance.

On the next night, Sawyer didn't mention her mistake, but the ABC correspondent covering the tornadoes in Alabama said on Sawyer's newscast, **"Their** [residents'] **trusted forecasters started spreading the word last Thursday, days before the storm."**

Sawyer said of the Occupy Wall Street movement (Oct. 10, 2011), **"As of tonight, it has spread to more than 250 American cities, more than a thousand countries...."** A thousand? Both the U.N. and the U.S. State Department list fewer than 200 countries.

More Sawyer: **"Good evening. There is a kind of collision course in the Gulf of Mexico tonight. Tropical Storm Alex, almost hurricane strength, is barreling toward south Texas."** (June 29) *A kind of collision course*? What kind of collision course is that? What kind of writing is that? A storm can't collide with a coast: only moving objects collide.

And grammarians say that when *kind of* and *sort of* are used to mean *somewhat,* they're unacceptable. Also, *there is*, *there are* and *it is* are all weak ways to start a story or a sentence. There are exceptions, of course. But *is* and *are* express no action.

Along with what's scripted, Sawyer has another problem: the unscripted.

When Hurricane Earl belted the East Coast recently, Sawyer was found slipping on the job. The ABC weatherman, Sam Champion, was saying, "**100 miles from the eye are hurricane-force winds....**" (Sept. 1) And he spoke of 30-foot waves. Maybe Sawyer wanted to reinforce what he was saying by repeating it—like a kindergarten teacher—or was just poking her oar into his boat. She chimed right in—and got it wrong: "**30-foot waves. And again, you said 100 feet** [he said *100 miles*] **from the eye of the storm, you'll still get hurricane winds?**" Champion ignored her fumble and replied discreetly, "**100 miles, that's right, from the eye of that storm.**"

Another unfortunate Sawyer presentation:

"**And now we want to show you the latest accomplishment from a man whose mind has amazed us time and again. He has Asperger's syndrome. His brain is simply acrobatic. Our Nick Watt watched him learn an impossible new language** [Icelandic] **at impossible speed** [one week]**.**"

Diane Sawyer

Then the mental marvel Daniel Tammet was shown performing on TV in Iceland, and Sawyer exclaimed: "**Unbelievable. How do you say 'wow' in Icelandic? And you can see more of Daniel Tammet's amazing abilities, along with other people capable of things you do not believe is possible** [isn't they?]—**tonight on a special *20/20*.**" (June 1)

But six days later, *TVNewser* reported that *20/20* had recycled the footage of Tammet from a 2004 British documentary, *Brainman*. *TVNewser* then quoted a statement made that day by ABC's *20/20*: "ABC News should have cited the documentary and made clear when it was recorded. We apologize for the errors." *Errors*?

The *TVNewser* article credited the Australian Broadcasting Corp. with breaking the story. Its *Media Watch* had quoted the producer of *Brainman* as saying the *20/20* report was a "gross distortion of facts."

I know of no one who suggests that Sawyer was aware of the Tammet story's provenance and of ABC's "errors." But Sawyer has broadcast a raft of errors. Even if her faulty scripts were written by someone else, she has read them on the air, thus giving them her imprimatur.

A grammatical misstep: **"And we turn next to court hearings today in a story you think you only see in the movies."** (Sept. 27) *Only* in that sentence is a misplaced modifier. The sentence should read, "you see only in the movies."

"The final report was in today about that drama that caused the beer summit at the White House." (June 30) No one *causes* a summit. And those two *thats* are too close to each other; change the first *that* to *the*.

"Emboldened by a judge's rebuke of that law yesterday, hundreds of opponents of the crackdown took to the streets today." (July 29) *Rebuke* means scold or reprimand. A person or a group can be rebuked, but not a law. *Emboldened* isn't a word to start a sentence with. Or maybe even use. Better: "Opponents of the crackdown were energized by a judge's ruling—and took to the streets today."

Another wrong word, this time in a story about Iran: **"You'll remember one young woman became the symbol for the revolt when she was shot dead by government forces."** (June 21) The demonstrations by the reformist Green Movement weren't a revolt. They were street protests.

Sawyer also said, **"He pled not guilty to all six counts."** (Aug. 30) The past tense of *plead* is *pleaded*, not *pled*. Stylebooks of The Associated Press, *Los Angeles Times*, *New York Times*, *Wall Street Journal* and *Washington Post* plead with staff members, Do not use *pled*.

"And now," said Sawyer, **"the second part of the *World News* investigation we first brought you last night about young American teenage girls in Portland, Oregon..."** (Sept. 23) Did Sawyer bring us the second part of the investigation *last night*? That's what she said. *Young... teens*? In contrast to *old teens*? Is that a story worthy of network coverage? If ABC could find a big city that has no child prostitutes, that might be worth a story.

After a correspondent reported on Greece's use of "Google Earth" to find pools whose owners had not paid taxes on them, Sawyer said, **"While the rest of us bite our nails about the world economy."** As we used to say when someone said something irrelevant or incongruous, "What's that got to do with the price of tea in China?" Besides, we don't all bite our nails. Anyway, the reference to nail-biting is a corny cliché.

Sawyer has latched onto two words that she must think will hold the attention of viewers: *startling* and *stunning*. She even used *startling* and *staggering* for the same story. Then, in reporting that story, ABC's medical editor, Dr. Richard Besser, used *alarming* (April 26). On another evening, she used *stunning* twice, both in relation to the same story (July 27). ABC correspondents also toss in those flashy adjectives.

Sawyer began a story this way:

"As we told you last night, the fishing waters of the Gulf are reopening, the surface oil fading. But is there oil in the creatures underneath?" (July 30) If you told us *last night*, why are you telling us again tonight? And telling us that before telling us what's new? In the world of broadcast news, *yesterday* is history.

When George Stephanopoulos sat in for Sawyer, he said, **"The war crimes trial of Liberia's former president, Charles Taylor, has become something of a Star Chamber."** (Aug. 9) *Something of a Star Chamber?* It's nothing of a Star Chamber. The Star Chamber was a notorious court in England abolished in 1641. At various times, its proceedings were arbitrary, closed to the public, and it tolerated torture to extract confessions.

> Whenever someone says, "to be honest with you," I wonder, Haven't you been honest with me till now?

Taylor is being tried by the United Nations-backed Special Court for Sierra Leone. The open trial is being held at The Hague, in the Netherlands; unlike defendants in the Star Chamber, those in the Special Court have the right of appeal. And as far as I know, no one there has been tortured.

On Sawyer's watch, ABC correspondents have also contributed to the stack of *World News*'s quirky and faulty scripts. A few more fumbles:

"Yeah, Diane, it is a welcome gesture from B-P, but I have to be honest with you. It dwarfs what B-P owes the people of the Gulf...." (David Muir, June 8) Whenever someone says, "to be honest with you," I wonder, Haven't you been honest with me till now?

On *World News Saturday*, which Muir anchors, a correspondent at the Gulf of Mexico said many local officials had seen no BP cleanup crews—but when President Obama arrived, several hundred cleanup workers showed up. Which led Muir to say, out of the blue, **"All right. Keeping** them honest, Matt." (May 29) What does that mean? Keeping whom honest? How? How can you tell they're honest? Were they previously dishonest?

When Muir sat in for Sawyer on July 2, a correspondent at the Gulf told of economic problems. Muir's tag: **"Feel so badly for those business owners."** ABC News should feel bad that no one caught the grammatical error. Someone who feels *badly* can be a piano tuner who has lost his touch. Otherwise, people feel *bad*.

Another Muir contribution: A correspondent said a policeman who acted quickly when a man tried to set off a bomb in Times Square would be honored at a dinner with the mayor of New York City. To which Muir added, **"As he should be."** (May 2) What shouldn't be is a mini-editorial.

Muir scored (or lost) points in ABC's intramural competition on July 30 when he responded to a question from Sawyer: **"Great question, Diane."**

When the ABC correspondent Sharyn Alfonsi was at the Gulf of Mexico, she reported on the skipper of a fishing boat: **"Yesterday morning, the father of four walked into the boat's wheelhouse and shot himself."** (June 24) Neither she nor Sawyer said whether he was slightly wounded or what. In fact, he was shot dead.

In another piece, Alfonsi said, **"Chris Smith wrote the cover story on Stewart for this month's 'New York' magazine."** (Sept. 17) Wouldn't you think someone on the *World News* staff, based in New York City, would know that the magazine is a weekly?

Another correspondent, Neal Karlinsky, said, **"Their fellow neighbors call them heroes..."** (Sept. 14) *Fellow neighbors*? Redundant.

The *World News* correspondent Pierre Thomas said a rape victim's story **"is going to make you angry."** (Sept. 14) Don't tell me what's going to make me angry. I'll tell you what makes me angry: scripts that predict my reaction—usually incorrectly. I'll be the decider.

(September 28, 2010)

ABC Anchor Fill-In Impaired by *Learning* Problem

Some of broadcast news's biggest names are among the biggest *learners*: they tell us they've learned this or learned that. And though they usually imply they've *learned* something important, whatever they've learned is often not new, or not true or not theirs alone.

A severe *learning* disorder became evident at ABC News on Feb. 6. ABC's senior White House correspondent, Jake Tapper, was anchoring *World News Sunday* at 6:30 p.m. ET when he introduced a story:

"We're learning more tonight about an unusual story of survival in Wisconsin. During the [correct: *a*] **blizzard, Joe Latta slipped in waist-high snow at the end of his driveway and then was buried when a snowplow pushed snow on top of him. He was stuck for four hours and feared he would die. But then a neighbor saw his hand."**

Learning more? Tonight? About an accident that happened four and a half days earlier? What was learned that hadn't been reported elsewhere days earlier? Tapper's story was ABC News's first about Latta's ordeal. So you might be tempted to call the ABC crew slow learners.

An article in Wisconsin's *Janesville Gazette* said Latta slipped in the snow about 5 a.m. CT, Wednesday, Feb. 2. The paper said a curious neighbor was looking through binoculars and noticed Latta's hand. Although Tapper told viewers, **"We're learning more tonight,"** he delivered a lot less than the *Gazette* and The Associated Press did the day after the accident.

After Tapper said a neighbor saw Latta's hand, he presented nine words from Latta and 33 words from his rescuer. Tapper then said Latta was treated in a hospital. End of ABC's story.

But Tapper didn't tell us Latta's age: 66. Or occupation: autoworker, retired. Or when Latta had the accident—four and half days before Tapper's newscast. Or even where Latta lives: Janesville.

Diane Sawyer had a curious *learning* experience:

7

"**Today** [Jan. 3], **we learned new details about what the Navy calls clearly inappropriate video shown to six-thousand sailors aboard a giant nuclear-powered aircraft carrier.**" And she called the skipper "**one of the Navy's most powerful commanders.**" The (now former) skipper's rank is captain. Was he one of the most powerful (whatever that means)? He commanded a carrier. But the Navy has 11 carriers—and a few thousand captains in various posts. And he's outranked by all admirals, 215 or so.

As for those *new details* Diane Sawyer promised: the only fact in the ABC package new to me was the captain's middle initial. In fact, what she called "**new details about what the Navy calls clearly inappropriate video**" had all been previously reported in one place or another, as had every other element of ABC's presentation.

The correspondent whom Sawyer introduced, Martha Raddatz, had been credited at abcnews.com with reporting, "**The U.S. Navy will temporarily relieve Capt. Owen Honors of his post pending investigation of the series of explicit videos he is said to have produced....**" Raddatz's article was posted at 3:26 p.m. ET. But Sawyer's evening newscast did not mention that news.

Three hours after ABC's posting, the NBC anchor Brian Williams said on *Nightly News,* "**Tonight, NBC News has learned what the punishment will be for the captain of an aircraft carrier....**" NBC's Pentagon correspondent went on to say the captain would be "**temporarily relieved of his command**"—as ABC's Raddatz had said. That news did deserve reporting at 6:30, but NBC's script would have been cleaner and leaner without the *learning.*

Another *learner,* NBC's White House correspondent, Savannah Guthrie, was co-host of the *Today* show's Sunday edition on Jan. 30, when she said, "**We've learned that the president spoke to Saudi King Abdullah, and the king told President Obama there should be no bargaining about the stability and security of the Egyptian people.**" Well, I, too, did a little learning: the AP moved a story from Riyadh, Saudi Arabia, at 4:40 a.m. ET that day about the telephone conversation. AP's lead: "The Saudi press agency says King Abdullah has told President Barack Obama that there should be no bargaining about Egypt's stability and the security of its people."

Nothing wrong with Guthrie's borrowing from the AP, not at all. That's why news organizations pay the AP for their output. But Guthrie's **"We've learned"** might make most listeners think NBC News had obtained something exclusively.

Two days later, Guthrie said on *Nightly News,* **"We've learned that Frank Wisner, who is a veteran diplomat, retired, was dispatched by the Obama administration to speak to Mubarak and did speak to him on Monday.** [The State Department had disclosed Wisner's being dispatched to Cairo more than 27 hours earlier.]

"The message from President Obama was, Don't run for re-election in September. That, of course, is exactly what Mubarak said today [Tuesday]...." Did Mubarak look in the mirror and say that to himself, "Don't run for re-election"? Guthrie said Wisner met with Mubarak on the previous day, Monday. The AP had also said that. But *The New York Times, Washington Post, Los Angeles Times, Wall Street Journal* website, Dow Jones News Service, Reuters and the BBC all said it was Tuesday. Which it was.

Everything that anchors or reporters tell us is something they've learned. So they should go ahead and report it. Have you ever heard a weathercaster say, "I've learned that the temperature is 70 degrees"?

If we were all subjected to less newscast hype, maybe we'd be less hyper.

(February 15, 2011)

ABC's David Muir: A Man of *Learning*

When you hear a newscaster say, **"Tonight we've learned,"** do you wonder what that means? And wonder whether the use of *learned* with *tonight* is merely a gimmick to make old news seem new? Or new news newsier?

An ABC anchor and correspondent, David Muir, used *learned* or *learning* several times last month on *World News*. And I wondered what in the world those words meant.

On Dec. 27, when he was sitting in for the regular anchor, Diane Sawyer, he said:

"And tonight we have learned that the U-S embassy in London was among the intended targets for a group of men arrested in Britain last week on terrorism charges. The nine men, ranging in age from 19 to 28, appeared before a judge today in London."

More than 15 hours before Muir's 6:30 p.m. ET newscast, The Associated Press moved a story from London at 2:59 a.m. ET headed: "British court holds 9 in US Embassy terror plot." By 3:11 a.m. ET, an ABC affiliate, WHTM-TV, in Harrisburg, Pennsylvania, had posted the AP article on its website. And the ABC network's own website posted a Reuters story from London transmitted at 9:02 a.m. ET.

The targeting of the U.S. embassy in London was worth mentioning on that night's *World News*, but Muir's **"Tonight we have learned"** tainted the story. If it's true that he didn't learn of the story until that night, he and the staff need NoDoz.

Nine days earlier, on Dec. 18, Muir's lead-in to a correspondent also turned out to be rancid:

"Tonight we've learned the Los Angeles police have been flooded with phone calls, emails, and visits to their website after these faces were published on the front page of the Los Angeles Times...."

Twenty-nine hours before Muir's newscast, the AP—at 1:08 p.m. ET, Dec. 17—moved a story from L.A. with this head: "LAPD Deluged with Calls in 'Grim Sleeper' Case."

ABC's own website posted the AP story more than 24 hours before Muir said, **"Tonight we've learned...."** And on the morning of Muir's evening broadcast, Dec. 18, *The New York Times* carried a story with a two-column head: **"Los Angeles: Deluge of Calls in 'Grim Sleeper' Case."**

On another newscast, on Dec. 5, Muir said:

"We're learning new details tonight about that [*that*? this is his first mention of it] **harrowing close call and rescue at a railway station. It happened in Madrid, Spain. Take a look."** [Please don't tell me what to do, particularly to look when I'm already looking.] Next, voice-over surveillance tape:

"A man falls onto the tracks. Onlookers on the opposite platform frantically try to alert the oncoming train. Finally, a man jumps onto the tracks. You see him pulling the person [*person*? he's a man] **across there just in the nick of time. The rescuer, we now learned** [*we now learned*?], **was an off-duty policeman. And get this** [please don't tell me to *get this*]: **He was just two months out of the academy."** Muir on camera again: **"Two months and putting himself to work."** Huh?

More than 25 hours before Muir said "**we now learned** [that the rescuer was an off-duty policeman fresh out of the academy]," CNN ran the footage on its 5 p.m. newscast on Dec. 4, the previous day, with this voice-over:

"All of Spain was riveted by this video of a dramatic rescue. Just look at this. [Looky here: please don't tell us to look at what we're already watching.] **A man fell off the train platform and onto the rails seconds before a high-speed train pulled into the station. An off-duty police officer jumped in** [*onto*] **the tracks—there he is—and dragged the man to safety. The officer had graduated from the police academy just two months ago. Unbelievable."** *Unbelievable* that he had attended the academy? Or that he had graduated? Or what?

And 24 hours before Muir's newscast, the anchor Lester Holt of NBC's weekend *Nightly News* also said the rescuer was an off-duty policeman who was a recent grad of the police academy: **"We have some video to show you that may make your heart race.** [Please don't worry about my heart; just tell me what happened.] **At a train station in Madrid yesterday, a man fell onto the tracks. Closed circuit video camera** was rolling when it happened. Passengers on the opposite side began screaming and gesturing to alert the operator of an oncoming train. Then an off-duty police officer, a rookie who had just graduated from the police academy, ran onto the tracks and pulled the man to safety just seconds before the train arrived. A very, very close call."

On the next day, ABC's *Good Morning America* said:

"And finally, an amazing rescue caught on video. A man fell onto the train tracks at a station in Madrid, Spain, on Friday." Voice-over:

"Now, passengers started waving immediately, trying to stop an oncoming train. And then an off-duty policeman jumped onto the tracks [and] pulls [don't mix past and present tenses; stick with one] the man to safety with just seconds to spare before that train rolls through. As you can imagine [imagine what?], here it is one more time. That off-duty cop was worried that a train was going to be coming from the other direction. But he still jumped down there. And this guy, this cop, is just two months out of the academy. He's fresh to the job, and immediately steps onto this...." *GMA*, too, said the rescuer was an off-duty policeman fresh out of the academy. In fact, said *off-duty* twice.

Yet, more than eight hours after *GMA*, Muir said of those facts—that the rescuer was an off-duty policeman just out of the police academy— "we now learned." When you think about it, you realize that everything on a newscast is something they've learned—from their own fact-finding and from wire services. If newscasters haven't learned of something, how could they tell us about it? But a newscaster's saying *we've learned* can lead viewers to presume the information is exclusive or hard to ferret out or especially important.

We can say that examining Muir's scripts has been a learning experience: we've learned how much *learned tonight* can mean. Or how little.

(January 4, 2011)

ABC's Muir Seems to Think Using *Tonight* Works Muiracles

David Muir of ABC News works the *tonight* shift. No matter when a story breaks—*yesterday, last night* or *today*—he seems intent on shifting it to *tonight*. So almost every story he delivers when anchoring *World News* becomes a *tonight story*. He persists in doing that even when his using *tonight* is a stretch—or far worse.

When Muir substituted for Diane Sawyer on Dec. 30, he said *tonight* 27 times. And correspondents sprinkled in five more *tonights*. In addition, the announcer contributed one *tonight*. As a result, the 30-minute broadcast offered 22 minutes of news—minus 33 *tonights*. That's an average of more than one *tonight* in every minute of news—a waste of time that could have been used for more news.

Muir introduced David Wright, a Washington correspondent, and used *tonight* twice, but Wright's first word was *today*. Wright talked about critics lambasting the administration, then said, **"Tonight, the White House communications director responded...."** Wright was wrong. The White House communications director had posted that response at 3:34 p.m. ET. That's not *tonight*. Not even close. Various news outlets soon carried the response—long before nightfall. (*Tonight* can be a good word to use, but only if it's needed and if it's true.)

When Muir introduced another Washington correspondent, Muir used *tonight* three times and sandwiched in an *evening*, **"We've learned this evening of another very similar plot a month ago to carry powdered explosives onto a plane."** *Learned this evening*? In fact, the AP moved that story more than 10 hours earlier. The *Detroit Free Press* website posted the AP article at 8:12 a.m. ET—more than 10 hours before Muir went on the air. The ABC correspondent on that story used *tonight* twice (not in connection with the *similar plot*), and when Muir thanked him, Muir added, **"Pierre Thomas on the case again tonight."**

Next, Muir asked a single question of an ABC consultant and wrapped up the interview with another gratuitous *tonight*, **"All right, Richard Clarke with us tonight."**

One of Muir's oddest *tonights* that night: **"We do move on tonight into a very deadly day for Americans in Afghanistan."** Pairing *tonight* and *today*? Yes, and he uncorked another oddity like that: **"Meantime, in the Netherlands tonight, where the suspect boarded that flight, they announced today they will now begin using full body scanners within three weeks...."**

Then he served up a sentence that starts with *tonight* and ends with *tonight*: **"Tonight, we're being told** [by whom?] **the T-S-A might crack down even more, and Eric Horng is monitoring this part of the story from Chicago's O'Hare tonight."** How many viewers know what TSA stands for? How many anchors know?

One of Muir's most misleading *tonights* that night: **"And as we continue here on** *World News*, **the major Tylenol recall that was under the radar until tonight."** *Under the radar*? (That cliché means *unnoticeable* or *undetectable*.) *Until tonight*? After that tease, Muir said: **"We are learning more tonight about a major recall from Tylenol that's apparently been in the works** [in the works? it was already under way] **for several weeks now. Johnson and Johnson is recalling Tylenol arthritis pain caplets....**[Correspondent] **David Kerley on the case tonight with why it took so long for so many to find out."**

Kerley said: **"In early November, Tylenol posted a small recall on its website. Twelve days ago, all six million bottles were recalled. But it wasn't until a nationwide F-D-A** [Food and Drug Administration] **medical alert just this Monday** [two days earlier] **that most people even learned the bottles had been pulled.... Tonight, the FDA said it is, quote, 'looking into the reason for the delay....'"**

Although Muir said the recall was *under the radar*, Johnson & Johnson had issued several press releases announcing the recall, including one on Dec. 19—11 days before that newscast—and one the previous month. On the day before Muir's broadcast, CNN carried an item on the recall—at 7:48 a.m. Also on that day, ABC's own website posted a story about the recall. And that evening—24 hours before Muir said the recall had been *under the radar*—NBC's Brian Williams carried the story on *Nightly News*.

In one of the ABC newscast's opening headlines on Dec. 30, Muir said: **"And the mystery at sea. The sea lions that suddenly disappear. Tonight, the before and after photos and the surprising menu that**

might hold the clue." The mystery, if any, is at San Francisco's Fishermen's Wharf. That's where the sea lions hung out. Disappeared *suddenly*? *Surprising menu*? Why be surprised that sea lions eat fish? Muir would have learned about that the previous evening if he had watched NBC's *Nightly News*. Referring to the sea lions, Brian Williams had said, **"They've likely just moved on looking for their favorite foods, which happen to be anchovies and sardines."**

Muir had introduced the package by saying, **"In San Francisco tonight, they're asking what happened to the sea lions."** He wondered, **"Could it be they were mad** [*angry*] **they ran out of a menu that would leave most of us holding our noses?"** Speak for yourself, Mr. Muir. The sea lions began leaving San Francisco's waterfront around Thanksgiving. (Did they go looking for turkey?) The *CBS Evening News* ran a package about the sea lions on Nov. 24, five weeks before Muir introduced the ABC story. CBS didn't mention the sea lions' diet or their departure. If the sea lions at Pier 39 ran out of food, maybe they just ran out for more.

Or perhaps they swam away because of pier pressure.

Muir: **"And finally tonight here, it was ten years ago this week, we were asking so many questions right here on this broadcast.... Tonight, our people of the decade...."** *Tonight* twice in one intro and *here* twice in one sentence.

No wonder Muir's motto seems to be "The Muir the merrier." But his *tonight*ing everything in sight does not leave me merry.

(January 12, 2010)

ABC Anchor Tampers with Clock and Calendar

One of the most abused words in broadcast news is *tonight*. The abusers are anchors and reporters who tell audiences that something happened *tonight* even though it didn't.

The time-twisting may be inadvertent, or it may be the result of misinformation or incompetence, even dishonesty. It's hard to say without the power of subpoena, the ability to put witnesses under oath and the right to grant them immunity.

An expert in inserting *tonight* in a script even when the story didn't break that night is David Muir, the anchor of ABC's *World News Saturday*. His sleight of hand (particularly the hour hand) makes time fly.

Recently, Muir said: **"We've learned tonight that those three American hikers seized last weekend by Iran have now been moved to Tehran. A sign of quick resolution of this case is unlikely.** [Says who? A *sign* is *unlikely*? What does that mean?] **They were arrested after wandering into Iran from northern Iraq."** He broadcast that item about 6:40 p.m., Aug. 8.

But almost 23 hours earlier, on Aug. 7, at 7:52 p.m., ABC's Martha Raddatz reported at abcnews.com, **"American hikers detained by Iran after allegedly crossing over from Iraq have been moved to Tehran, a U.S. official tells ABC News...."** Raddatz is ABC's senior foreign affairs correspondent. Four other staff members were credited with contributing to her 241-word story. Among them: Jim Sciutto, ABC's senior foreign correspondent.

Raddatz's report was widely circulated, picked up that night by FoxNews.com, HuffingtonPost.com and other sites, including the website of KGO-TV, the ABC station in San Francisco. (The three detainees are graduates of UC Berkeley.) And cnn.com ran a link to the Raddatz story posted by foxnews.com.

The other day, I searched the internet, but I found no articles, including those of wire services, originating on Aug. 8—the date of Muir's newscast—about the hikers' being moved to Tehran.

Muir said the hikers were grabbed **"last weekend."** Wrong. A companion of the three hikers had stayed behind in Iraq, and he blogged on July 31, a Friday, that he had received a phone call from one of the hikers at 1:33 p.m., Iraq time, saying he and the other two hikers were being taken into custody by Iranians. That means the three hikers were detained about 6:33 a.m. ET, Friday. Hardly the start of the weekend. Not even close. According to *Webster's New World College Dictionary*, the weekend runs from Friday night or Saturday to Monday morning.

Muir began his script by saying, **"We've learned tonight."** Isn't he suggesting that the story he's about to report is new—and maybe exclusive? Every story that anchors report is something the newsroom learned. So an anchor could lead into any story by saying, "We've learned...." If someone in the newsroom hadn't learned it, how could an anchor report it?

News junkies need news fixes throughout the day. But they don't need news that has been doctored.

(August 18, 2009)

Scripts That Need
an Editor Who Edits

ABC's *World News* may be the most-watched evening newscast on television, but it's certainly not the most-edited. It's a truism that every writer needs an editor. That's triply true in broadcasting, where many scripts are written in a newsroom that's a noiseroom—written under pressure, often in haste.

But unless a qualified copy editor reads scripts, many mistakes aren't caught and corrected. For us, though, mistakes that get on the air can be useful: mistakes are often our best teachers. So let's see what we can all learn from a sampling of *World News*'s slipups. A few nights ago, the anchor, Charles Gibson, said:

"Well, President Bush today addressed the issue of global warming today [*today* twice!]. **The President is calling on 15 major nations** [have you ever heard *major nation*?] **to set a goal for reducing greenhouse gas emissions. This is a major change for the White House and comes just days before the President goes to the meeting of major industrialized nations...."** (May 31, 2007)

Gibson used *major* in that item three times. And that night, he used *major* twice more: **"Just how major is this arrest?"** (you call that a question?) and **"The President made his proposal on a day when a major debate over global warming erupted at NASA...."** Gibson even outscored Joseph Heller and his Major Major Major Major.

In the same newscast, a correspondent also used *major*: **"It's part of a major effort to negotiate ceasefires...."** All told, *major* was used in the newscast six times, probably in an effort to make stories sound more important. But to paraphrase Sir William S. Gilbert, Where everything is major, nothing is major.

In another story that night, Gibson said, **"Robert Alan Soloway did today plead not guilty to the charges lodged against him."** *Did today plead?* Ungainly, unnatural, unconversational. You and I would write,

"Robert Soloway pleaded not guilty today to identity theft." You and I would never tell anyone, "I today got up early." Or "I today swore off newscasts."

Gibson again that night: **"Next, we turn to Iraq, where the U-S military's number two commander, Lieutenant General Ray Odierno, made a dramatic assertion today, saying that he believes 80 percent of the Sunni and Shiite insurgents can be convinced to lay down their arms."** Convince can be followed by *that* or *of*, not *to*. The word needed is *persuaded*.

On a previous broadcast, Gibson said, **"There is a major scandal rocking the world of NASCAR just days before the most prestigious race of the season, the Daytona 500."** (Feb. 14, 2007) The main problem: starting with *there is*, a dead phrase. Better: "A scandal is rocking the world of NASCAR...." I didn't call it *major*. After all, do networks report minor scandals? Sometimes, but *major* is so overused that it has lost much of its sock.

"If you happen to fly through the Phoenix airport today, there was a new machine being used to screen passengers at the security checkpoint, and this one has privacy advocates rather upset." (Feb. 23, 2007) I didn't go through Phoenix that day, so does that mean the new machine was not being used? As for *rather*, Strunk and White say in their *Elements of Style* that writers should avoid qualifiers: "rather, very, little, pretty—these are the leeches that infest the pond of prose, sucking the blood of words."

"If you or anyone you know are flying tonight, we have information on airport delays and arrivals." (Feb. 13, 2007) That sentence needs more than first aid; it needs reconstructive surgery. *Anyone* is singular, so *are* should be *is*. When subjects are joined by *or*, the verb should match the part of the subject closer to it. But if you shifted *you* to follow *or*, you'd have an equally awkward sentence. Maybe: "If you're going to fly tonight—or anyone you know—we have information...." No, that doesn't sound right. And opening with *if* is not promising; *if* is the weakest word in the dictionary. Better: "For you or anyone else flying tonight, we have information...." But I'd skip that *you* stuff: only one viewer in a thousand might be flying that night. And all those already aloft—or sitting on a runway—wouldn't even hear the newscast. The best solution might be to skip that story.

"And in Iraq today," Gibson said, **"a helicopter owned by the private security firm Blackwater U-S-A crashed in central Iraq.** [*Iraq* twice in one sentence? Yep.] **Five civilians were killed.** [Were they on the plane? On the ground? Or what?] **A senior Iraqi defense official said the aircraft was shot down over a predominantly Sunni neighborhood, and an insurgent group did claim responsibility."** (Jan. 23, 2007) Why not *claimed*?

"Finally tonight, our 'Person of the Week.' The Library of Congress, this coming Wednesday, will present the first annual Gershwin Prize for Popular Song...." (May 18, 2007) Rather than *this coming Wednesday*, why not use the shorter *next Wednesday*? The Associated Press stylebook says: "An event cannot be described as annual until it has been held in at least two successive years. Do not use the term *first annual*. Instead, note that sponsors plan to hold an event annually."

World News correspondents also broadcast flawed stories:

"Yes, there have been many weighty questions about the hamburger, but perhaps none so contentious as from whence it came." (Feb. 20, 2007)

Whence means *from where*, so *from whence* is redundant. You might recall *from whence* in Psalm 121 in the King James Bible. But henceforth, forget about it—forget about *from whence*, not the Bible.

"The relative calm this time comes as the Mahdi army...appears to be laying low." (Feb. 16, 2007) Should be *lying low*. In *Mrs. Bluezette's Grammar Guide: Writing Tips for Broadcast News*, Mona Scott says, "'Lie' means to recline or occupy a position or location." And 'lay' means to set something down. It always takes an object." Anyone who still has trouble with *lie/lay* should check a grammar or a dictionary.

"SWAT teams held mock drills before the school day even started." (Oct. 10, 2006) *Mock drills?* Mock turtle soup uses no turtle, so I take it that a mock drill is not a drill at all. A drill is a make-believe run-through, like a fire drill. Or an abandon-ship drill. A mock drill? No such thing.

"The president of B-P North America told us today that he never received any warning of problems that were years in the making." (Aug. 9, 2006) *Never!* Then the correspondent asked him on camera, **"Were you ever warned about a serious corrosion problem at Prudhoe Bay?"** His answer: "Not that I'm aware of." Well, that's not *never*.

"The draft agreement was reached after 16 hours of talks today between the six nations involved." (Feb. 12, 2007) Mention of more than two nations, or two people, or two of anything, requires *among*, not *between*.

"The key to resuming operations in a storm like this one, advance planning, although ultimately, weather is unpredictable." (Dec. 1, 2006) *Advance planning* is redundant. No one plans for an event or an eventuality after the fact.

"One out of five from those with less than five-thousand residents, many of them poor communities." (Feb. 20, 2007) *Less* should be *fewer*. The AP stylebook: "In general, use *fewer* for individual items, *less* for bulk or quantity." So it'd be correct to say, "My car uses less gas, but I go out on fewer calls.

"The headlines say it all: 'Subway Superman.'" (Jan. 3, 2007) How can two words *say it all*?

"There is a reason why Alaa and Saif and so many other Iraqi journalists risk their lives...." (May 18, 2007) *The New York Times* stylebook says: "Both *because* and *why* are built into the meaning of *reason*. So avoid *the reason is because* and *the reason why*. Write, 'The reason is that the mayor got more votes....'"

"Instead, 180-million dollars were spent gutting and rebuilding it." (Sept. 25, 2006) Should be *was spent*, not *were* spent.

More time should have been spent on all those *World News* scripts. A good copy editor would have fixed those scripts before they were broadcast. And seen to it that they were cleaned up and cleared up.

Skilled editors are essential because they don't take anything for granted. They scrutinize copy, check facts, question murky meaning, straighten out word misuse, tighten loose construction, brighten dull copy, repair grammatical glitches and make sure scripts are written smoothly and in broadcast style.

Editors who edit and know how to edit make a big difference. If a copy editor were to make the scripts for *World News* the most-watched, she'd be taking an important step. But let's not call it *major*.

(June 2007)

When *Now* is Not Now
on ABC's *World News*

When a newscast doesn't have a copy editor, it saves money. But it doesn't save copy. Let's look at some scripts from ABC's *World News* and see for ourselves.

World News scripts are not reviewed by a copy editor but by what a staff member told me were "a variety of people." Recently, the anchor—and managing editor—Charles Gibson said on his 6:30 p.m. network newscast:

"Good evening. There was a tragic incident in Iraq today that is a stark reminder that while the demands on U-S forces in Iraq may be diminishing, the mental stress on service members remains high. A soldier this afternoon opened fire in a clinic in Baghdad that was treating military personnel for stress and suicide prevention. Five American soldiers were killed...." (May 11, 2009)

The script's first sentence is toothless—no bite. It has four linking verbs, which express no action. *There was*, the opener, is a dead phrase. The script's next verb is *is*. Any form of *to be* (*is, are, was, were*) is a linking verb. The script's *was* and *is* are followed by another linking verb, *may be*, and still another linking verb, *remains*.

A linking verb connects a subject with a word or expression that identifies the subject or describes it. Although *there was* is dead, there are exceptions. Bryan A. Garner says in his *Modern American Usage* that *there is* is acceptable if a writer's only recourse is to use the verb *exist*.

In Baghdad, a dramatic scene had unfolded with the shootings. But not in that script. Another reason the script's first sentence is flat is the lack of an action verb like *hit*, *shoot* or *kill*.

Better: "A U-S soldier in Baghdad shot five U-S soldiers dead." *Dead* is a good word to end a sentence. It's one syllable. Its last letter is a hard consonant. *Dead* packs the impact of a strong punch in the head. And Strunk and White's *Elements of Style* says, "The proper place in the sentence for the

22

word or group of words that the writer desires to make most prominent is usually the end."

Tragic and *tragedy* are two of the most overworked (and rarely justified) words in broadcast news. *Tragedy* is defined in Webster's *New World College Dictionary*: "A serious play or drama typically dealing with the problems of a central character, leading to an unhappy or disastrous ending brought on, as in ancient drama, by fate and a tragic flaw in this character, or, in modern drama, usually by moral weakness, psychological maladjustment or social pressures."

The dictionary's fifth—and last—definition of tragedy: "a very sad or tragic event or sequence of events; disaster."

The last sentence of the ABC script says the Baghdad clinic was treating military personnel for *stress* and *suicide prevention*. Someone can be treated for suicidal impulses. But no one can be *treated* for *suicide prevention*. The verb *treat* applies to only one noun, *stress*, but not to *prevention*. A competent copy editor would have cleaned up that copy.

After a correspondent elaborated on the five Baghdad homicides, Gibson wrapped up the story with three words: **"A tragic accident."** *Accident?* Sounds as though Gibson hadn't been listening, not even to himself. If *accident* was ad-libbed and a slip of the tongue, it points up the peril of not having his every word on the teleprompter.

When Walter Cronkite anchored the *CBS Evening News*, a writer would type daily: "And that's the way it is [with the date]. This is Walter Cronkite, CBS News. Good night." Cronkite certainly knew his name and his nightly sign-off, but nothing was left to chance. An anchor can always have an inexplicable mental lapse, so ad-libs are risky.

Was it necessary for Gibson to call the deaths tragic again? You can call the death of every soldier in war tragic. Many local newscasts, at least in New York City, seem to report every day at least one *tragic* fire or *tragic* death. But the late singer Beverly Sills said, "Let's keep tragedy in the opera, where it belongs." In the opera or in the theater.

Gibson also said:

"Of all the images to emerge from the unrest in Iran, none has gotten more attention than a video showing the death of a young girl seconds after she was shot at a protest. Her name is Neda...." (June 22, 2009) Her name *was* Neda. If she had survived, we could say her name *is* Neda. Also, the 26-year-old victim was a young woman, not a young girl.

"There is late-breaking news from Washington, where at least two people have been killed in a Metro train collision near the Washington,

D-C – Maryland border." (June 22, 2009) A train that was standing was hit by a train that was moving, so the crash was not a collision. A collision requires two objects that are both moving. The next night, Gibson again called the crash a collision.

"Much of the criticism centers around their using expensive corporate jets." (June 11, 2009) Should be centers *on*.

"As expected, the World Health Organization [WHO] **has raised the alert level for the H-1-N-1 or swine flu to level six, so it's now a full-scale pandemic."** (June 11, 2009) As expected? By whom? By WHO?

"In a decision that could reverberate in school districts across the country, the Supreme Court issued a ruling on special education students today. [Not newsy. *Issued a ruling* = ruled. Rather than speculate on what *could* result, it's preferable to start with what *did* occur.] **It was a six-to-three decision, and the court made it easier for parents of special-needs kids to get the public to pay for their children's private school."** (June 22, 2009) Whether the vote was 6-3, 8-1 or 9-0, the decision has the force of law, so it's best for a writer to defer the vote, certainly not report it before telling what the decision was.

The best pattern for the first sentence (at least) in a script is S-V-O—subject, verb, object. Start with the subject, then go to the verb (the closer the verb follows the subject, the easier for listeners to follow) and then the object. Moreover, that script needs a makeover: "The U-S Supreme Court made it easier today for special-needs students to go to private schools with their tuition paid by the public."

Ideally, a correspondent in the field would send her proposed script to the executive producer, who would sign off on it and turn it over to the copy editor for examination. But that didn't happen when a correspondent in ABC's New York bureau said on *World News,*

"Whomever gets custody would be entitled to a large share of the Jackson estate." (June 26, 2009) *Whomever*? Whoever approved that script should go to the back of the class, and take along everyone who played a part in its being broadcast: the correspondent, the executive producer and the managing editor. *Who* and *whoever* are used for subjects in a sentence; *whom* and *whomever* are for objects.

Another correspondent said on *World News,* **"In southwest Michigan, a trio of tornadoes toppled trees...."** (June 21, 2009) Tornadoes don't travel in trios. *Trio* is best used to refer to three tenors (or sopranos, or a combo) or three instrumentalists—perhaps, in this case, three wind players.

The anchor of *World News Saturday,* David Muir, is skilled in mak
ing a not-so-fresh story sound new: he often turns it into a *tonight* story.
On May 9, he said, **"In Boston tonight, a trolley operator says he
crashed because he was text messaging."** In fact, that morning's *Boston
Globe* reported that the operator had admitted text messaging almost 24
hours before Muir's newscast. In some cases, Muir's technique bends the
truth—or blurs it, or blots it out.

When Muir sat in for Charles Gibson on Friday, July 3, Muir again
used the device for a story about Michael Jackson:

**"And tonight we're learning just how deadly and dangerous some
of those drugs are."** *Tonight we're learning?* Sounds like a late-breaking
exclusive. Muir then introduced a correspondent who said ABC News
had learned that among the drugs seized by police in Michael Jackson's
rental home was Diprivan. But more than five hours earlier, CNN said
The Associated Press was reporting that Diprivan had been found in the
home; and in CNN's next hour, its chief medical correspondent spoke at
length about the drug.

After the ABC correspondent finished his report from Los Angeles,
Muir said, **"We're learning more tonight about the memorial service
that will be held in that arena...."** *Learning more tonight?* Muir went
on to say the memorial service would be held in the Staples Center at 10
a.m. PT, Tuesday. ABC's website had reported all that information the
previous day.

Muir said 17,500 seats would be given to the public. CNN had reported that information about five hours earlier. Muir also said the police had said they would need 2,500 officers **"to control the estimated
750,000 people who will try to get in anyway."** ABC News's website
had reported those last two numbers the previous day, July 2. It turned
out, though, that during the memorial service, the city stationed 3,200
police officers outside the Staples Center. But only about 1,000 fans and
curiosity seekers showed up outside—about 749,000 fewer than the number Muir had said were estimated to show up. Muir never did say who
made the estimate.

Muir also said the registration website for tickets to the Jackson funeral had crashed because of 500 million Internet hits. At 5:48 p.m. ET, July
3, the website of the *Los Angeles Times* reported that number. And CNN,
on its 6 p.m. ET newscast, carried the number and attributed it—120,000
hits a second—to an unidentified PR agency. Might a PR agency err? Or
exaggerate? Your guess is as good as mine—or theirs. Muir should have

attributed that huge number to the PR agency or whoever was ABC's source. As the wit Steven Wright has said, "42.7 percent of all statistics are made up on the spot."

At the start of that segment, Muir said, **"We're learning more to-night about the memorial service."** *Learning* implies that what was absorbed was true. You can't properly say, "I learned today that 2 plus 2 equals 5." What Muir said about the date, time and place of the Jackson service was accurate, but his other info was wrong or questionable. And with the possible exception of the "500 million hits," ABC didn't dig out that info that night. And certainly couldn't have *learned* what wasn't so.

On the Saturday *World News,* July 11, Muir twisted the time big-time. At the end of a story about a surgical technician accused of misusing dirty syringes, Muir said, **"And tonight, in that newest case, authorities in the Denver area now say up to six-thousand people may** [should be past tense, *might*] **have been exposed to hepatitis C by that one addicted technician."** Authorities say *now*? The release of that number, 6,000, was neither *now* nor *new*. Nine days earlier, on July 2, the AP moved a story from Denver that said, "About 6,000 patients are being advised they may have been exposed...."

How would a professional copy editor deal with all those scripts and that kind of writing? No pro would ever sit still for it. Or stand for it.

(July 13, 2009)

World News Scripts That Need Work

Word news about *World News*: An ABC News correspondent reported from Hanoi, **"The president was greeted as a friend of Vietnam today, promoting capitalism and trade in a country which fell to communism in 1975."** (ABC's *World News*, Nov. 17, 2006)

Vietnam did not fall to communism in 1975. After the communist Viet Minh defeated French troops at Dien Bien Phu in 1954, the former French colony was partitioned into two countries. The North became communist, the South became non-communist. In 1975, North Vietnam conquered South Vietnam, and since then Vietnam has been one country—and under communist rule.

The correspondent's sentence doesn't sound right. The participial phrase **"promoting capitalism..."** should be close to the subject it modifies, *president*. But that would separate president from *was greeted*. Needs rewriting. And *which* should be *that*.

Let's look at more ABC *World News* excerpts that fell flat, fell down or fell apart. The anchor, Charles Gibson, said: **"Good evening. The U-S mission in Afghanistan, fighting terrorist elements in that country, often takes second billing to Iraq.** [Second billing to Iraq or to the U.S. mission in Iraq?] **But tonight, there are significant developments there.** [There where? And *there* twice in one short sentence?] **Four U-S soldiers have died in Afghanistan today."** (June 22, 2006)

The shift of time—from *night* in the second sentence to *today* in the third—seems odd. The second sentence speaks of significant developments *tonight*, but the next sentence tells of the four deaths *today*. In fact, more than 11 hours before *World News* went on the air that night, ABC's *Good Morning America* reported correctly that the four deaths had occurred the day before.

Also: *terrorist elements* = terrorists. Delete *in that country*; the anchor had mentioned only one country. Further, when you use the present perfect tense (*have died*), you don't use *today*. Better: "were killed."

Gibson made another abrupt shift from *tonight* to *today*:

"Good evening. We will get to our headline stories in a moment, but there is late news breaking in Washington tonight that could have enormous political implications. There is word today that Senator Tim Johnson, a Democrat from South Dakota, has suffered a stroke...." (Dec. 13, 2006)

Late news breaking? The story broke at least two and a half hours earlier. NBC's *Nightly News* called it a *developing* story. CBS's *Evening News* told the story without *breaking* or *developing*.

At 4 p.m. that day, Sen. Johnson's office announced his hospitalization. The AP and Reuters moved stories within minutes. And CNN broadcast the news shortly after 4 p.m.

As soon as stories break, they start developing. Aren't stories about Iran, climate change, U.S.-China trade and many more still developing?

A persistent problem in leads: *there is*. It's a dead phrase. When used in an opening sentence, it should almost always be deleted. *Is* conveys no action; it just is.

More *World News* excerpts:

"There is a new study out today that indicates those under 18 years of age could lose weight just by getting more sleep." (Feb. 7, 2007) Delete *there is*. Better: "A new study says...."

"There is not a prescription drug in your medicine cabinet that hasn't been reviewed and approved by the F-D-A. But tonight there are troubling questions about how well the F-D-A is doing its job...." (Sept. 22, 2006) The double negative in the first sentence can confuse viewers. Strunk and White tell us in their *Elements of Style* to put our statements in a positive form.

Better: "Every prescription drug in your medicine cabinet has been approved by the Food and Drug Administration. But a new report about the F-D-A raises troubling questions." Still better: "A new report says the Food and Drug Administration is sick and needs some strong medicine."

"There are more politicians taking preliminary steps toward running for president." (Nov. 13, 2006) That's easy to fix. Delete *there are*: "More politicians are taking preliminary steps to running for president."

"Federal health officials say tonight that lettuce was the most likely cause of the E. coli outbreak linked to Taco Bell restaurants." (Dec. 13, 2006) The key word in that sentence is *lettuce*. That's said to be the likely cause of the outbreak. But in the script, *lettuce* is mired in the middle. That's no place for a word that should be spotlighted. The best way to do that is to follow a rule set down by Strunk and White: "The proper place in the sentence for the word or group of words that the writer desires to make most prominent is usually the end." Now let's apply the rule to the faulty script: "Federal officials say the most likely cause of the E-coli outbreak at Taco Bell restaurants was lettuce."

Several more tips on writing and language, also inspired by *World News* scripts:

"A war of words broke out on the day after President Bush unveiled his newest plan to stabilize Iraq." (Jan. 11, 2007) *War of words* is a cliché. The English poet Alexander Pope (not to be confused with Pope Alexander) used that metaphor in 1725. Can you imagine how many times *war of words* has been used in 282 years? It's long past the time for a ceasefire.

George Orwell said long ago, "Never use a metaphor, simile, or other figure of speech which you are used to seeing in print."

He also said:

- Never use a long word where a short one will do.
- If it is possible to cut a word out, always cut it out.
- Never use the passive where you can use the active.
- Never use a foreign phrase, a scientific word, or a jargon word if you can think of an everyday English equivalent.
- Break any of these rules sooner than say anything outright barbarous.

Back to *World News*: **"Later today, St. Margaret's will open its door to the public for viewing as Ford's casket lies in repose...."** (Dec. 29, 2006) A coffin doesn't lie in repose. The deceased does. And how about treating him respectfully and making it "Mister Ford"? Or "former President Ford"?

"The priest and the nun who had to choose between their love for God and one another." (Feb. 6, 2007) That headline needs repair. Two persons love *each other*. More than two love *one another*.

"Our Phoenix affiliate, K-N-X-V, first broke this story." (June 19, 2006) *First broke* is redundant. If a reporter is the first to report it, she's credited with breaking it.

"He came under fire from some fellow evangelicals who objected to one of his invited guests." (Dec. 1, 2006) *Invited guests* is a redundancy. A guest is someone who has been invited.

"Joe Lieberman, the powerful senator and former vice presidential candidate from the state of Connecticut has been defeated...."

(Aug. 9, 2006) Connecticut is a state, so delete *the state of*.

"As this month draws to a close, we note that 70 U-S troops have been killed in Iraq during the month of April." (April 28, 2006) April *is* a month, so delete *the month of*.

"And, believe it or not, this school is set to reopen in two weeks' time." (Jan. 25, 2007) A week is a measure of time, so delete *time*.

"Starting Monday, the Democratic Congress plans to closely scrutinize the President's 2008 budget." (Feb. 3, 2007) *Closely scrutinize* is redundant. *Scrutinize* means "to examine closely."

More wasted words on *World News*:

"And in San Francisco, in domestic news today, one of the most highly anticipated product rollouts in memory...." (Jan. 9, 2007) Telling listeners that a story from San Francisco is domestic news is a waste of time. Better: "A long-awaited product was introduced today in San Francisco." Better yet: "Apple has now introduced a long-awaited product, the iPhone."

"Some news tonight for computer users." (Jan. 29, 2007) Poor way to start a script. For viewers who aren't users, isn't that a turnoff?

"Political news next. Another day, another entry in the presidential race. Delaware Senator Joe Biden is the ninth Democrat to jump into the candidate pool. But tonight he might be wishing for a do-over...." (Jan. 31, 2007) Why waste time labeling stories? The category is obvious.

"Ford convinces almost half its labor force to take a buyout." (Nov. 29, 2006) The Associated Press stylebook says: "You may be convinced *that* something or *of* something. You must be *persuaded* to do something." Bill Walsh, copy desk chief of *The Washington Post*'s business desk, sums it up, "*Persuade* involves action, *convince* involves thought."

Spelling, too, is a problem on *World News*. A business columnist for *The New York Times*, Joe Nocera, was identified in a super as "Joe Nocero." And someone else was ID'd that night (Jan. 3, 2007) as a "dietician." Correct: *dietitian*. Another night, *World News* labeled a man on the screen as a "Prof Emiritis." (Jan. 23, 2007) Correct: *emeritus*. And yes, *Prof* needed to be followed by a period, which is the way we treat abbreviations.

All of which illustrate the point that presenting news well is not so simple as ABC.

(February 2007)

NBC NEWS

The *Tonightly* News

The *Overnight* Life of Brian

Brian Williams is not a disagreeable man, not at all, but recently he disagreed with himself. Publicly.

On Saturday, April 2, in his 6:30 p.m. ET newscast, he said:

"There is other news tonight from Iraq, where insurgents attacked the infamous Abu Ghraib prison in western Baghdad. It happened at sundown [there!]. **Sixty insurgents opened fire...."**

Twenty-four hours later, Williams told his Sunday night audience:

"But now to some of the other news of this day and an N-B-C News exclusive on that massive overnight attack on the Abu Ghraib prison in Iraq...."

Overnight? Not only did the anchor contradict what he had said 24 hours earlier, but he also misstated the time—and not for the first time.

Reuters had moved a story from Baghdad at 2:47 p.m. ET, Saturday, saying the attack on Abu Ghraib began around 10 a.m. ET, Saturday. At 3:34 p.m. ET, the AP quoted a U.S. officer as saying the attack lasted about 40 minutes. (Sunday's *New York Times* confirmed the time of the attack.)

In the practice of journalism, which is in the realm of nonfiction, an attack that took place around 10 a.m. ET, Saturday, cannot accurately be described on Sunday night as an *overnight* attack.

Just what does an anchor mean when he says something happened *overnight?* That it happened after midnight? That it happened at night? That it lasted all night? And whose *overnight*, ours or theirs? Even when defined loosely, *overnight* cannot be properly applied to an event that happened 32 hours earlier.

We do use *overnight* elastically in certain idioms, such as *overnight success*. So maybe we could call that *Nightly News* presentation—and misrepresentation—an overnight failure.

(April 2005)

32

Brian Williams: *Nightly* Problems

Does this script make sense—or am I dense?

Brian Williams said, **"It will take place across the country tomorrow morning, and if you didn't know it was coming, there's no way you would know."**

If I didn't know it was coming, I wouldn't know what? Know that it was coming? Know that it had arrived? Know what it is?

Williams broadcast that snippet from a script recently on NBC's *Nightly News.* He's also the managing editor. I was told about the script by a television network producer in Australia, Matthew McGrane, who said he was baffled. I hadn't seen that newscast, but I've confirmed the text delivered by Williams:

"We are back this Monday night with 'NBC News In Depth,' an American milestone. It will take place across this country tomorrow morning, and if you didn't know it was coming, there's no way you would know. It wasn't all that long ago [delete *all that*]**, November 20th of** [delete *of*] **1967, President Lyndon Johnson was giving a speech at the Commerce Department in Washington. The crowd started to applaud, noticing what was going on behind him.** [Better: "The crowd noticed what was going on behind him—and began to applaud."] **The President turned around just as the huge digital counter above him, state of the art** [cliché] **at the time, cranked the estimated U-S population to 200-million. A lot of Americans thought we had grown**

Brian Williams

33

just about as big as we ought to get, but, of course, we didn't stop there. Well, tomorrow morning at 7:46 a.m., Eastern time, and don't ask us how they estimate it, the U-S population will click over to 300-million...." (Oct. 16, 2006)

The NBC script referred to 7:46 a.m. in the morning. A.M. is the abbreviation for ante meridiem, which means "before noon." So *a.m. in the morning*, as journalism students are taught, is tautological. [Thanks to sharp-eyed reader Gil Haar for setting me straight on what *a.m.* stands for.]

An understandable rewrite of that loopy lead:

"Tomorrow morning, the U-S population will reach an estimated 300-million. In 39 years, the population has risen by 100-million." Instead of using "1967," I did the math for the listener.

The next night, Williams said, **"There is, as expected, news tonight about that American milestone that we were just at the cusp of when last we spoke last night. This morning, at 7:46 a.m., and again don't ask us how anyone figures this out...."** If there's news, why not tell us what it is instead of taking the time to tell us there's news when we already know we're watching a newscast?

As expected? Who expected him to repeat what he told us the night before? *As expected* is a news-appetite depressant. So is that clunky writing. And again the redundant *7:46 a.m.* and *morning*.

How often does *Nightly* use *tonight* when it's not tonight? Almost nightly, it sometimes seems. Just the other night, on Oct. 31, Williams said, **"We've learned tonight that after 50 years in the business, Bob Barker says he will retire this coming June...."** *We've learned tonight?* The AP moved a story about the retirement in mid-afternoon. It showed up at *Nightly*'s newsroom at 3:39 p.m. ET, more than three hours before Williams said, **"We've learned tonight."**

Another question occurs to me when I watch *Nightly News*: what does Williams mean when he introduces a story by saying **"There's word tonight"**? Let's examine one such story:

"There's word tonight a notorious Utah polygamist who's been on the run and [insert *on*] **the F-B-I's list of America's most wanted has now been captured."** (Aug. 29, 2006) Sounds to me as though Williams is suggesting the story broke that night. But more than eight hours before that newscast, at 10:17 a.m. ET, the AP reported the capture occurred the night before.

At best, *there's word tonight* is ambiguous. Otherwise, you'd expect an anchor to say merely, "A notorious polygamist on the F-B-I's list of most wanted has been captured." (The polygamist *was* wanted, so there was no need to say he was on the run.) As for the phrase **"There's word tonight,"** it's past time to put it on a list of the most unwanted.

Another questionable *"Nightly"* script:

Although the newscast is called *Nightly News,* it could easily be called *Tonightly News.* The word *tonight* is sprinkled throughout scripts liberally. On Nov. 1, 2006, Williams used *tonight* twice in one sentence—after using it in the preceding sentence: **"And for more on where this day-long political saga stands as we speak tonight, we go to Tim Russert. Tonight finds our Washington bureau chief in Orlando, where he is moderating the Senate debate at the University of Central Florida tonight."** Yes, Williams began and ended the second sentence with *tonight.* While we're at it, let's look at some other flawed excerpts from *Nightly News:*

"The North is threatening to do it again, blow off another nuclear weapon, if not several more." (*Nightly News,* Oct. 17) *Blow off?* Dictionaries say it means to ignore, or to outperform in a contest, or to end a relationship with, or to fail to attend. The writer probably meant *blow up.* Or *set off.* Or *explode.* Or *detonate.*

After the anchor's lead-in, a correspondent said, **"N-B-C News has been told by U-S officials that North Korea's military has informed China it intends to explode not only one nuclear test but a series of underground nuclear tests."** A test isn't exploded; a bomb is. Further, the use of *not only* calls for *but also.*

"There's health news to report tonight." (Nov. 2, 2006) So report it—without delay. Pronto, Tonto.

"But today the president assured them, they'll be back there in just a few months' time." (Aug. 2, 2006) A month is a measurement of time, so there's no need for *time.*

Another *Nightly* script: **"There is a follow-up on our top story here** [delete *here*] **last night about the rapidly deflating** [better: *slumping* or *weakening* or one of many more possibilities] **housing market. Last night we reported on that sharp drop in existing home sales. Well, today we learned** [everything newscasters say on the air is something they've learned] **new home sales also have dropped sharply, down four-point-three percent last month. That is the largest percentage drop since February. The inventory of unsold homes, sitting on the market across the country, also climbed to a new record high."** (Aug. 24, 2006) Lead with news, not a recap of yesterday's news. News is what's new. *New record* is an old redundancy; if the inventory climbed to a new high, that *is* a record.

We'd better rewrite the script; using only facts found in the original, we'll ditch *there is*—a dead phrase—and make it newsy:

"New home sales dropped sharply last month—down four-point-three percent. That's the largest drop in five months. And the number of new homes on the market across the country rose to a record high. Sales of existing homes, reported yesterday, fell sharply."

The original is 74 words; the rewrite is 41—shorter, sharper, stronger.

The previous evening, Williams said, **"The news today** [isn't today's news what a newscast is all about?], **sales of existing homes fell four-point-one percent in the month of July to their lowest level since January of 2004."** July *is* a month, so *month* is superfluous. Similarly, you wouldn't say, "I'm going to paint my car the color orange." You'd say "I'm going to paint my car orange"—and skip *the color*. Also: do the math for the listener; instead of citing January 2004, it's preferable to say the sales had fallen to their lowest point in two and a half years.

That script was broadcast August 23, so *July* was the previous month. In conversation—and broadcast writing should be conversational—we'd refer to July as "last month."

Another departure from conversationality on *Nightly*:

"Now to the White House, where President Bush today signed into law new rules for interrogating and putting suspected terrorists on trial. But can the new law itself pass the legal test?" (Oct. 17, 2006) *The legal test*? Is that what students face in law school? No need to mention the White House or *today* in the lead-in as long as the correspondent went on to say both *White House* and *today*.

The anchor put *today* before the verb. That's almost always wrong. We don't talk that way. We don't say, "We today are going to a picnic." Or "I tomorrow am going to the dentist."

Makes you wonder: where was the editor? And how about the managing editor?

(November 2006)

Brian Williams: Lack of Copy Editor Causes Problems

When we watch NBC's *Nightly News*, we hear things we shouldn't be hearing. But some things we should be hearing, we don't hear.

A professional copy editor would spot the gaps and lapses. And if the copy editor missed them, the managing editor—the anchor Brian Williams—should spot them. So let's look at some of these lapses in excerpts from Williams's scripts—and gather a few tips on journalism along the way:

"With the recession causing Americans to cut down on just about everything, it turns out passport applications are way down, a full 25 percent lower than last year." (March 26, 2009) A *full* 25 percent? We've heard of a full plate, a full glass and a full life, but a *full* 25 percent? Sounds like an effort to make 25 percent seem more robust.

"As several of the organizers and musicians explained, because instruments and human hands perform poorly in such cold weather, because it was such a momentous occasion, they could not take the chance at [should be *of*] **sounding badly."** (Jan. 23, 2009) *Sounding badly*? Sounds terrible. Should be *sounding bad*. We use the adjective *bad* when a verb functions as a linking verb. Linking verbs include forms of *to be* (*am, are, was, were, will be*) and verbs associated with our five senses: *look, smell, feel, taste, sound*. So whoever let that script slip by is entitled to feel bad—not *badly*.

"And today marks a sad milestone, an anniversary in the popular culture of this country. This is otherwise known as 'the day the music died.' Fifty years ago today, Buddy Holly, Richie Valens and the 'Big Bopper' all died when their small plane went down after a concert on a snowy night in Clear Lake, Iowa...." (Feb. 3, 2009) *Sad*? Sad for whom? Audiences don't need an anchor to tell them when news *is* sad. But that crash happened 50 years ago.

Journalism students are taught not to characterize news as good or bad, happy or sad. Or *amazing, shocking, disturbing* or *alarming*. Listeners can decide for themselves how good or bad the news is. Chances are, they don't watch newscasts with a clipboard, checking off each story as either good news or bad news.

Sad to say, Williams didn't identify one of the three crash victims: "The Big Bopper" was Jiles P. Richardson, a singer and songwriter. With a little Googling, I found that "the day the music died" refers to the lyrics of a song memorializing that crash of half a century ago, "American Pie" by Don McLean.

How much of *Nightly News* does Brian Williams write? He's quoted as saying in *Power Performance: Multimedia Storytelling for Journalism and Public Relations* (by Tony Silvia and Terry Anzur), published in 2011: "I am still forced to write my copy because I can't read anything cold. I have almost a kind of dyslexia when it comes to reading someone else's writing. It's not that mine is better, but how could they know what I was going to say? How could they possibly know how I was going to tell this story? I'm compelled to write and put everything in the broadcast in my own words...."

When Williams reported that space junk had threatened three astronauts on the International Space Station, he said, **"The grapefruit-sized piece of an old rocket motor floated safely by, thankfully."** (March 12, 2009) Fortunately, Williams doesn't express his thanks after every bit of good news, every rescue, every safe landing. But he does interject *thankfully* from time to time. He uncorked two *thankfullys* last month (March 2009), three last September and three in July. In most months he uncorks only one, thankfully.

In a recent story about the cruise ship that foundered off Italy, Williams said, **"Thankfully, it was close to shore."** In the very next sentence, he used one of his favorite phrases, ***"In plain English**, the Costa Concordia shouldn't have been anywhere near those rocks."* (Jan. 16, 2012) Two weeks later, Williams again summoned *in plain English* for duty on *Nightly News*: **"In plain English, Dick Clark's American Bandstand was great...."** (Feb. 1, 2012)

In plain English, I've been hoping to hear more of the newscast in plain English.

"Fire is also making news in China tonight, where a huge blaze in downtown Beijing engulfed a luxury hotel under construction and damaged the new headquarters of China's state television. It was a bizarre sight at first. The suspected cause is a fireworks show that went up just before the building went up in flames. No reports,

thankfully, of deaths or injuries so far." (Feb. 9, 2009) Everything on a newscast is *making news*, right? The fire began the previous day about 8:30 p.m., Beijing time, and was put out by 2 a.m., Beijing time. When that's converted to ET, the fire was out by 1 p.m. That evening, Williams said, at 6:30 p.m. ET, the fire was *making news in China tonight*. In Beijing when *Nightly News* went on the air, it was 7:30 a.m., the next day.

"Wall Street took all of today's news in stride...." (March 6, 2009) Taking something *in stride* is such a cliché. Ever hear of someone's not taking it in stride?

"The state of New York has a new U-S senator, Kirsten Gillibrand, appointed today by Governor David Paterson...." (Jan. 23, 2009) *Has* is a linking verb, so it expresses no action.

Strunk and White say in their *Elements of Style,* "The proper place in the sentence for the word or group of words that the writer desires to make most prominent is usually the end." And their sentence is an example of the construction they suggest, with *end* at the very end. So let's sharpen the script: "New York's governor has chosen a new U-S senator—Kirsten Gillibrand. She's taking the seat of Hillary Clinton, the new U-S Secretary of State...."

> In plain English, I've been hoping to hear more of the newscast in plain English.

"The news from Alabama [where a man shot 10 people dead] **was followed by news from Europe. Another mass shooting, this one today by a teenager, a former student at a high school in Winnenden, Germany. Correspondent Robert Moore from our broadcast partners, I-T-N, is there for us tonight with the latest. Robert, good evening."**

Robert Moore: **"Brian, good evening. Yes, this was a horrifying sequence of events that has shaken Germany to the core. It began at 9:30 this morning when a former student at this school, dressed in black, carrying his father's stolen pistol** [his father didn't steal the pistol; in fact, his father had registered it with the police], **walked into the school and simply opened fire. He killed many of the students, most of them women, by shooting them in the head at very close range. The police tonight have issued a poignant detail, saying when they found the bodies of those students many of them were actually carrying and still clutching their pencils** [if the students were clutching them, that says they were carrying them]. **After that, he fled the school. He was pursued by** more than one-thousand German police officers. Eventually he was cornered, and then he decided, we [*we?*] believe, to shoot himself, although there were earlier reports he had been shot by a police marksman. Certainly tonight, Germany is a nation bewildered. Because, behind all of this, there is no clear motive. Brian."

WILLIAMS: "Robert Moore in Winnenden, Germany, for us tonight. Robert, thanks." (March 11, 2009)

What's your reaction to that coverage? If you don't have anything bad to say, read it again. The problems: neither Brian Williams nor the reporter told us how many people the German teenager shot dead: 15. Nor did anyone provide the shooter's age; a teen can be anywhere between thirteen and nineteen. The shooter was 17. (The ABC and CBS newscasts that evening carried the age and the number of dead.) All of which again prompts us to ask: How can a network put on a first-rate newscast without a first-rate copy editor? I'm not running down *Nightly News*'s copy editor, because *Nightly* doesn't have a copy editor. Scripts are reviewed by any available senior producer, not by a full-time, qualified editor—a pro.

"Tonight, we have another story sent in from one of our viewers, also from New England, about a woman performing a badly needed service and Making A Difference in the lives of her grateful customers. Her story tonight from NBC's...." (March 26, 2009) Two *tonights*. And not the only item that night with twin *tonights*. Come to think of it, the profusion of *tonights* on *Nightly News* prompted someone (namely me) to suggest renaming it the *Tonightly News*.

"Two years ago, Ann first discovered everyday life there to be a struggle simply to survive. And now Ann has gone back again [this is her second trip, so, no she wasn't going back *again*] traveling to Chad and its border with the Darfur region." (Feb 19, 2009) *First discovered* is a redundancy: *discover* means to be the first.

"We're covering the world tonight, starting in Israel." (Feb. 10, 2009) *Covering the world?* After 45 words about Israel and 64 about Iran, *Nightly News* carried no other foreign coverage. (The only Williams covering the world that night was Sherwin.)

"We bring another week to a close and with apologies. Tonight, again, there are some grim numbers to report, starting with jobs in January down almost 600-thousand." (Feb. 6, 2009) *Apologies?* If an anchor starts apologizing for delivering bad news, he'll be one sorry guy. But how about apologizing for some of those scripts—and getting a copy editor?

(March 31, 2009)

Brian Williams Trips
on the *Learning* Curve

In the world of network news, Brian Williams may well be the *earningest* man around—and also the *learningest.*

His use of **"NBC News has learned"** (and **"We've learned"**) seems to imply that NBC dug up a story and is the first to report it. At its best, the term is ambiguous; at worst, it's false. Why is *learned* so popular with Williams and other newscasters? Maybe they think it helps to grab listeners by the ears and hold them.

Several of broadcast news's biggest names are the biggest *learners:* they tell us they've learned this or learned that. And though they usually imply they've *learned* something important, what they've learned is often not new, or not true or not theirs alone. And Williams has *learned* about many a story long after it broke.

Take a White House announcement. On June 1, 2011, Williams told his audience: **"We've learned an Army Ranger will be receiving the Medal of Honor, the nation's highest military decoration, for his heroic actions in combat in Afghanistan. He is 31-year-old Sergeant First Class Leroy Petry from Santa Fe** [in which state? The Santa Fe in Texas or Ohio? New Mexico? Even Minnesota has one; The Associated Press stylebook lists 30 large cities that don't need to be accompanied by states; Santa Fe is not one of them], **married father of four. He lost a hand throwing a live grenade, saving three American lives, including his own.** [An enemy's grenade had landed near Petry. When he threw it back, it detonated and blew off his hand.] **Petry will receive the Medal of Honor from President Obama in a ceremony July 12th. He will be only the second living Medal of Honor recipient since the Vietnam era. There are 84 living recipients now."**

Although Williams introduced the story with **"We've learned,"** CBS News had posted a story about Petry's award 24 hours earlier—at 6:20 p.m., May 31. The AP moved a story a few minutes later, at 6:31 p.m. ET, on May 31.

41

On May 26, Williams also had a learning experience: **"NBC News has learned that Pakistan has agreed to let the C-I-A send a forensic team into the compound where bin Laden was killed by those Navy SEALS to search for any al-Qaida materials that might have been left behind—items that could be buried in the walls, buried on the grounds. Pakistan's cooperation here** [where is *here*?] **may be a sign that tensions are easing a bit over that secret mission and the kerfuffle it caused."** (May 26, 2011)

NBC News has *learned?* That slyly suggests that NBC was breaking the news. Not so. More than four hours before Williams's newscast, *Newsday*, the Long Island newspaper, posted an AP story about the Pakistani development at 2:14 p.m. In fact, five hours before Williams said NBC News had *learned* of the story, a National Public Radio (NPR) blog reported that news at 1:34 p.m. As for Williams's script, *search* is too far from *forensic team*. (The closer the verb follows the subject, the easier for the listener to follow.)

> NBC News has *learned?* That slyly suggests that NBC was breaking the news. Not so.

The previous night, on May 25, Williams used the same *learning* gimmick, **"From our Pentagon outpost, NBC News has learned President Obama has made his pick for chairman of the Joint Chiefs of Staff, Army General Martin Dempsey...."** *NBC News has learned* sounds like an NBC News exclusive. An hour and a half before Williams went on the air at 6:30 p.m. ET, the AP moved the story on Dempsey's selection. The NBC script's *made his pick* sounds like *tabloidese*, which is not a compliment.

As for Williams's liberal use of *learned*, every story on *Nightly News* is something NBC's news division has learned. Even some NBC correspondents use **"NBC has learned."** On Nov. 25, 2009, Williams said, **"We first learned word of the president's upcoming** [*upcoming* makes some listeners think of an undigested meal] **trip to Copenhagen this morning from NBC's Savannah Guthrie."** *Learned word?* Those two words don't go together. At 6:10 a.m., usatoday.com had posted a brief AP story that the president would be going to Copenhagen. At 1:16 a.m. ET, Xinhua, the Chinese news agency, had posted a brief story.

Williams went on to say of Guthrie, **"Tonight she's learned something else...."** Then Guthrie said: **"NBC News has learned that the president has made the decision** [it was *a* decision; better: *has decided*] on strategy for Afghanistan and troop levels....He will make this announcement Tuesday night, as you said [a time waster], 8 Eastern Time, at West Point....Now [unneeded] we still don't know the exact number [no need for *exact*] of additional troops the president will send. It's expected to be in the tens of thousands, military officials expecting a range near 30-thousand...." A single number is not a range. A range in that case might extend, say, from 25,000 to 35,000.

Despite all that *learning*, the equivalent of blaring trumpets, her report didn't break any news. Eight hours before her report—at 10:26 a.m. that day—*The New York Times* posted a story saying the president was going to announce his decision at 8 p.m., Tuesday, at West Point. Subsequent postings elaborated. Seven minutes before the *Times*'s first posting about West Point, politico.com posted a much longer story. Both the ABC and CBS evening newscasts that day reported the Obama-West Point story while Williams was reporting the results of his *learning*. Guthrie has recently been promoted to co-host of the third hour of the *Today* show.

When George Mitchell, President Obama's chief representative to the Middle East, resigned, Williams said on his *Nightly News* (May 13, 2011) that Mitchell is a former secretary of state. Not so. Mitchell has never been secretary of state. Has Williams corrected that misinformation? Not yet.

(June 14, 2011)

How Brian Williams Beats The Clock

Brian Williams is often ahead of his time.

When Sir Edmund Hillary died in New Zealand about 9 a.m. on Jan. 11 there, the time in New York City was about 3 p.m., Jan. 10.

But Williams said in a tease that night, **"When Nightly News continues here this Thursday night, the death this evening of one of the best-known explorers in the world."** *This evening? 3 p.m. this evening?*

Although NBC's *Nightly News* originates live at 6:30 p.m. ET, Williams, the anchor and managing editor, opened his newscast on July 12 by saying, **"Late tonight, the Associated Press reported the following item, and we'll quote here...."** After reading the AP's 33-word sentence, he said, **"End of quote."** *Late tonight?* At 6:30 p.m.? In fact, the AP had moved the sentence he quoted at 4:46 p.m. ET—an hour and three-quarters before Williams said it had moved *late tonight*.

Even though Williams credited the AP, it's rare for a newscaster, particularly a network newscaster, to deliver AP copy verbatim—copy written for the eye, not the ear.

On Nov. 30, Williams said, **"The bulletin** [source unidentified] **we received in the newsroom tonight read like this, quote, "The granddaughter of motorcycle daredevil Evel Knievel says the 1970's icon has died."**

Received *tonight?* An AP item with that very lead (word for word), which Williams said was received in his newsroom that night had been posted on a Knoxville, Tennessee, website (KNOX.com) at 4:13 p.m. ET. Which means the AP moved the story in the afternoon, not that night.

As for that script's *quote*, use of that word in scripts has been criticized by experts for at least 60 years. In 1947, *A Manual of Radio News Writing* said: "Thoughtless use of such hackneyed terms as 'quote' and 'end quote' tend to interrupt the listener's thought. They have a barking, staccato sound no matter how softly they are spoken."

The first news director of CBS, Paul W. White, wrote in *News on the Air* in 1947, "Remember that since the word 'quote' is foreign to the ear as far as ordinary conversation is concerned, it probably always is disturbing to the listener...." And in 1948, *News by Radio* said, "Such phrases as 'and I quote' and 'end quote' are shunned by skillful writers."

When the singer Robert Goulet died in Los Angeles on Oct. 30, his website said he had died at 10:17 a.m. Other sources also reported he died that morning. But the next day, Brian Williams reported the death occurred not *yesterday* but *last night.*

If a news event doesn't meet his standards for timeliness, he's not reluctant to advance the hour hand and turn day into night. Williams's biggest stretch in time that I heard last year occurred in March. A Garuda jetliner made a hard landing in Jakarta and burst into flames. Twenty-one people were killed. Time there in Indonesia: 7:14 a.m., March 7. We're 12 hours behind, so the time here was 7:14 p.m. ET, March 6.

Yet, the next night in this country, March 7, Williams said the accident happened *today.* Wrong. He was co-anchoring in Baghdad, which is eight hours ahead of Eastern Time. Thus, the time in Baghdad was 2:30 a.m., March 8. So his *today* in Baghdad was even wronger.

Williams may not be obsessed with hours and days, but he is sensitive to the passage of years: He has declared an end to several eras. He said the death of Ken Lay, the founder of Enron, ended an era. And when Dan Rather left CBS News, Williams described that, too, as the end of an era.

With the death of Brooke Astor, Williams said another era had come to an end. He said she had been a "living link to another time and to the vast family fortune of John Jacob Astor." An era had come to an end? I'd say Brooke Astor, 105 years old, had come to an end.

When Evel Knievel died, Williams called him a **"cultural icon who helped define the early 1970s."** (Were they *that* bad?) *The Economist* observed: "Statistically, most of his 300-odd jumps were successes. But he was famous for the number of times he miscalculated the distance, or his speed, or mistimed things...." *The Economist* went on to say his two most-watched jumps were both "disasters." And he was a cultural icon?

As for disasters. Williams broadcast this script on Aug. 13: **"In plain English, the wings fell off Wall Street earlier today, and as the Dow Jones plunged downward 340 points, there were fears about where it was all headed. That was right before it swooped up before ending the day down just a little bit...."** *Plunged downward?* That's an aggravated redundancy. *Swooped up?* An editor should have swooped down on that *up. Before...before?* Twice in one sentence. What kind of plain English is that? *Earlier today?* Of course. If it hadn't happened earlier, you wouldn't know about it. Ironically, *in plain English* is one of Williams's favorite expressions. After using it in that script, he used it again that month—twice.

Earlier today? Skip *earlier.* Every *today* story we report happened earlier today, or else we wouldn't know about it.

I've heard of wings falling off an Aeroflot plane, but falling off Wall Street? In plane English, the wings fell off that script.

Williams also used *today* twice in one sentence—and with *tonight*, a jarring combination and a grammatical wreck: **"In Iraq tonight, we've learned today three U-S soldiers were killed by a roadside bomb south of the city of Baghdad today. And there are two very different versions of an incident today in Ramadi, a center of Sunni violence west of the city of Baghdad...."** (Feb. 28, 2007) Thank you, Mr. Williams, for telling us in your first sentence that Baghdad is a city—and, in your second sentence, reminding us that it's a city.

Forever and a day is a long time, but Brian Williams has accomplished what seems impossible: he compressed "forever" *into* a day. On Dec. 13, he told his audience:

"Some of the biggest names in baseball, the best players of what will now be known forever as the steroids era, tonight stand accused of cheating by taking drugs."

But the next night, *the steroids era* that Williams said would last forever ended: **"Now to our other big story tonight,"** he said, **"the fallout from what's already being called the steroid era in major league baseball."** So overnight, the *steroids era* dissolved into the *steroid era*— and lost its *foreverness.*

To dredge up a weather-beaten cliché from *Nightly News* (Dec. 11, 2007), those faulty scripts are only the *tip of the iceberg.*

(January 15, 2008)

Network Newscasts Mess
With the Clock Big-Time

Poor Shakespeare. He once wrote that night follows day. So he wouldn't be able to hack it in some broadcast newsrooms. In those shops, night does not follow day: night blots out day.

Let's look at a recent case of blotting, and of bending and twisting time:

On Thursday, Sept. 25, at 4:37 p.m. ET, the AP reported an earthquake on Hokkaido, Japan. The AP said the time on the island when the quake hit was about 4:50 a.m., Friday. Japan is 13 hours ahead of ET, so the time in New York City was about 3:50 p.m., Thursday. That's the time that governs for newscasters in Manhattan because they're expected to present the time according to where they are.

More than two and a half hours after the quake, on his 6:30 p.m. broadcast, the NBC anchor Tom Brokaw said on *Nightly News*, **"There was a very strong earthquake in Japan tonight...."** *Tonight?*

Was is a linking verb that expresses no action, and *there was* is a dead phrase. Better: "A strong earthquake has shaken Japan." Or "A strong earthquake shook Japan this afternoon." A half-hour later, at 7 p.m., CNBC said, **"The latest on today's big earthquake in Japan."** But later, **"Tonight's magnitude eight reinforced Japan's earthquake awareness with a powerful jolt."**

Dictionaries define *evening* and *night* rather loosely, but where I come from, 3:50 p.m., about three hours before sunset, is too early for *evening* or *night*. At 3:50, most people in this country are still at work. But those excused at 4 p.m. wouldn't say, "I'm getting off work early this evening." And certainly not "I'm getting off work early tonight." They'd probably say *today* or *this afternoon*.

At 6:30 p.m. ET, *Marketplace*, produced by Minnesota Public Radio, said, **"In the wee small hours of Friday morning in Japan, which is to say this afternoon in the U-S, an earthquake registering a preliminary**

47

seven-point-eight on the Richter scale hit the northern Japanese island of Hokkaido."

ABC's *World News Tonight* said at 6:30 p.m., **"A powerful earthquake shook northern Japan today."** (CBS's *Evening News* carried the
story the next night.)

PBS's *NewsHour* said, **"A powerful earthquake shook northern
Japan early Friday morning...."** But the next night, *NewsHour* said,
**"Northern Japan began returning to normal today, despite the world's
strongest earthquake in two years. The pre-dawn shock wave damaged some buildings...."** Better: "pre-dawn shock wave yesterday...."

Earlier, CNN's 5 p.m. newscast said, an hour after the quake, **"Only
moments ago, a huge earthquake hitting** [should have used the verb
hit] **northern Japan, a magnitude preliminary read seven-point-eight
rocking the northern Japan island of Hokkaido, authorities fearful
there is a possibility of a tsu-
nami in this northern Japanese island."** Me no liking
tenseless, incomplete sentences
like that. And no liking *northern* three times. And *Japan*(ese)
three times. And *island* twice.
And *moments ago* even once.

> Anything that happened *today* happened *earlier today* or we wouldn't be able to report it. But the quake didn't happen at any time *today*.)

The Fox News Channel said on its 5 o'clock program, **"Panic in Japan. A seven-point-eight Richter-scale quake hits the northern Hokkaido area...."** I couldn't find wire copy that mentioned or suggested
panic. Makes you wonder: was the panic in the Fox newsroom?

CNNfn's 6 p.m. newscast said, **"Tonight, a powerful earthquake has
hit northern Japan...These are the pictures of the interior of that office as the earthquake struck this afternoon."**

At 11 p.m., Canada's CTV said, **"The northern Japanese island
of Hokkaido took a powerful hit today.** [A North Korean missile?]
**An earthquake with some dramatic effects, but no apparent loss of
life...."**

The next day, Friday, Sept. 26, CBS's *Morning News* said, **"The strongest earthquake anywhere in the world this year hit Japan earlier
today."** (Anything that happened *today* happened *earlier today* or we
wouldn't be able to report it. But the quake didn't happen at any time
today.)

Shortly after 7 a.m., NBC's *Today* said, **"In northern Japan, more** than 300 people were injured this morning in a powerful earthquake." *This morning*? Maybe that's why they call the show *Today*.

At 7:50 a.m., Minnesota Public Radio's "*Marketplace*" said, again correctly, "**Japanese officials are still adding up the costs of the damage from a series of strong earthquakes that rocked the northern island of Hokkaido yesterday.**"

At 5 p.m., Friday, 24 hours after the quake, CNN said: "**Earthquake hits Japan. The world's most powerful quake in more than two years hit northern Japan before dawn....**"

At 6:30 p.m., Friday, CBS's *Evening News* said: "**Emergency officials in northern Japan say damage from a powerful earthquake was surprisingly light. The magnitude-eight quake shook office buildings, touched off an oil refinery fire and pushed a tsunami wave along the coast, but there were only a few hundred injuries.**" *Only*? When was the quake? *Today*? *Yesterday*?

At 10 p.m., Friday, 30 hours after the quake, CNN said, "**In Japan tonight, quite a large earthquake, even by Japanese standards.**" And later: "**Other news tonight: in northern Japan, people are being pummeled by aftershocks from an earthquake earlier today....**" *Earlier* makes me surlier. Didn't someone there read the wires and that morning's newspapers? As for *pummeling* (beating someone, as with fists) earthquakes don't pummel people. People pummel people.

What would Shakespeare say about all that fudging and fiddling with facts? Well, if he were still alive, he'd be very tired. But he might quote Polonius's advice to Laertes in *Hamlet*:

"This above all: to thine own self be true, And it must follow, as the night the day, Thou canst not then be false to any man."

(October 2003)

Brian Williams: *History-Maker*

Brian Williams already stands out in this year of the Olympics: He set a record, apparently, in the men's singles, free-style, indoor competition for tossing around the word *tonight.*

In one sentence, he used *tonight* four times. In the first 33 words of a 53-word sentence on NBC *Nightly News* of Jan. 24, he said, **"We have a crowded broadcast tonight from our backdrop here tonight, as Tim Russert and I prepare for tonight's GOP presidential debate, to medical news on ovarian cancer, to our lead story tonight...."** And, in a display of stamina, he again said *tonight* in each of his next two sentences.

But history-making events are not unusual on *Nightly News.* About once a month, on average, Williams, the anchor and managing editor, describes an event as *historic,* or *history making* or a *history-maker.*

Williams likes *history* enough to use it twice in one sentence: **"The Iowa caucuses** [the day before] **are history, and no matter where the race goes from here, Barack Obama and Mike Huckabee are now in the history books as the winners."** (Jan. 4) *Now in the history books?* Any publisher who could bring out a history book that fast—in less than 24 hours—would be what Williams calls a *history-maker.*

Several nights later, Williams said, **"Good evening from Manchester, New Hampshire, where the primary here tonight will go into the history books."** (Jan. 8) *The primary here tonight?* The primary lasted all day. People were still voting, the polls hadn't closed, the votes hadn't even been counted yet. *Will go into the history books?* Who knows?

As for the term *history-maker,* it's a cringe-maker: **"And, Tim, on this next and final question about how people plan to vote, I know the answer is also a history-maker."** (Oct. 18, 2006) What does that mean—if anything?

And **"It** [a hurricane] **hit that coastline as Category 5, as strong as they get, a history-maker, the strongest storm there in two decades** [better: *20 years*]." (Aug. 21, 2007)

Historians are the ones who decide what makes history, and they don't do it every day by 6:30 p.m., ET.

After a beagle was the first of its breed chosen top dog at the West-minster Kennel Club Show, Williams wrapped up the story by saying, **"And in this exciting election year for all of us humans, this made dog history last night at Madison Square Garden."** (Feb. 13) *Dog history*? Here's a dog mystery: Williams called the winning dog *proud, noble* and *very happy. Proud? Noble?* How could Williams tell? Was that beagle a talking dog?

They say history repeats itself. Well, on *Nightly News, history-making* can also repeat itself. Williams introduced a correspondent by saying, in part, **"The U-S Supreme Court today ended its 2007 term with a history-making ruling."** (June 28) After the correspondent reported the ruling, Williams said, **"All right, Pete Williams, who was in the chamber today for what will go down as this history-making decision of the Supreme Court for us tonight."** Why *all right*? Was the decision *for us*? Or was Pete Williams at the Court *for us*? Or what?

Not only does Brian Williams use *tonight* far too often, but he also puts it in the wrong place often: **"And the White House has just tonight announced the president will travel to the Middle East in January."** (Dec. 4) *Has just tonight announced?* Doesn't sound conversational—or English. Psst: In December, we refer to January as *next month.*

One goal newswriters should have is to make their writing conversational, and in conversation we don't put the time element (*today, tonight, tomorrow*) before the verb.

Another oddity: Williams told Ann Curry, **"You had to know while you were there touching those children, recording these pictures, that this work would be impactful around the world."** (Nov. 19) *Impactful?* Bryan A. Garner, a leading expert on English, says in *Modern American Usage* that *impactful* is "barbarous." Garner also says, "Whatever its future may be, *impactful* is, for now, a word to be scorned." (When Ann Curry sat in for Williams on Aug. 8, she said, **"You're looking at just one glimpse of the damage...."** A glimpse is "a brief, incomplete view or look." So no one can look at a glimpse, not even glimpse a glimpse.)

Also to be scorned by newscasters is the labeling of stories as *great*—or anything else. Yet, sometimes Williams calls a story great: **"There is a great story to go with every veteran...."** (Feb. 17, 2006) *Great* story?

Every veteran? Deserters? Goof-offs? Those discharged dishonorably? Vets who served honorably but did nothing interesting or outstanding?

Whenever I hear Williams call a story *great*, I wonder about all the stories he doesn't call *great*. Does he regard them as just so-so? Or substandard? And I wonder whether the correspondents on the un-great stories should start polishing their résumés—and praying.

Besides calling a story *great*, Williams said, **"You're about to see and hear a powerful piece of reporting."** (Nov. 29) But he has said that only once. Which raises questions about his opinion of the work of all the other NBC News reporters.

Sometimes Williams calls a story *big* or characterizes it another way: **"And we begin here tonight with an awful story to have to tell you about."** (Dec. 5, 2007) A sniper in Omaha had shot eight people dead, then killed himself. But Williams didn't *have* to tell us. Williams also called that news **"devastating."** Viewers don't need help from an anchor to realize that the news is bad.

Interesting night *out of* South Carolina? Where do people talk that way?

As in that script, he says from time to time he's forced to report a story: **"Tonight, we continue our coverage of the disaster, the unfolding human suffering going on in Haiti, except this evening, we must begin with a big story in this country that may affect this nation's foreign policy, health care policy, perhaps the remainder** [he means *the rest*] **of the Obama presidency."** (Jan. 20, 2010) *Must?* Sounds as if someone is holding a gun to his head.

Three weeks later, Williams again mentioned compulsion, **"Sadly tonight, we have to begin our reporting from here with a tragic story."** (Feb. 12, 2010)

One of the oddest scripts ever on *Nightly*: **"Microsoft tonight says, it is true by the way, hackers somehow got into its computer system and stole the codes to top secret software. Tonight the F-B-I is on the case, and Microsoft, which has a business relationship with NBC News, is trying to sort out what the hackers really found out."** (Tom Brokaw, Oct. 27, 2000) What makes that so odd is the anchor's saying **"it is true."** And *by the way* makes it seem incidental. Have you ever heard an anchor say a story is true? Aren't they all true? The theft of the codes had been reported in that morning's *Wall Street Journal*, and shortly an Internet newsletter said the FBI was investigating.

Substituting for Williams, Harry Smith said, **"Three young men found guilty and convicted."** (Aug. 19, 2011) *Guilty* and *convicted* say the same thing.

Back to Brian Williams: **"And in a country with enough problems** [that phrase could be used every night]**, he turned a corner of this nation into a nightmare late yesterday afternoon when he left home with four weapons and went on an awful rampage through three separate towns."** (March 11, 2009) Aren't all towns separate, except for twin cities?

Some of Williams's closings are also odd: **"Well, it could be an interesting night out of South Carolina."** (Jan. 26) Interesting night *out of* South Carolina? Where do people talk that way?

The importance of scrutinizing every word in a script is pointed up in a joke told by Harold Evans in his *Newsman's English:*

A London fishmonger had a sign that said: FRESH FISH SOLD HERE. A friend persuaded him to rub out the word FRESH; he was expected to sell fish that's fresh. Then the friend persuaded him to rub out HERE; he was selling it there in his shop. Then the friend urged him to rub out SOLD; he isn't giving it away.

Finally, the friend persuaded him to rub out FISH; you can smell it a mile off. But you shouldn't be able to say that about network newswriting.

(March 6, 2008)

Network Newswriting
That's Snoozewriting

There's a persistent problem in the air: *there is*. What's the problem? It's a wordy, wobbly way to start a script. The subject of a story is not *there*, and *is* is a linking verb, which expresses no action. It's best to lead with a solid noun and a strong verb. Although *there is* is a dead phrase, some network newscasts rely on it often.

"There is news out of Iraq tonight. A series of deadly attacks across that country today killed as many as 30 people, including two unidentified American soldiers." (Brian Williams, NBC *Nightly News*, Feb. 24, 2005) Several problems besides *there is*: no need to say there's news; it's a newscast. And news comes *from* a place, not *out of* a place.

Also: no need to call the attacks *deadly*. If they killed so many people, they must have been deadly. Rather, *fatal*. *Deadly* means capable of causing death or likely to cause death; *fatal* describes events that have caused or will cause death.

And no need to say the U.S. soldiers were unidentified. Even if the newsroom had their names, they almost certainly wouldn't have used them. And why the word *tonight* in the first sentence, then the shift in the next sentence to *today*?

"There is new information tonight about William Rehnquist, the Chief Justice of the United States Supreme Court, who is battling thyroid cancer." (Brian Williams, *Nightly News*, Dec. 10, 2004)

Some old information for that anchor: William Rehnquist's title is Chief Justice of the United States.

No need to announce that the newscast has new information. What else would a newscast offer? Old information? Slightly used information?

"There is health news to report to you tonight." (Brian Williams, *Nightly News*, Dec. 2, 2004)

Why tell me you're going to tell me? Just tell me. Better: "A new study says almost half of all Americans were taking at least one prescription drug."

"There is history throughout the American South." (Brian Williams, *Nightly News*, Dec. 10, 2004) Who'd have ever suspected it?

"There is news on the economy tonight. It turns out it grew faster than first thought at the end of last year." (Brian Williams, *Nightly News*, Feb. 25, 2005) Better: "The U-S economy grew faster in the last quarter than previously thought."

"There's some very good news tonight from off the coast of South Carolina. A young Atlantic right whale that was tangled in fishing gear was freed by rescuers..." (Lester Holt, *Nightly News*, Dec. 31, 2004) Journalism 101 teaches us not to characterize news as good or bad, glad or sad. Don't tell listeners what to think of the news. Just deliver the news, and let listeners decide for themselves whether it's good, or bad, or indeterminable.

"There is sad news tonight in American politics, the death of U.S. Representative Robert Matsui of California." (Lester Holt, *Nightly News*, Sunday, Jan. 2, 2005) The news is sad for his family, friends, neighbors, colleagues, constituents and admirers. But not for those of us unfamiliar with him.

What is sad is that kind of newswriting. In the *Golden Book on Writing*, David Lambuth writes, "The habit of beginning statements with the impersonal and usually vague *there is* or *there are* shoves the really significant verb into subordinate place instead of letting it stand vigorously on its own feet."

When is the phrase *there is* defensible? The grammarian Bryan A. Garner asks that question in his *Modern American Usage* (2003). His answer: "When the writer is addressing the existence of something. That is, if the only real recourse is to use the verb *exist*, then *there is* is perfectly fine." He offers an example: "There is no positive relationship between aid levels and economic growth."

On another *Nightly News* program that Lester Holt anchored, he said: **"And a sad note to report tonight about a popular attraction in Washington. The national Christmas tree has died and was cut down this weekend. Federal officials say the blue spruce succumbed to transplant shock...."** (May 6, 2012) *Sad?* Let listeners decide whether they're sad. Or glad. Or mad. Yes, as the poet Joyce Kilmer wrote, "Only God can make a tree." But who's saddened by that tree's death? Just don't tell any weeping willows.

Let's look at a few other faulty scripts from the same newsroom.

"There is court news tonight." (Brian Williams, *Nightly News*, Feb. 23, 2005) I swear, someone did say that.

"And there are fresh reports tonight that the U.S. is engaging in a kind of risky business, sending terror suspects to foreign countries for questioning and, it is alleged, for torture..." (Brian Williams, *Nightly News*, March 7, 2005) *Fresh* reports? An NBC correspondent then told the story of one former detainee, a Canadian born in Syria who was arrested at JFK airport and flown by Americans to Syria for questioning. Interesting but not new: Three weeks earlier, the *New Yorker* of Feb. 14 ran a 9,000-word article called "Outsourcing Torture." The first 600 words were about the Canadian.

"And the chairman of the Federal Reserve, Alan Greenspan, made news today when he told an advisory panel in Washington that replacing the income tax with a new consumption tax, like a national sales tax, would help the U.S. economy." (Brian Williams, *Nightly News*, March 3, 2005) Everyone in a newscast makes news—whatever that means. So let's ditch the meaningless cliché and go straight to the news: "Federal Reserve Chairman Alan Greenspan said today that replacing..."

> The best way to approach a story with a new development is to present the development as news, not waste time with any preliminaries.

"On Wall Street today, stocks were slightly lower." (Brian Williams, *Nightly News*, Dec. 10, 2004) *Were*, like any form of *to be*, is a linking verb, so it conveys no action. Better: "On Wall Street, stock averages slipped." Or *dipped*.

"California drenching. A violent storm system on the West Coast tonight brings more damage and misery." (Brian Williams, *Nightly News*, Feb. 22, 2005) California wasn't drenching. California was being drenched. And the storm didn't *bring* damage; it *caused* damage.

"There is word tonight of a late development at the Pentagon. Tonight, our correspondent..." (Brian Williams, *Nightly News*, Jan. 6, 2005) Many, if not most, major stories have new developments every day, sometimes every hour. The best way to approach a story with a new development is to present the development as news, not waste time with any preliminaries. *Tonight, tonight?* I heard you the first time.

"In Colorado tonight, the University of Colorado's president, Elizabeth Hoffman, announced today she is stepping down..." (Brian

Williams, *Nightly News*, March 7, 2005) *Tonight, today?* Inspired by Cole Porter?

"Right up until tonight, it had recently been so peaceful in the Middle East between Israel and the Palestinians. In fact, all of the talk was of a new era of cooperation. That was right up until word arrived late tonight of a suicide bombing. It happened in a popular area of bars and nightclubs near the beach in Tel Aviv. There are dozens of casualties. And tonight all eyes [*all eyes?*] are on two things: the death toll and what effect this will have on what was the beginning of a new era. We begin here tonight with NBC's...." (Brian Williams, *Nightly News*, Feb. 25, 2005) *We begin here?* He began that script 92 words earlier. And said *right up until* twice. *New era* twice. And *tonight* four times.

Word arrived late tonight? The newscast began at 6:30 p.m. ET; the bombing occurred around 11:30 p.m., Tel Aviv time—4:30 p.m. ET. That's hardly *tonight*, let alone *late tonight*. (The AP and Reuters moved bulletins before 5 p.m. ET.) A correspondent also used *late tonight* wrongly on the 6:30 p.m. newscast on March 15, and a substitute anchor did so on March 21.

But the news about those lame scripts is good: everyone responsible has an opportunity to learn.

(March 28, 2005)

When a *Hit* Is Amiss

The man who threw a "pie" at Rupert Murdoch was able to get into the hearing room because he apparently wasn't subjected to a pie detector.

Eventually, the pieman's aims became clear, but his aim was off. Although Brian Williams didn't attend the Parliamentary hearing in London on July 19, his presentation that night was striking. At the top of his newscast, the NBC anchor told his *Nightly News* audience:

"On the broadcast tonight, the most humble day of Rupert Murdoch's life, he says. But then he went on to say he does not accept blame for the hacking scandal. Then he was hit by a pie in the face. Then his wife struck the attacker...."

Williams went on to say:

"Both Murdochs tried to stay above the fray, then the fray came to them in the form of a guy with a cream pie aimed right at the face of the patriarch. It was that kind of day. It's been that kind of scandal." And it's that kind of script. In his opening, Williams set a possible record by using *then* three times in successive sentences—and starting two straight sentences with *then*.

Even though Williams said Murdoch was "hit by a pie in the face" [better: *hit in the face by a pie*], two NBC siblings, cnbc.com and MSNBC, said the protester did not hit Murdoch in the face. Just after 6:30 p.m. ET, about the same time Williams began to talk, the guest host on MSNBC, the Rev. Al Sharpton, said, **"The man tried to pie Murdoch but wasn't successful...."** *Tried.*

About 90 minutes before Williams went on the air, MSNBC's Chris Matthews said, **"A man tried to hit him** [Murdoch] **with a plate full of shaving cream."** *Tried.* At 7:02 p.m. ET, msnbc.com posted an article saying a man *tried* to attack Murdoch. At 7:22 p.m., MSNBC posted an article that said Mrs. Murdoch "leaped forward to smack a protester from smashing a pie into her husband's face." *Smack* someone from *smashing*? And an hour after Williams's *Nightly News,* an MSNBC anchor said the protester **"attempted to smash Rupert Murdoch in the face with his pie."** *Attempted.*

At 1:49 p.m. ET, cnbc.com posted an article by a senior editor that said the protester "attempted" to strike him [Murdoch] with a pie plate filled with foam. *Attempted.*

On the next day's *Today* show, shortly after 7 a.m., ET, Ann Curry said the protester **"tried to hit him in the face with a pie."** *Tried.*

What about the network newscasts that compete with Williams's? On the *CBS Evening News*, Bob Schieffer said **"someone hit him with a cream pie."** But nothing about Murdoch's being hit in the face.

On ABC's *World News,* the anchor, Diane Sawyer, said, **"a heckler with a pie tried to attack her husband."** *Tried.* An ABC correspondent in London said, **"...it was so fast it was hard to see what happened."** Later that night, though, on ABC's *Nightline*, a correspondent (David Wright) said a **"shaving cream pie"** had been **"stuffed in** [Murdoch's] **face."**

On PBS's *NewsHour*, a correspondent said a man **"rushed at Murdoch with what appeared to be a plate of white shaving cream."** But nothing about scoring a hit.

The Associated Press didn't say Murdoch was hit in the face. All day, in updates, the AP used *tried* or *attempted.* The AP's twin byline included the AP's London bureau chief. A half hour before Brian Williams went on the air, the AP moved a short version of the Murdoch story in "AP News in Brief" at 5:58 p.m. ET. The story said, "He stayed seated when a prankster tried to throw a foam pie, splattering his suit jacket...." *Tried.*

Bloomberg said Murdoch *was* hit in the face. The news service moved an article that said, "A man standing behind Murdoch came from his left and leant into him and pushed a plate of the substance into his face, according to a Bloomberg reporter in the room."

CNN, too, said Murdoch had been hit in the face. One of CNN's producers in London, Jonathan Wald, wrote at cnn.com: "He [the protester] said, 'You're a naughty billionaire,' plunging a plate with some gunk in it firmly in Murdoch's face." Wald said Murdoch was hit "squarely in the face."

Just after 11 p.m. ET, a substitute anchor, Dr. Sanjay Gupta, told CNN viewers, **"Take one media mogul, one pie in the face, a right hook and a stiff upper lip, and you have pretty much summed up the day in Britain's Parliament and Rupert Murdoch's phone-hacking scandal...."**

Howard Kurtz, the host of CNN's weekly program monitoring the media, *Reliable Sources*, wrote at the website of Daily Beast at 12:53 p.m. ET, "The sober hearing got a jolt when a protester tried to throw a pie at the senior Murdoch...." *Tried*. Kurtz is the Washington bureau chief of Daily Beast and *Newsweek*.

How about the BBC? Right after the attack, the British broadcaster said Murdoch "was apparently hit in the face with a plate of shaving foam...." But at its website later, the BBC said, "[A] man tried to throw a foam pie at Rupert Murdoch." No mention, though, of hitting Murdoch in the face. At 6:16 p.m. ET, Reuters said the protester *tried* to hit Murdoch but didn't say Murdoch was hit in the face.

All three U.S. national newspapers—*The New York Times*, *Wall Street Journal* and *USA Today*—said the protester had *tried* to hit Murdoch in the face.

A Canadian newspaper, the *Globe and Mail*, also said the protester had *tried* to hit Murdoch with the "pie." Canadian Press, a national news agency, and CBC (Canadian Broadcasting Corporation), a national public broadcaster, also said *tried*.

The newsweeklies—*Time*, *Newsweek* and *The Economist*—ran stories about the attack on Murdoch, but none said the "pie" had hit him in the face.

The British newspaper *Guardian*, credited with breaking the phone-hacking story, said the protester had *tried* to throw a plate of white foam into Murdoch's face. The *Financial Times* blog also said *tried*. A *Times* of London blog said *attempted*. The *Telegraph*'s blog said, around noon ET, "The man slapped the pie on to Rupert Murdoch's shoulder; Wendy [Murdoch] then grabbed it from him and pushed it into the assailant's face."

Except for CNN, Bloomberg and ABC's David Wright, the news outlets cited here did not say the attacker hit Murdoch in the face with a pie. But anyone who says the "pie" did hit Murdoch in the face has a much more dramatic story.

"The majority is always wrong," Ibsen said. But this majority's near-unanimity and reputation have me sold. No wonder Brian Williams's presentation about Murdoch—**"hit by a pie in the face"**—stands out. But, as we've seen, it doesn't stand up.

(August 8, 2011)

Network Script Gets a
Hard Look—and Crumples

When a correspondent says she (or her network) has *learned* something, what do you think that means? That her story is exclusive? She did some original reporting? She found something special? She did learn something or other?

Well, let's see what *we* can learn. We'll focus on the 6:30 p.m. edition of NBC's *Nightly News* on Saturday, Oct. 18, when the anchor, John Seigenthaler, said:

"Back in this country, new information tonight about the man who may be responsible for planting box cutters and other banned items on passenger jets, and his warning that airport security doesn't work. NBC's Rehema Ellis has that story." Then she spoke:

"Tonight, N-B-C News has learned that F-B-I investigators have questioned and released a 20-year-old college student suspected of breaching airline security. He was not charged, but he will appear in court on Monday. [Excuse me: we don't know whether he *will* appear; he's *scheduled* to appear.] **Government sources tell N-B-C News that Nathaniel Heatwole, whose parents live here in Damascus, Maryland, is responsible for placing the modeling clay and box cutter knives** [a box cutter *is* a knife] **like these on board two Southwest Airlines planes. The items, discovered on Thursday, led the Transportation Security Administration to order an immediate inspection of the nation's seven-thousand passenger planes."**

Next, the correspondent said:

"Tonight W-N-B-C-T-V is reporting that this may not be the first time Heatwole has carried items like these on Southwest Airlines. The station reports that in April of this year Heatwole allegedly passed the security screeners at two different airports [all airports are different] **with similar items and left them on the planes. The items were found by Southwest Airlines maintenance workers, who reported them to**

security, including T-S-A officials, and an investigation was launched. W-N-B-C-TV reports that Heatwole does [why the present tense?] **the same thing again at the same airports in September, but officials say this time he sent** [why the abrupt shift in tense?] **what they characterized as 'a polite email' to the T-S-A...."**

Sounds as if NBC News and NBC's flagship O&O (owned-and-operated station), WNBC-TV, have this story alone, that they own it. But before we bestow any laurels, let's root around a little and see whether the *Nightly News* story is new, true and exclusive.

Twenty-two hours before NBC's network newscast, the AP moved a story—at 8:23 p.m., Oct. 17, the day before the *Nightly News* presentation—about a new development in the case. The story said the FBI announced it had found the person who planted box cutters and other items on Southwest Airlines planes. The story said he was a 20-year-old North Carolina man and that an FBI statement said agents had interviewed him. The FBI did not disclose his name.

More than ten hours before *Nightly News* went on the air, a CNN correspondent said, at 8:01 a.m., **"The F-B-I and Transportation Security Administration officials say that** [delete *that*] **they were able to find a 20-year-old North Carolina student that** [*who*] **actually** [adds nothing] **put these devices onto Southwest Airline planes."** The CNN correspondent told about the flights, the box cutters and the clay, and he said a Bush administration official asserted the e-mails **"detailed locations, times, and places where the contraband was put on board the airplanes."**

The CNN correspondent also reported, **"They say there is no terrorist threat at all...."** Then the anchor said, **"Very serious matter."** To which the correspondent responded, **"Very serious matter."** That appraisal was a big help. Unseriously.

Five hours before the broadcast of NBC's *Nightly News,* the AP moved a story at 1:25 p.m. that began:

"The man suspected of hiding box cutters on two airline flights warned the government in an email of his intention to conceal similar suspicious items on six planes and provided dates and locations for the plan but was not considered a threat, a senior Bush administration official said Saturday."

The AP said the website of a North Carolina newspaper, *Greensboro's News & Record*, quoted a 20-year-old man as saying the FBI had questioned him the previous day about the case. The AP went on to give the man's name, age, hometown, the name of his college and his court date.

At 2:12 p.m., the CNN anchor said they now had the man's name, and the correspondent credited an article posted at the website of the *News & Record*. At 4:06 p.m., he reported the name of the man's college (in Greensboro), the name of his hometown and other elements of the story.

At 5:29 p.m., an hour before *Nightly News* went on the air, the AP moved its fourth story that afternoon about the man, corrected the misspelling of his first name and provided additional details.

Shortly after 6:30 p.m., a correspondent on the *CBS Evening News* delivered the essentials. He said the FBI had questioned the man and gave his name and age and the name of his college.

As for ABC News, two days later, *World News Tonight* led with the story of the student: **"We're going to begin tonight** [as soon as an anchor opens his mouth, I know he's beginning] **with an F-B-I document that landed with a thud in newsrooms all across America today.** [Sounds ominous.] **In this job, we see a lot of F-B-I material.** [What? What kind?] **But today, when the government charged a young man, Nathaniel Travis Heatwole, with carrying concealed weapons onto two Southwest Airlines flights some time ago, the F-B-I's affidavit tells a remarkable story...."** The

If you go back to the top for a minute and re-read the *Nightly News* script, you'll see that the stories run by the AP, CNN and CBS make it clear that the NBC story was not new or exclusive.

FBI affidavit *landed with a thud in newsrooms all across America*? Let's get real. Did it even land with a thud in the only room it was presented, the courtroom? In any case, that script may help us: now that we know the man's middle name, we won't confuse him with any other Nathaniel Heatwole.

If you go back to the top for a minute and re-read the *Nightly News* script, you'll see that the stories run by the AP, CNN and CBS make it clear that the NBC story was not new or exclusive. And that NBC's original reporting, if any, was negligible. New information? Almost none. Certainly, none of any consequence. The anchor's lead-in provided nothing new, and the correspondent's first 190 words offered only one tidbit I found nowhere else: "a polite email." Later, she quoted a note found on a plane: **"Ha, ha. I did it again."** I couldn't find that quotation anywhere else. As far as I could tell, those were the only possibly new bits of information.

The NBC correspondent said the TSA had ordered an immediate inspection of the nation's 7,000 planes. But the order had been canceled. That very morning, on NBC's *Today,* a spokesman for the TSA told an anchor about the cancellation. The TSA had announced the cancellation the night before.

Even so, a wrap-up of the Heatwole case was certainly news worth using, but not in language suggesting that NBC had done something special. It's true, as the correspondent said in her script, that NBC did learn something (by reading the wires and newspapers?). But so did we.

We see—despite NBC's chest-thumping presentation—there's a lot less to the script than meets the ear. As is sometimes the case there and elsewhere, the newscast seemed more intent on promoting the story and itself than in reporting it.

Lesson learned.

(November 2003)

Network Anchor Makes
Time Fly at Warp Speed

When is an anchor's *tonight* not tonight? Too often.

News tends to break during our daytime, but too many anchors regard *today* as a dirty word. No matter what, they don't want to use it. Instead, they use *tonight*. And some even change *yesterday* to *today* and *last night* to *overnight*.

But the most frequent alteration is the conversion of *today* to *tonight*. Conscientious reporters try to freshen a *today* story by finding a follow or a late update, but in most such cases, *tonight* is inappropriate. Even when the story has not been advanced, some anchors go right ahead and say something happened *tonight*, though they must know *tonight* is untrue.

Yet, not all untrue *tonight*s are false. Some *tonight*s end up in scripts through inadvertence, or indifference or incompetence. No explanation can justify the misuse of *tonight*, but the worst cases are those in which writers have misrepresented the time element intentionally. Where I come from, we call it lying. I'm tired of being lied to. And I wish I didn't have to take it anymore.

Tonight in a script may seem to make the news newsier, but I resent being misled. I resent being taken for a numskull. I want to be able to trust anchors I spend time with. But when I hear a *tonight* that's wrong or find out later that it was wrong, I can't help wondering what else in the newscast might be wrong.

Let's look at a wrong lead-in that's typical of the time-twisters:

"In Israel, a dramatic development tonight: the emergence of a videotape of that country's most wanted fugitive." (John Seigenthaler, *Nightly News,* Aug. 27, 2005) Starting with *in* and a place-name is weak. Every story occurs somewhere, but a *where* is hardly a grabber.

The anchor did not say, "Tonight, we report a dramatic development in Israel." That would have been true. Right after the weekend anchor said *tonight*, the correspondent on the scene contradicted him: **"Now**

he's resurfaced on a shadowy videotape stamped with Hamas approval and broadcast last night...." *Last night*! When the correspondent spoke—accurately—in Gaza, the Hamas tape had already been released the previous night, Aug. 26.

The time in Gaza is seven hours ahead of ET, so the videotape had been released in our ET afternoon, the day before NBC News made it a *tonight* event.

More than 25 hours before the anchor told of the development *tonight*, ABC News posted at its website an AP story about the videotape at 4:51 p.m. ET, Aug. 26.

And NBC's affiliate in the San Jose-San Francisco area, KNTV-TV, ran part of the fugitive's videotape on its 11 p.m. newscast, Aug. 26.

But the next day, *Nightly News* made it a *tonight* story. Is that what they mean by *making news*?

(October 2005)

Former NBC Writer Slams Brian Williams's Scripts

Brian Williams is not only first in the evening news ratings, but he also rates first with me.

What I mean is, so far this year I've written two articles about him for my website. In 2006, I wrote one article about him. And in the past few years, I've also written more than one article about the newscast he anchors, NBC's *Nightly News*. After all, people would rather read about a winner (in the ratings) than a loser.

Although the articles have been widely noted and quoted, neither Brian Williams nor anyone else at NBC News has written to me to comment. Or complain. Or cheer me on.

Now, though, I've received an e-mail from a former NBC News writer-producer, Charles Coates. He's a retired journalism professor, the author of *Professional's TV News Handbook* and a friend. Because his letter is pertinent, I've posted it at my website.

My most recent article, posted on March 6, "Brian Williams: History-Maker," includes a dozen excerpts from scripts delivered by Williams on *Nightly News*. That article is apparently what prompted Coates to e-mail me; this is his entire message:

"I never wrote like that for Huntley, Brinkley, Chancellor or Brokaw (or MacNeil or Vanocur or McGee or Gabe Pressman or Bill Ryan or Frank Blair). First, I lack the imagination to do it. And second, they would not have read it."

(March 24, 2008)

NBC's Pete Williams
Catches a Mistake: *Mine*

Pete Williams, who covers the Justice beat for NBC News, recently spotted a mistake I made. He spelled it out in a letter, which he gave me permission to print:

> Mr. Block —
>
> I've been reading your delightful critiques of the writing on the three evening network newscasts, and I'd like to ask a question about one of your comments regarding a correspondent's script in an ABC broadcast.
>
> You write:
>
> "'Iraqi officials say the gunmen were part of a religious cult composed of Shias, Sunnis and foreign fighters.' [Jan. 29, 2007.] The whole comprises the parts; the parts compose the whole. So *composed of* should be *comprising*."
>
> It could certainly be said that a play comprises three acts, or that three acts compose a play. I've always thought of it this way: that comprise means "includes these things and no others" and that compose means "make up."
>
> Why, then, would it not be proper to say that the play is composed of three acts—that the play is made up of three acts?
>
> The error that Fowler and the other authorities warn against is *comprised of*.
>
> In the ABC example, *comprising* would certainly be a more elegant way to phrase it, but is *composed of* really an error? And might it not be more conversational?
>
> Respectfully,
> Pete Williams
> NBC News Justice Correspondent

I goofed. Yes, *composed of* in that ABC script was perfectly acceptable. What was really goofy: I already knew that. I had previously written about *compose* and *comprise*, and I'd also spoken about them. But apparently my brain's synapses and dendrites misfired. When I was writing that faulty sentence in my article, maybe I blacked out. Or blanked out. Certainly, the correct usage was something I blocked out.

I apologize to my readers, and I salute Pete Williams. He has written a letter that's kind and gracious. It can serve as a model for any reader, or anyone else for that matter, in writing a letter to point out a mistake.

Williams began his letter with a compliment, so I was pleased and eager to read further. He said he'd like to ask me a question. That sounds innocent enough, not alarming. Or threatening. Next, he reminded me of something I had written in my latest article. Then he demonstrated his knowledge of the subject I had written about. He didn't accuse me of committing a crime against humanity; he merely asked his question. And he ended the letter gently with two more polite questions.

Although Williams caught my mistake, he didn't write a nasty gotcha letter. He didn't bash me or trash me. He even signed off with "respectfully."

Gotta respect a man like that.

(July 2007)

CBS NEWS

Mistakes Happen—
and Happening Now

Scott Pelley: Wearing Two Hats
Can Cause Headaches

The managing editor of the *CBS Evening News* needs to keep a sharper eye on the scripts broadcast by the anchor, Scott Pelley. But Pelley *is* the managing editor. Unfortunately, Pelley the anchor slips many faulty scripts past Pelley the editor and puts them on the air.

A reporter recently wrote, "Pelley says he personally edits every script in his broadcast." And the reporter quoted Pelley as telling him, "There is no part of the broadcast that doesn't go through my hands."

The reporter is Tom Crabtree of WSPA-TV, a long-time newsman at the CBS affiliate in Spartanburg, South Carolina. His article is posted at the station's website, www2.wspa.com.

Let's look at some scripts that Pelley broadcast:

"It's not quite the fountain of youth, but researchers tell us tonight they have found new clues to the aging process." (Nov. 3, 2011) *Tell us tonight?* The previous day, Nov. 2, *The New York Times* published a long article about the findings. Neither Pelley nor the CBS medical correspondent credited the Mayo Clinic. The *Times* did. So did the article posted by cbsnews.com at 10:42 a.m., Nov. 3, eight hours before Pelley said researchers **"tell us tonight."**

Pelley had another problem on the *Evening News*: **"In a practical sense, what is a doctor and a patient supposed to do with this information?"** (Nov. 1, 2011) *Is?* Should be *are*.

When not anchoring, Pelley is a correspondent for CBS's *60 Minutes,* where he also had trouble with subject-verb agreement. **"There's almost a thousand agents representing N-F-L players...."** (Oct. 9, 2011) Correct: *There are*. Better: "Almost a thousand agents represent N-F-L players."

Both Pelley the anchor and Pelley the managing editor slipped up again on the *Evening News*: **"That begs the question: can the airport be fined under the passenger bill of rights?"** (Oct. 31, 2011) *Begs the* *question* doesn't mean "raises the question." A grammarian at *The New York Times* reminds us that it means "to use an argument that assumes as proved the very thing one is trying to prove." Which is why editors beg their reporters not to misuse "beg the question."

Pelley: **"The district attorney in Orange County, California, said today he will seek the death penalty in yesterday's mass shooting at a beauty salon."** (Oct. 14, 2011) But it wasn't *yesterday*; it was two days before.

"Drama at the manslaughter trial against Michael Jackson's doctor." (Oct. 31, 2011) Trials aren't held *against* anyone. It was the trial *of*.

"There was news in Libya today." (June 7, 2011) Isn't there news from Libya every day? Go ahead and report the news instead of eating up time announcing your newscast has news?

After a correspondent delivered a report from Libya, Pelley said delightedly, **"Original reporting. Barry Petersen, thank you."** (Sept. 1, 2011) Isn't *original reporting* routine? Pelley had never mentioned *original reporting* before on the air, and he hasn't mentioned it since.

When Pelley moved into the anchor chair in June, CBS advertised: "What if you can have the world-class original reporting of *60 Minutes* every weeknight? Well, now you can." CBS didn't talk up *original reporting* again until August when it released a video that boasted that CBS invented *original reporting*. But David Shedden, library director of the Poynter Institute, quickly said, "No one person or network invented original reporting on TV."

Pelley: **"There's news tonight on a story that Sharyl Attkisson broke on this broadcast."** (June 15, 2011) News about a story? Besides, starting a story with *there is* or *there are* is usually not good. (There are exceptions.) *Is* and its various forms—*are, were, was, has been, will be*— are linking verbs, so they don't express any action.

Pelley again: **"Good evening. Herman Cain, the front runner for the Republican presidential nomination, could not have been more clear about it. He said, quote, I have never sexually harassed anyone. Endquote."** In that script, Pelley violated a broadast newswriting no-no by saying "quote" and "endquote." The first news director of CBS, Paul W. White, wrote in *News on the Air,* a book published in 1947, "Remember, that since the word 'quote' is foreign to the ear as far as ordinary conversation is concerned, it probably always is disturbing to the listener." In the same year, Burton Hotaling wrote in *A Manual of Radio News Writing,* "Thoughtless use of such hackneyed terms as 'quote' and 'endquote' tend to interrupt the listener's thought." In 1948, Mitchell Charnley wrote in *News by Radio,* "Such phrases as 'and I quote' and 'end quote' are...shunned by skillful writers." R. H. MacDonald said in his *Broadcast Manual of Style* (1994), the use of *quote* and *unquote* is "a holdover from the ancient days of sending news by telegraph when the sending operator wanted to be certain the receiving end knew the limits of the quoted material." There are various ways to avoid *quote* and *unquote*: "as she put it," "in her words," "as he called it." Robert Papper says in his *Broadcast News Writing Stylebook,* "Few statements are so strong that we need to quote them." And the AP's 1972 *Broadcast News Style Book* said using direct quotation in stories is "lazy writing."

More Pelley: **"It now looks like the United States will not default for the first time in its history."** (Aug. 1, 2011) Whatever else that ambiguous sentence may say, it does say that for the first time, the U.S. will not default.

"How some people are living in their homes for free, next." (Pelley, June 29, 2011) *For free* is a solecism. Free = at no cost. No need for *for.*

More misusage: **"Casiano tried to convince the villagers to come to a meeting...."** (Oct. 4, 2011) *Convince* can be followed by *that* or *of*; *persuade* is followed by *to.*

"This story is amazing. A court case in southern India has led to an astounding discovery." (July 5, 2011) Journalism 101: Don't characterize news as good or bad, amazing or astounding, shocking or disturbing; just tell the story. On the same newscast, Pelley said, **"News today of an astounding public school cheating scandal."** *Astounding*? Such scandals are abounding. But on June 12, he used *astounding* in two sentences in a row. In his *60 Minutes* story about *The*

Scott Pelley

King's Speech, Pelley said, **"Wow, what an astounding thing. What an astounding thing."**

More gee whizzery: gaining fast in frequency on the *Evening News* is *incredible*. After the medical correspondent delivered the report about mice and the aging process, Pelley said: **"Jon, thank you very much. Incredible."** (Nov. 3, 2011)

Major has also become a major word in Pelley's newscasts. He used *major* twice on Aug. 18, 2011, and three correspondents also used it. Even an interviewee used it. When everything is *major*, nothing is *major*.

Then there's Pelley's *we-we* problem. Apparently he doesn't want to seem self-centered, so instead of saying *I*, he says *we*: **"With the economy struggling, we were surprised today when we were booking flights for the holidays. Some of the prices we were getting seemed to have climbed so high so fast that we asked Anna Werner to find out what's going on with the airlines."** (Oct. 12, 2011) Four *we's*. Whee! Mark Twain said, "Only kings, presidents, editors, and people with tapeworms have the right to use the editorial 'we.'"

Another problem: Pelley's on-air thank-you's to correspondents. He varies from a simple "thank you" to "thank you very much." But in acknowledging a reply from a correspondent, he unloosed a **"thank you, very, very, much.**" (Jan. 4, 2012)

More Pelley: **"We got word today that the nation's largest bank—Bank of America—is about to charge a fee of five dollars a month for the privilege of making a purchase with a credit card."** (Sept. 29, 2011) *We got word*? Sounds as if CBS had an inside source, but, in fact, the AP moved the story six hours earlier, at 12:34 p.m. ET. Pelley's script could have skipped **"we got word"** and started, "The nation's largest bank...."

Pelley asked an aviation expert, **"What will this mean for pilots going forward?"** (Dec, 21, 2011) *Going forward* has the thud of business-speak. Not only does it sound like Wall Street jargon, but it's also excess baggage. If Pelley had ditched *going forward*, his question would have meant the same thing. But he seems fond of *going forward*. Several years ago, a *Financial Times* columnist dismembered *going forward* and observed, "No one would ever say: 'Will you marry me going forward?'"

Pelley is also fond of *learned*. He uses that word often: **"As you know already, North Korea attempted to send a rocket into space, but it ended in failure last night. We've learned that less than two minutes after the launch, the first stage burned out roughly as planned and splashed down 100 miles west of Seoul, South Korea...."** (April 13,

2012) *As you know already?* Betcha never heard an anchor say that before. Would you be inspired to stay tuned if an anchor said you already know what he's about to tell you? In any case, how does Pelley know what six million viewers know? Better: "North Korea tried to send a rocket into space last night but failed." Relying on the CBS script's information, the rewrite is tighter, gets to the point faster, and stresses the key word, *failed.*

The rocket was fired shortly before 7 p.m. ET, April 12, the night before. At 7 p.m., April 12, CNN reported the rocket failure. So why didn't Pelley find a second-day lead rather than a last-night lead? At least, Pelley didn't call the rocket breakup *breaking news.*

When newscasters learn something, they can go ahead and report what they've learned with no need to say they've learned it. Everything they broadcast is something they've learned, right? After you look out a window, would you ever say, "I've learned that it's raining"? When newsies use *learned,* they generally mean they've acquired information no competitor has.

We got word? Sounds as if CBS had an inside source, but, in fact, the AP moved the story six hours earlier, at 12:34 p.m. ET.

In another learning experience, Pelley said: **"A major terrorist plot was stopped just in time at the Afghan defense headquarters in Kabul. CBS News has learned that 11 explosive vests were found yesterday near a parking lot where Afghan soldiers were supposed to board 11 buses...."** (March 27, 2012) CBS News *has learned?* Sounds as if CBS had obtained inside information. By 6:30 p.m. ET, when Pelley began his newscast, every newshawk and newsdove on the planet would have—or could have—already learned about the 11 vests. An Afghan website (Khaama Press) posted the story at 11:20 a.m., Kabul time (2:50 a.m. ET). NBC News's website posted the story at 4:54 a.m. ET. CBS News itself posted it no later than 6:09 a.m. ET, perhaps earlier. The AP, UPI, BBC, ITV and Sky News ran the story at various times from the middle of the night till the middle of the day (and beyond). So Pelley couldn't help learning it.

Pelley: **"In Pakistan, there is a power struggle brewing that you should know about....So this will bear watching in the days ahead."** (Jan. 11, 2012) If I need to know about it, please watch it and keep me posted. I don't even care about the power struggle in this country— between advocates of wind power and advocates of solar power

"The speech happened over the weekend." (June 21, 2011) Speeches don't *happen*. Accidents happen. Speeches take place. Or occur. Someone (perhaps Pelley) let Pelley down twice in one short sentence: **"He pled guilty to a minor misdemeanor."** (*60 Minutes,* August 21, 2011) The past tense of *plead* is *pleaded*, not *pled*. *Minor misdemeanor?* A misdemeanor is a minor offense.

The m.e. of the *Evening News* let the anchor down another time: **"The economy is hitting young Americans especially hard, according to the Census Bureau today."** (*Evening News*, Sept. 22, 2011) In broadcast newswriting, when attribution is needed, attribution precedes assertion. Knowledgeable broadcast newswriters know that attribution is never tacked on the end of a sentence, which is print style. *Television News Writing*, a 1958 book by the staff of CBS News, said, "...always say who before you say what someone said or did...The viewer is entitled to know the authority for a statement or action first so that he can gauge what importance to attach to it as the newscaster relates it." The *BBC News Styleguide* says that more colorfully: "Broadcasters should always identify the source of an assertion before making it...You would not say to a friend: 'I am a dissolute, disreputable failure, a moral vacuum with no discernible redeeming features. That's what my wife said last night.' You would naturally put the attribution first: 'My wife says I'm a dissolute....' That's the way we speak, and it's the way we should write news stories."

Pelley also has a weakness for strained transitions: **"...the T-S-A says that starting this week, children under 12 won't be subjected to patdowns as often as they have been, and they will no longer be required to remove their shoes."** He stretched those shoes when he introduced the next item: **"We wondered whether the candidates were going to be throwing shoes at the Republican presidential debate last night."** (Sept. 13, 2011)

Right after an *Evening News* correspondent reported on wildfires and firefighters, Pelley tried to tie the next item to the previous item: **"There was a bit of a fire of sorts in Miami today. The Martins suspended their new manager for five games after he caused an uproar in the city...."** (April 10, 2012) No, the Martins didn't fire him. What gave away Pelley's puerile game was his use of *a bit* and *of sorts*. Maybe Pelley was impelled to say what he did by a burning sensation.

"How did murderers get to work at the governor's mansion as trustees?" (Jan. 12, 2012) Although the workers were trusties—convicts worthy of trust—Pelley called them trustees, a term for someone who hold legal title to a trust. A corporate director is also a trustee. So is someone to whom something is entrusted.

A grammatical glitch: **"Swept away, millions of tons of tsunami debris is headed for U-S shores.** (Feb. 28, 2012) Subject-verb disagreement. The tons of debris *are.*

Pelley: **"If you reach the point of having a successful manned flight, what will you have proven?"** (*60 Minutes*, March 18, 2012) The AP stylebook says, "Use proven only as an adjective: *a proven remedy.*" The verb needed in that excerpt is *proved.* Other stylebooks say the same.

Pelley: **"When we were reporting the results in Iowa last Tuesday, the big surprise was how well Rick Santorum did. But New Hampshire is a very different place. Bill Whitaker is with the former Pennsylvania governor tonight. Bill?"** (Jan. 10, 2012) An even bigger surprise: hearing that Santorum had been governor of Pennsylvania. He had been a senator there, never governor.

From what we've seen, Pelley the anchor *needs* Pelley the managing editor to start governing.

(November 9, 2011)

Anchors', Reporters'
Use of Confirmed Questionable

Ever wonder about anchors' saying a story has been *confirmed*? Wonder what they mean by *confirmed*? Wonder why they use that word at all? Wonder whether it's as meaningless, or misleading, or mendacious, say, as *exclusive*, or *breaking news* or *happening right now*?

The *CBS Evening News* presents many stories, but seldom does the anchor Scott Pelley say CBS has *confirmed* a story. In one recent week, though, Pelley twice told viewers that CBS News had confirmed a story.

In the first of the two stories, Pelley said, about 6:50 p.m. ET, **"CBS News has confirmed today that** [Sen. John] **Kerry will help the president prepare for his three debates against** [Mitt] **Romney...."** (June 18, 2012) Better to skip *CBS News has confirmed today that* and plunge straight into the news, as in this sentence: "President Obama has chosen Senator John Kerry to play the role of Mitt Romney to help the president prepare for his debates with Romney."

At 4:33 p.m. ET, 2 hours and 20 minutes before Pelley spoke of confirmation, the CBS News website itself reported the "Obama campaign" had "confirmed to CBS News" Kerry's role.

More than six hours before Pelley went on the air, *The Washington Post*'s Philip Rucker and Dan Balz had broken the story: "President Obama has tapped Sen. John Kerry, the 2004 Democratic presidential nominee, to play Republican Mitt Romney in mock debate rehearsals, Obama campaign officials and the senator's office confirmed Monday."

At 12:22 p.m. ET, Rucker tweeted the posting of the story and tipped off the world.

At 3:43 p.m., among many other websites that posted the news (some were updates), politico.com said "an Obama campaign official confirms to Politico" the selection of Kerry.

At 4:20 p.m. *The Wall Street Journal* posted the story.

At 4:39 p.m., *New York* magazine quoted the announcement by the Obama campaign.

At 4:55 p.m. thecaucus.com, the politics and government blog of *The New York Times*, posted the story.

At 5:21 p.m., The Associated Press quoted a Democratic officlal as saying Kerry had been chosen.

At 5:33 p.m., Reuters posted the Kerry story.

Four nights after Pelley *confirmed* the Kerry story, he called that verb into service again: **"Pentagon correspondent David Martin has confirmed this evening that Syria shot down a Turkish jet fighter over the Mediterranean Sea."** (June 22, 2012) *Confirmed?* The shootdown wasn't exactly a secret. It had been reported repeatedly much of the day by the AP, AFP and Reuters (among others); and they provided abundant attribution.

At 11:37 a.m. ET, Reuters said Syria had shot down the Turkish jet. At 2:02 p.m. ET, *International Business Times* reported that Syria had acknowledged shooting down the Turkish jet. And at 5:16 p.m. the CBS News website posted an AP story quoting Turkey's prime minister as saying Syria had shot down the Turkish jet.

Ordinarily, broadcast writers treat AP copy as though it were written by a staff writer and did not need confirmation unless. Unless what the AP is reporting seems highly unlikely.

So Pelley *confirmed* two stories no longer in need of confirmation.

When an anchor announces that his newsroom has confirmed a story, it eats up precious time and raises questions:

How about all those other stories not *confirmed?* Are they only hearsay?

Why did Pelley announce the confirmation of those two stories but of no other items on those newscasts? Or any other newscast that month?

Don't reporters confirm *all* stories before broadcasting them?

Once a reporter pins down the facts and determines a story is true, the anchor can go ahead and report it as a fact.

An anchor's saying his team *confirmed* a story sounds as if they had done something above and beyond what's called for. Declaring a story *confirmed* may strike some viewers as a noteworthy accomplishment. And to some viewers, *confirmed* may sound as though the anchor is breaking the news.

Confirmed was also put to work on a weekend edition of the *CBS Evening News*. The anchor, Jeff Glor, said (July 15, 2012), **"In this country, the Food and Drug Administration is under fire tonight...."** Under fire even on a Sunday night?

Glor then introduced a correspondent, Jan Crawford, who is CBS's political correspondent and chief legal correspondent. She said: **"Well, Jeff, I mean, this is really quite a story that's been uncovered by the New York Times.** [Don't sell it, tell it. The *Times* had posted the article the previous day, sometime before 4:59 p.m.—the time of the first comment.] **I mean** [*mean* again?]**, think about this.** [If you *think on these things*, (to lift a line from the New Testament), Crawford didn't say whether she was adding any information to the *Times* account.] **According to the Times, the F-D-A was secretly monitoring e-mail accounts of its own scientists...the Times discovered some 80-thousand pages of documents the F-D-A secretly monitored. Confirmed by CBS News, they include a letter the scientists wrote...."** *Confirmed* what? Confirmed the count of the 80,000+ pages? Confirmed the contents? Confirmed that the story was dug up by the *Times*?

Diane Sawyer, anchor of ABC's *World News*, and Brian Williams, anchor of NBC's *Nightly News*, also announce, infrequently, that their newsrooms have confirmed stories. And some of their correspondents, too, sometimes say they've confirmed a story. They might use *confirm* to give heft to a bland or routine story. Or to make it seem they're adding fresh work to a story already reported.

Brian Williams, on his 6:30 p.m. newscast, said: **"First, Herman Cain, the current front-runner,** [how about making this a complete sentence by inserting *is*?] **forced to answer allegations of sexual harassment first reported by the website Politico. Tonight NBC News has confirmed that two women accused Cain of inappropriate sexual conduct while he was C-E-O of the National Restaurant Association, and that at least one of them received a financial** [settlement]." (Oct. 31, 2011) Why acknowledge Politico's story unless you believe what Politico reported is true? And if you accept it as true, why say you've confirmed it? So why is he telling us that?

Politico had posted the nub of its story about 24 hours earlier. Politico went on to say its information had been confirmed by "multiple sources." At 8:26 p.m., The Daily Beast reported the Politico story. At 9:24 p.m., the Huffington Post picked it up. At 10:09 p.m., CBS News posted an article about Politico's story and the Cain campaign's denial of the allegations.

At 11:04 p.m., the AP moved an article about Politico's story that carried Cain's denials of misconduct. And at 10:58 p.m., the British *Guardian* ran the story and quoted Politico as saying that at least two women had accused Cain of improper behavior.

On Oct. 31, when Brian Williams said NBC News had confirmed that two women accused Cain, Cain or members of his staff had been denying any misbehavior since the night before. And on the day of Williams's broadcast, The Daily Beast said in its online blog: "Cain spent Monday morning [Oct. 31] denying he was ever accused of sexual harassment against two women in the 1990s. Then he acknowledged the allegations but said they were 'false' and 'baseless' while saying he knew 'nothing' of a cash settlement." So that evening Williams was confirming what was already widely known.

One of the most unusual confirmations by an anchor occurred on June 8, 2011. Diane Sawyer told viewers about the criticism of Congressman Anthony Weiner, with some other Democrats calling for his resignation. She said allies were abandoning him but that one exception was his wife. Then the correspondent Claire Shipman said Weiner's wife, Huma Abedin, is **"facing even more unwelcome scrutiny of her private life tonight: ABC News has confirmed she's expecting her first child with embattled husband Anthony Weiner."** Remember that word *embattled*. At 5:11 p.m., an hour and 19 minutes before the ABC newscast, *The New York Times* reported Mrs. Weiner's pregnancy. The *Times* attributed the news to three unnamed people "with knowledge of the situation." Weiner himself, the *Times* story said, "has admitted to engaging in salacious online conversations with at least six women."

Twenty-nine minutes after the *Times* story was posted, at 5:40 p.m., the ABC News website said: "ABC News's Devin Dwyer reports: Embattled [the word later used by Shipman] Rep. Anthony Weiner of New York and his wife...are expecting a child, ABC News has learned. News of the pregnancy, which was first reported by the New York Times, comes as the couple..."

First reported by the New York Times? Was ABC acknowledging that it *learned* about the pregnancy by reading the *Times?*

Even before Dwyer (or a colleague) read *The New York Times* story, other websites were posting the news and crediting the *Times* with breaking the story. Some of those who credited the *Times* before Shipman said ABC News had confirmed the story: NPR, TMZ, Mediaite, *People* and *The Washington Post*.

I wonder how ABC News *confirmed* the story so fast—by finding Mrs. Weiner's OB/GYN and questioning her (or him) or re-reading the *Times* story?

After poking around the Internet for this article about the use—and misuse—of *confirmed*, I find my darkest suspicions confirmed.

(July 18, 2012)

60 Minutes Story About Singer Hits False Note

Ever hear something on the air that stops you cold? And makes you wonder, "Could that be true?" That happened to me recently while watching CBS's newsmagazine, *60 Minutes*. A correspondent began his story:

"Just what is it that sets Placido Domingo apart from the greats of the operatic stage? Well, look up 'applause' in the Guinness Book of Records, and you'll see that an audience cheered him after a performance for an hour and 20 minutes nonstop. Fair to say no audience in history has ever seen anything quite like it, and for opera, that's just the problem. After Domingo, then what?" (May 16, 2004)

What stopped me was *nonstop*. And how could the correspondent, Scott Pelley, know that no audience in history has ever seen anything quite like it? Has a central registry been keeping stats on all gatherings since the Stone Age?

Curious, I followed Pelley's suggestion and looked up *applause*. Turned out, though, the index to *Guinness World Records 2004* does not list *applause*. And no *clapping*, no *curtain call*s. Nor does the index of last year's *Guinness* list *applause*. And no *Domingo*, either. Same for the index of the 2005 *Guinness*: no *applause*, no *clapping*, no *curtain calls*, no *Domingo*. The correspondent referred to the *Guinness Book of Records*, but the book has not carried that title for five years.

You can find the purported event through the index of the 2002 *Guinness*—but not by looking up *applause*; there is no such entry. You need to look up *Domingo*. The entry credits the *longest applause* to him for "1 hr. 20 min. through 101 curtain calls after a performance of Otello... at the Vienna Staatsoper...." Then you'll see a date for the performance: July 30, 1991. The year is right, but *Guinness* has the month wrong. The correct date: June 30.

At first, my raising questions about the *60 Minutes* story seemed like a trivial pursuit. But the more I poked around, the more my search became a

82

reportorial challenge: tracking down sources and trying to sort out conflicting information, all in an effort to find the cause of Pelley's bad start.

Back to our fact-finding expedition: Domingo's *longest applause* in 1991 might have occurred too late for inclusion in the 1992 *Guinness* but probably not too late for the 1993 *Guinness*. Yet, if you look up *applause* in the '93 index, you're referred to *clapping*. And that leads to: "Most curtain calls. On 24 Feb. 1988, Luciano Pavarotti...received 165 curtain calls and was applauded for 1 hr. 7 min. after singing the part of Nemorino in...Donizetti's *L'elisir* [correct: *L'Elisir*] *d'Amore* at the Deutsche Oper in Berlin...." But no mention of *Domingo*.

Even so, the Guinness website currently includes both Pavarotti's and Domingo's ovations. Of Domingo, the site says: "Thunderous clapping echoed around [how about *inside*?] the Vienna Staatsopher [no *h*] on the warm summer evening of July [*sic*] 30, 1991, for one hour and 20 minutes, setting a new record [my goodness, Guinness, *new record* is redundant] for the world's longest applause ever [*ever*? anywhere? for anything?]. The audience, who [*which*] had just reveled in a performance of a lifetime by Placido Domingo in Othello [*sic*], responded by rising to their feet and clapping through encore after encore—101 curtain calls to be exact." (*Encore*? An encore is a plea by an audience for an additional performance, or it's the performance itself. Guinness doesn't specify.)

The first time a Guinness book reported the 1991 Otello ovation—the "longest applause"—came in the 1998 edition, seven years after the event. The Domingo item was printed right below *Pavarotti* and his curtain calls. The Domingo entry also ran in the next two editions. The 2001 book skipped it, but it reappeared in 2002, then disappeared.

If you accept the Guinness website's entries, Pavarotti's audience in Berlin apparently applauded twice as fast as Domingo's audience in Vienna: the Berliners registered one curtain call every 24.3 seconds, more than two a minute; Viennese registered one every 47.5 seconds. How did Berlin outclap Vienna, 2-1? Maybe the Berliners clapped more briskly. Maybe the Viennese clapped in waltz time. Or the scorekeeper's stopwatch malfunctioned.

An on-stage observer of the Otello in question—and a leading participant, too—was the baritone Sherrill Milnes. He recalled, as quoted in *Placido Domingo: My Operatic Roles*:

> There were 58 curtain calls [after Domingo's first *Otello*, in Hamburg, Germany, in 1975], but believe it or not, this is not the most we got after an *Otello*. That record goes to the last of a run

of performances at the Vienna State Opera in 1989 (*Guinness* said *1991*), which also happened to be the last performance of the season. Again, Katia [Ricciarelli] was Desdemona, and the conductor was Michael Schoenwandt. Right from the start, we felt a sort of electricity in the air, the feeling that tonight the stars are in the right place—a Sternstunde [great moment], as it's rightly called in German—and by the end of our Act II Otello-Iago duet, the place exploded! It went berserk! And at the end, we took our bows, the soli, the tutti, and half an hour or 40 or 50 curtain calls after, we were still there. By then we were all getting tired of smiling, the way that you do at wedding receptions, and finally an hour and a half and 101 curtain calls later, we got away!

Although Domingo sang the title role in the Vienna Otello, that account did not single out Domingo as the recipient of the audience's plaudits. Rather, in that account, in the book (by Helena Matheopoulos, published in 2000), Milnes spoke of the cast's sharing the acclaim. He used *we* and *our* several times and *tutti* (Italian for *all*).

In 1989, the year Milnes was talking about, *Schoenwandt*—according to Tenorissimo.com—did not conduct a Vienna *Otello*. But the site, which calls itself Domingo's official website, notes he conducted the *Otello* there on June 30, 1991. (PlacidoDomingo.com also calls itself Domingo's official site.) Tenorissimo.com quotes the *Hamburger Abendblatt* of July 2, 1991, as saying Domingo received 80 minutes of bravos, flowers and standing ovations.

But a newspaper in Vienna—not cited by the Domingo websites—described the ovation there on June 30, 1991, as a salute to the stars and a tribute to the departing director of Vienna's State Opera. In its review on July 2, *Die Presse* said there had been 101 curtain calls in an hour and a half. That's 10 minutes longer than reported by Guinness and the German paper.

The first paragraph in the *Die Presse* review also said the audience had put the final touch to the end of an era. And said many friends of the director's had come to thank him one more time. Above the article, the head focused on the departure of the director.

Otello ordinarily runs two hours ten minutes. Which means the "longest applause" ran more than half as long as the opera. Did the entire audience hang around all that time or only a claque?

Eight months after the "longest applause," in February 1992, a British magazine, *Classic CD*, ran an article saying Domingo had received "the world's longest standing ovation, one hour and 50 minutes." In Barcelona. In 1986.

Since 1991, more than 20 other magazines (all linked from Tenoris-simo.com) have carried long cover stories on Domingo. In only one did I find a reference to a record: *Télérama* of Dec. 9, 1998. The French magazine said Domingo had made it into "the Book of Records" (not further identified) after receiving an ovation of 75 minutes and 87 curtain calls. In Vienna. In 1986.

In 1994, the BBC published Placido Domingo's *Tales from the Opera*. But one tale it didn't carry was that of Domingo's "record" of 1991. So I recently e-mailed the author, Daniel Snowman, in London, and asked in a P.S.: "Which singer has had the longest applause for a performance? Which opera? Where? When?" Snowman turned the question around and asked me, "What's the answer to your PS???" I told him I didn't know. He responded, "I remember Placido telling me in 1983 that he and [Mirella] Freni had eighty-odd curtain calls over a period of one-and-a-quarter hours at the end of a Vienna *Bohème*!" Snowman had written about that ovation in his *The World of Placido Domingo*, published in 1985.

Snowman's recollection is echoed in *Placido Domingo* by Cornelius Schnauber, published in 1994: "Just how enthusiastic the Viennese audience can wax over Domingo is demonstrated by the fact that he once received a seventy-five-minute ovation and 83 curtain calls following a performance of *La Bohème* there. This one event assured him a place in the *Guinness Book of World Records* as being the singer with the longest applause in the history of opera." But Guinness has never proclaimed the *La Bohème* ovation a record.

I asked Dr. Schnauber, an associate professor at the University of Southern California, whether that "record" (of 1983) still stands. He e-mailed: "Yes, it is still a record."

What does the Vienna Staatsoper itself have to say? I sent an e-mail asking who held the record there for applause. The reply (from Brigitta Wutscher in the press office): "It is not possible to answer your request in a real honest kind because the time of applause was never measured."

So I wrote back and asked her, again in English, about curtain calls. No reply. But my translator, Annette Leyssner, a German student in the Graduate School of Journalism, Columbia University, phoned Vienna's Staatsoper and spoke with a man in the press office. Then she e-mailed me: "As far as they are concerned, Ljuba [Welitsch] got the most [curtain calls] for *Salome*. But they were not very precise and said it was in the Fifties...they keep no official statistics [but the curtain calls] went on for 'about 45 minutes.'"

Again I asked Brigitta Wutscher about the record for curtain calls at Vienna's Staatsoper, this time with the help of my translator, who e-mailed my questions in German. That brought a reply. My translator e-mailed me: "Wutscher says 'it is said' that the *La Bohème* under Karajan got [the] most curtains in 1977. She is not sure if it's true, as they keep no statistics."

Thus, the Staatsoper's press office gave two different answers about curtain-call records there, one suggesting a *La Bohème*, the other a *Salome*. But both press people said they do not keep such records. And neither person at the Staatsoper mentioned Domingo's *Otello* in Vienna in 1991—the one that Pelley was apparently alluding to.

Still another book, *The Private Lives of the Three Tenors: Behind the Scenes with Placido Domingo, Luciano Pavarotti and José Carreras*, published in 1996, discusses the careers of the singers, but it mentions neither Domingo's "longest applause" nor Pavarotti's "most curtain calls." The author was Marcia Lewis. (She's the mother of Monica Lewinsky. That's another story.)

Likewise, *Placido Domingo: Opera Superstar* by David Goodnough, published in 1997, says nothing about the purported *nonstop* applause.

The 1997 *Guinness Book of Records* carried an item about Pavarotti's curtain calls in 1988, but even by 1997, Guinness still had not printed one word about Domingo's applause in 1991. If you look up *applause* in the '97 *Guinness*, you're referred to *clapping* and *curtain calls*. But when you go to the first page listed for *clapping*, the word *clapping* doesn't appear. Yet you will find on that page Pavarotti's "most curtain calls."

Right after the Pavarotti item, the 1997 hardcover *Guinness* gives half a page to about 350 words on Domingo—and his photo. On the bottom half of the page, a photo of the Three Tenors—Domingo, Pavarotti and José Carreras—is accompanied by 175 or so words. The lead of the Domingo article: "Most roles performed, most recordings made, and the biggest-selling CD in classical music history; good things do come in threes for Placido Domingo." A page of pure puffery. Yet nothing about Domingo's "longest applause." Not until the next year, 1998, did an item about that applause (in 1991) debut in a Guinness book.

At the Guinness website, a man identified as Keeper of the Records says: "I maintain a vigilant watch to guarantee the accuracy and relevance of each and every Guinness World Record™, and my team of researchers operates with unswerving impartiality and commitment to veracity. A fact may only become a Guinness World Record™ when it's tested, verified and elevated above all suspicion."

The 29-volume *New Grove Dictionary of Music and Musicians*, published in 2001, has no entry for *applause, curtain calls* and *Guinness*. It says Domingo is "particularly identified with Verdi's *Otello*" but says nothing about his "longest applause." The four-volume *New Grove Dictionary of Opera* is also silent about it. This *Grove* was published almost 18 months after the Vienna *Otello*, but it quoted Guinness as saying the record for most curtain calls was held by Pavarotti.

Today, the online *Grove,* incorporating the 1998 edition of the opera dictionary, also quotes the Guinness item about Pavarotti's "record." Still nothing, though, about Domingo's (or anyone's) "record" for applause.

Let's review the key elements in the erroneous *60 Minutes* excerpt:

- Pelley, the *60 Minutes* correspondent, said you can find the Domingo-centric applausathon in the *Guinness Book of Records* by looking up *applause.* But you can't. Domingo's "record" is not mentioned in the three latest editions (2003, 2004 and 2005). Nor is the *Guinness Book of Records* the title of those editions. As we've also seen, *applause* is not even in the index of the latest edition to carry the Domingo item, *Guinness World Records 2002*.

- Both the 2002 *Guinness* and the Guinness website list the date of the "longest applause" as July 30, 1991. Correct: June 30.

- The Guinness website makes several other errors: it renders *Otello* (the correct spelling of the Verdi opera) as *Othello* (Shakespeare's spelling) and misspells Staatsoper. I e-mailed Guinness twice and asked about the Domingo and Pavarotti items. No reply.

- The press office at the Vienna Staatsoper, where the "longest applause" supposedly took place, says it keeps no records on the length of applause or the number of curtain calls.

- Guinness says the applause was for Domingo. And *60 Minutes* credits Guinness for that information. Yet, the way the singer Sherrill Milnes is quoted in *Placido Domingo: My Operatic Roles*, the applause was not for Domingo alone. And the contemporary account in Vienna's *Die Presse* said explicitly the ovation was not only for Domingo but also for his co-star and the departing director of the state opera.

- Guinness says the applause lasted an hour and 20 minutes. But Milnes, who sang in that *Otello*, is quoted as saying it lasted an hour and a half. Vienna's *Die Presse* says the same thing.

- Although the applause in Vienna's Staatsoper after that *Otello* was, by several accounts, extraordinary, most of them agree it was not intended for one person. An exception: Guinness's belated—and inaccurate—recounting.
- Pelley said the audience cheered Domingo for an hour and 20 minutes nonstop. I haven't found anyone else who says it was nonstop. Not even Guinness has called the applause nonstop.
- Pelley ended his opening by asking portentously, "After Domingo, then what?" My answer: Don't worry. Even after the King of Tenors, Enrico Caruso, made his final exit (in 1921), opera survived. From what I hear, it's still going strong.

Does it really matter whether the CBS correspondent got everything in his story right? After all, it wasn't the story of the century. And he didn't commit a hanging offense. But on a program produced by a network's news division, especially a program with the standing that *60 Minutes* enjoys, I expect everything to be true. Presenting a non-fact as a fact breaks faith with listeners who expect accuracy. (One fact not in dispute: Domingo is one of the greatest singers of our time, if not the greatest.)

Now it's time for the fat lady to singe; yes, she can scorch.

Was Domingo's "longest applause" plausible? And was that applause or applesauce?

(October 15, 2004)

Alas, Poor Couric

Now that critics have commented on Katie Couric's CBS debut—her legs, her set, her wardrobe, her makeup, her delivery, her sign-off and her perkiness, let's take a look at her words and see how Katie did. Or didn't.

In Katie's first week as anchor—and managing editor—of the *CBS Evening News*, one word that popped up on her newscast repeatedly was *exclusive*. She used it most often in connection with her interview with President Bush. She began promoting it on her first night, Tuesday, Sept. 5—the night before her "exclusive interview."

How exclusive was her *exclusive*? NBC's Brian Williams had what he called an "exclusive conversation" with President Bush on Aug. 29, eight days earlier. And on Sept. 7, Charlie Gibson had an interview with the president that ABC called *exclusive*.

Two of the leading national newspapers, *The New York Times* and *The Wall Street Journal* probably break more heavyweight stories than any other national news organizations, yet they never call them *exclusive*. A *Chicago Tribune* columnist wrote last week that he asked a network news executive the difference between an *interview* and an *exclusive interview*; the exec is quoted as replying, "Nine letters."

Katie trumpeted her first *exclusive* on her first CBS newscast: a photo of what she called *Vanity Fair*'s **"newest cover girl,"** Suri, the daughter of Tom Cruise and Katie Holmes. The magazine, Katie Couric said, **"has the baby picture everyone has been waiting for, and tonight so do we."** *The baby picture everyone has been waiting for? Everyone?* Include me out.

Another word that got a good play on the program: *unprecedented*. Couric used it twice the first night to describe a story by CBS's chief foreign correspondent, an interview with the Taliban 10 miles from a U.S. base in Afghanistan. In the opening headlines, Couric said the correspondent **"has an unprecedented encounter with al-Qaeda's best friend"**;

in her lead-in, Katie said the correspondent had **"unprecedented access to some Taliban fighters in one of their new strongholds….Here's her exclusive report."** Again, both of those high-octane words: *unprecedented* and *exclusive*.

The gist of the report: the Taliban are making a strong comeback. Even if CBS could be certain that no one else, including Middle Eastern networks, had interviewed the same group there, does CBS's coverage deserve a word, *unprecedented*, that's applied to the momentous? And deserved twice?

The next night, Sept. 6, Couric introduced another correspondent by saying, **"I really think this next story is going to knock your socks off."** Please don't tell me what effect you think a story is going to have on me; just tell me the story. I'll decide for myself whether it's socko.

That night, after chatting with her predecessor, Bob Schieffer, she said, **"Great to see you."** And at the end of a package, **"I just love that story."** Please don't gush all over me.

> Twice during her first week, Katie said *needless to say* and then went ahead and said it. If something is *needless to say*, why say it? *Needless to say* is needless to say.

On Friday, Sept. 8, she used *exclusive* twice, this time to describe an interview she had conducted for *60 Minutes*. In the interview, she spoke of a **"toxic brew"** that she said was *unprecedented*.

On her first night, Couric teased: **"Still ahead…it may be a record discovery of black gold** [where I come from, we call it oil] **in the Gulf of Mexico, but does it mean you'll be yelling 'Eureka' at the gas pump?"** No. I don't own a car. Even if I did, and even if the discovery in the Gulf led eventually to more gas at the pump. I'd have no reason to shout *Eureka*. But I might mutter, "That's highway robbery."

The discovery in the Gulf may not result in more gas any time soon—or ever. The next day's *New York Times* said: "It will take more than a year of drilling to confirm the value of the find…. The analysts cautioned that there was little likelihood the report would give drivers much relief at the pump because full production might not come on line for five years or more. By itself, it also appears that the discovery could make little more than a dent in the country's energy dependence."

In her *exclusive* interview with President Bush, Couric asked, **"Can** you give us any indication about what kind of information you were able to glean from these, quote-unquote, 'high-value targets'?" Avoid yes-or-no questions. And don't ask for an "indication"; ask for information. *Quote-unquote* is moldy.

No less an expert than CBS's first head of news, Paul W. White, "Please, please don't use 'unquote.'"

In *Writing Broadcast News Shorter, Sharper, Stronger* (advt.), I quote more than 20 authors of broadcast journalism manuals, stylebooks and textbooks who have echoed that advice.

Twice during her first week, Katie said *needless to say* and then went ahead and said it. If something is *needless to say*, why say it? *Needless to say* is needless to say.

She also tossed in—instead of out—a few clichés: **"But in the war on terror, you have to wonder, is it back to the drawing board?"** (Sept. 5) *Back to the drawing board* should have been sent back to the keyboard. So should *state of the art* (Sept. 6) and *political firestorm* (used by a correspondent on Sept. 7). Two days later, Couric reported *a storm of controversy*. And on *60 Minutes*, Sept. 10, she spoke of a *firestorm of criticism* and used another cliché—*added insult to injury*. Two nights later, on Sept. 12, she repeated a cliché (*picture-perfect*) she had used on her first night.

But let's give her a pass: she's new on the job.

(September, 2006)

Couric: When *Exclusive* News is
Not Exclusive—and Not Even News

"We're beginning tonight with a CBS News exclusive," Katie Couric said on May 16, 2007—**"another scandal in the aftermath of Hurricane Katrina. Many survivors of the killer storm are now getting sick,"** she said on the *Evening News,* **"and their government-provided trailers may be to blame. Nearly two years after Katrina, 86-thousand families are still living in FEMA** [Federal Emergency Management Agency] **trailers, and every day more and more of them are developing health problems. We have two reports tonight, beginning with our chief investigative correspondent, Armen Keteyian."**

Before we look at what he said, let's look again at what she said; she's the anchor and the managing editor:

"Many survivors...are now getting sick." True—but far from new. And certainly not exclusive. *Now getting sick?* Ten months earlier, msnbc.com ran an article, on July 25, 2006, titled: "Private testing finds high levels of formaldehyde; residents report illnesses." The residents were living in FEMA trailers.

Two weeks before Couric broadcast that lead-in on May 16, 2007, Dan Rather said on his program on HDNet, **"Now we're learning that some of these trailers appear to be toxic. And some of the people who moved into these temporary shelters say the trailers have been making them sick."** *Now* we're learning?

Rather's 20-minute (or so) *Toxic Trailers* began, on May 2, with Gulf Coast residents Paul and Melody Stewart of Bay St. Louis, Mississippi. Among others who figured in *Dan Rather Reports* that night were Becky Gillette and Dr. Scott Needle.

Three months earlier, Gillette, Dr. Needle and the Stewarts had been quoted in a long article posted at the *Nation*'s website (thenation.com) on Feb. 14. The article was titled "Dying for a Home: Toxic Trailers Are Making Katrina Refugees Sick."

Amanda Spake wrote in the article: "Along the Gulf Coast, in the towns and fishing villages from New Orleans to Mobile, survivors of Hurricane Katrina are suffering from a constellation of similar health problems. They wake up wheezing, coughing and gasping for breath. Their eyes burn; their heads ache; they feel tired, lethargic. Nosebleeds are common, as are sinus infections and asthma attacks. Children and seniors are most severely afflicted, but no one is immune." The author also mentioned Angela Orcutt, a teacher, and her three-year-old son, Nicky.

Four months after that article ran, Dr. Needle and both Orcutts showed up in the *exclusive* CBS package of May 16, 2007. After Couric's intro, presented above, Armen Keteyian featured snippets of interviews with them. He also interviewed a supervisor at a factory making trailers.

Keteyian said Dr. Needle, a pediatrician, was the first to notice that Nicky Orcutt was not alone in becoming ill. But the article at thenation. com in February said the doctor was "one of the first" to notice an unusual number of illnesses among trailer residents. Dr. Needle also appeared in Rather's story on May 2, 2007.

Keteyian said CBS **"has discovered this internal FEMA document that cites cancer as a potential job hazard for those just inspecting the trailers."** He also caught up with FEMA's top administrator, David Paulison, on Capitol Hill. Paulison said he hadn't heard that dozens of children were sick. Then a CBS Washington correspondent reported on several aspects of Katrina.

Dr. Needle, Becky Gillette, and Paul and Melody Stewart appeared in print together in a long article posted by msnbc.com on July 25, 2006. Seven months later, all of them, except Gillette, were quoted in the *Nation*'s article. Rather included Gillette in his story, along with Dr. Needle and the Stewarts.

Two nights after Keteyian's first report, Couric returned to the trailer troubles and again called CBS's story *exclusive*. She credited it with **"exposing an emerging health crisis."** And again she began by saying she was beginning:

"We're beginning tonight with a CBS News exclusive, a follow-up on our report exposing an emerging health crisis for thousands of survivors of Hurricane Katrina. As we reported earlier this week, many people living in trailers provided by FEMA are getting sick. Tonight we can tell you FEMA has known for a long time that the trailers are toxic but did little about it. CBS News chief investigative correspondent Armen Keteyian, who first broke this story, has the

follow-up tonight." (*First broke* is redundant. If you break a story, you *are* the first.)

Tonight we can tell you? With that, Couric seemed to imply that she was the first to bring that information to public attention. In fact, FEMA issued a news release on Aug. 8, 2006, headed, "FEMA To Test Methods To Reduce Formaldehyde In Travel Trailers."

The msnbc.com article of Aug. 4, 2006, by Mike Brunker, said FEMA's director of mobile home operations in Mississippi asserted the agency "has determined that there is a problem with elevated formaldehyde levels in 'two or three' of the at least 10 brands of travel trailers [supplied by FEMA after Katrina]."

Ten days later, on Aug. 14, 2006, cnn.com reported, "Last week, FEMA also announced it will begin testing its trailers for toxic levels of formaldehyde after people in the trailers complained of sickness and local officials and environmental groups raised concerns."

> A story CBS broke? Please, give me a break. The real story is that a network anchor persists in calling an old story new.

But, as widely reported, FEMA was not responsive, and Rather said on May 2, 2007, **"FEMA hasn't been listening."**

After Couric's lead-in on May 18, Keteyian said: **"Twenty-one months after Hurricane Katrina virtually blew the Gulf Coast off the map, some 86-thousand families still call these FEMA travel trailers home. As we reported earlier this week, formaldehyde fumes seeping from these trailers pose a serious health risk to some young children. On Wednesday, the man in charge at FEMA, David Paulison, had this to say on Capitol Hill."**

Paulison said on camera: "The formaldehyde issue was brought to our attention, and we actually went out and investigated. We used EPA and some other agencies to do testing. We've been told that the formaldehyde does not present a health hazard."

Two months later, on July 19, Couric said on the *Evening News*:

"A lot of people were outraged by our exclusive CBS News investigation two months ago, which found that thousands of Hurricane Katrina victims are living in trailers that are just plain unhealthy. Well, today the outrage spread to Congress, where House members accused FEMA of a cover-up. Two years after Katrina, 76-thousand

FEMA trailers are still being used to house families who lost their homes. Many of the trailers have high levels of formaldehyde, which can result in dangerous respiratory problems. Chief investigative correspondent Armen Keteyian's reporting triggered today's congressional hearing."

Then Keteyian reported:

"The chairman of the hearing, Congressman Henry Waxman, blasted the disaster relief agency for receiving multiple warnings about dangerous levels of formaldehyde in FEMA trailers that could lead to asthma, sinus infections and other breathing problems...."

Four nights later, on July 23, Couric was still crediting CBS's "chief investigative reporter" with breaking the story:

"And now an update on a story Armen [Keteyian] broke back in May about the health problems of Katrina refugees living in FEMA trailers. Congress heard reports last week that thousands of the trailers contained dangerously high levels of formaldehyde. But today FEMA said it will continue to sell and donate the trailers while government health officials test them."

A story CBS broke? Please, give me a break. The real story is that a network anchor persists in calling an old story new. And calling it *exclusive*. Give me another break.

(August 2007)

Couric: Time Twisting, Time Wasting and Other Problems

Although Katie Couric is her newscast's managing editor, she broadcasts many scripts that needed more editing. And she introduces correspondents whose scripts also needed more editing. Let's look at some of them and see what we can learn:

Some scripts suggest that Couric needs a new clock or new calendar. On March 21, a Wednesday, she said, **"The Coast Guard has just made a huge drug bust."** *Just?* The correspondent she tossed to went on to say, **"Acting on an intelligence tip, Coast Guard cutters and aircraft moved in Sunday on a 300-foot cargo ship off the coast of Panama...."** *Sunday*! The correspondent had it right; the seizure took place three days before Couric's newscast.

Further, the correspondent's sentence violated broadcast style. He began it with a participle, which is not conversational. No one would say at the dinner table, "Feeling hungry this afternoon, I grabbed a candy bar."

In the program's opening headlines, Couric said:

"Tonight, a major victory in the other war, the war on drugs. The Coast Guard boards a suspicious boat and makes one of the biggest drug busts ever, seizing tons of cocaine that was destined for the United States." Correct: *"were destined."* Better yet, delete *were* and make it: "tons of cocaine destined for the United States." Also, a 300-foot vessel, as the correspondent described it, is not a boat. A boat is a small craft, one that can usually be carried aboard a ship.

Then another *major victory*: Couric said, **"Saudi Arabia is claiming a major victory tonight in the war on terror."** (April 27, 2007) When she said that, it was 1:30 a.m. in Saudi Arabia. I doubt that they were claiming anything at that hour. In fact, the story had broken more than 12 hours earlier.

"A State Department report tonight says terror attacks worldwide are up sharply, along with the death toll." (April 30, 2007) The State

Department released that information at 4:15 p.m., not *tonight*. (NBC's *Nightly News* said, "Tonight the new report is out," ABC's *World News* said, "Today, the State Department released its worldwide survey....")

A tricky time element also figured in a lead-in delivered by Harry Smith, sitting in for Couric: **"An insurgent group with ties to al-Qaeda claimed responsibility tonight for the suicide bombing at the Iraqi parliament...."** (April 13, 2007) In fact, the insurgent group claimed responsibility for the bombing more than 12 hours earlier.

More scripts delivered by Couric:

"And there's a major recall to tell you about tonight." (March 16, 2007) Please don't waste time and tell me you're going to tell me. Just go ahead and tell me. (*Major* is a major word on all network evening newscasts.) *Tonight?* Why keep repeating that word? Viewers already know it's *tonight*. On May 8, Couric's newscast used *major* four times.

Couric: **"Did the U-S military try to rewrite history? That was the allegation on Capitol Hill today as...."** (April 24, 2007) That wasn't an allegation; that was a question. Another script, another question:

Couric began a story this way: **"And 18 seconds. Did you know that, on average, is how long doctors let patients describe their symptoms before cutting them off? Eighteen seconds."** (March 16, 2007) One second. That's how long Couric should have looked at that script before rewriting it. Or having it rewritten. The problem is, it backs into the story and opens with the key fact. No one speaks that way or tells a story that way. Would you ever say: "Dead. That's what Terry Taser is tonight. Dead"? As for question leads, how many viewers hurry home to watch the news so they can hear the latest questions?

That 18-second figure needs attribution. The doctor Couric interviewed did not use it, but he had used it elsewhere. In any case, the script was DOA.

"General Petraeus said the U-S military, quote, 'can never sink to the level of the enemy.'" (May 7, 2007) Using "quote" is an awkward way of introducing a quotation. "Quote" is an ugly word. People don't use it in ordinary conversation. Better: "General Petraeus said the U-S military—in his words—'can never sink to the level of the enemy.'" Still better in almost all cases: paraphrase the quotation.

"And here at home, Virginia Governor Tim Kaine made good on his promise to close the legal loophole law that allowed...." (April 30, 2007) *Legal loophole law?* Sounds strange. *Here at home?* Virginia is not my home.

"In two short weeks, we'll know if France will have its first woman president." (April 23, 2007) All weeks are the same length.

"It all began here just over a year ago and sent shock waves across the nation." (April 11, 2007) *Shock waves*? What might be shocking is that a network evening newscast would use a cliché older than Methuselah. (Time to find some younger clichés.)

"If you're wondering what to pack these days and what products you can't bring on a plane, it has changed again." (Sept. 25, 2006) What is the antecedent of *it*? Also: You *take* products on a plane. *Bring* and *take* are used in relation to the speaker: "Please bring me another glass," but "Please take that glass away."

"Coming up next: more and more of our food comes from China, but how safe is it? You might not like what we found out." (April 26, 2007) What I dislike is an anchor's telling me what my reaction to a story might be.

> *Shock waves*? What might be shocking is that a network evening newscast would use a cliché older than Methuselah.

"And don't forget: for more on the Virginia Tech story, including the very latest details and pictures, you can go to our website...." (April 16, 2007) The *latest* is the latest. Nothing can be later than the latest, not even *the very latest*.

Some of the faulty scripts on the *Evening News* were broadcast by correspondents:

"Investigators bugged more than 90 phone lines, sifted through 27,000 hours of video...." (April 30, 2007) Phones are tapped, not bugged.

"After three years, Tiger Woods [a South China tiger named for the golfer] **and the others are successfully able to hunt for themselves."** (March 27, 2007) *Successfully able* says the same thing twice.

"Shortly after the vote and one day after House Speaker Nancy Pelosi chided Mister Bush to take a deep breath...." (March 29, 2007) *Chide* means "scold mildly." It isn't followed by "to." You can *persuade* someone to do something, but you can't chide him to.

"And she wasn't thrilled about him going." (March 16, 2007) Should be "*his* going." Reason: a pronoun preceding a gerund should usually be possessive.

"The government has no appetite for regulating the food companies now, so parents better watch what their kids eat...." (March 29, 2007) Should be *had better*. "Sadr has been laying low since the troop surge began...." (April 9, 2007) Should be *lying* low. We'll review *lie* and *lay* in Part 5, "Networks Mangle and Strangle Language."

"You hear these kind of boasts...." (Sept. 14, 2006) Should be *this kind of boast* or *these kinds of boasts.*

"In a sworn affidavit, Goodling claims a senior official...." (March 26, 2007) *Sworn affidavit* is redundant. An affidavit is a sworn statement. If it isn't sworn, it isn't an affidavit.

And if scripts aren't edited rigorously, they aren't ready for broadcast, certainly not by a network.

(May 2007)

Producer Says My Article
About *Evening News* Had Errors

A senior producer in CBS's investigative unit, Keith Summa, has written to me and pointed out what he called "errors" in my article "Couric: When *Exclusive* News is Not Exclusive—And Not Even News."

Below are his letter and my point-by-point reply.

Dear Mr. Block:

As a former journalist, we know you are as concerned about accuracy in reporting as we are at CBS News. So, we would like to address some errors in your blog posting of August 2, 2007, concerning our series of reports on the *CBS Evening News* with Katie Couric about the formaldehyde problem with FEMA trailers.

You wrote that our stories were neither exclusives nor news. However, as the following list of details about our reportage makes clear, they were exactly that:

The *CBS Evening News* reported, for the first time, on never-before-seen documents that revealed FEMA itself had testing data showing that formaldehyde fumes in trailers were at dangerous levels.

The *CBS Evening News* reported, for the first time, that FEMA was warning its own employees that merely inspecting the trailers exposed one to the risk of "cancer" from the formaldehyde.

The *CBS Evening News* reported, for the first time, information from a supervisor at a factory that manufactured the trailers that they were made with shoddy materials and often manufactured too quickly.

The *CBS Evening News* interviewed, for the first time on this topic, FEMA administrator Paulison during which he said he didn't know why the children are getting sick.

Most news organizations qualify new or never seen or reported before information relating to any news event as exclusive. And in this case, we weren't the only ones with this understanding. After our first broadcast, others in the press, as well as elected officials, pointed to our reporting as new information that required action from FEMA. Senator Landrieu, after viewing us, called for an investigation into the formaldehyde problem.

The day after our first story aired, Congressman Jindal, quoting data from it, called for a Congressional hearing. When Congress held hearings on this issue on July 19, Congressman Waxman's staff called CBS News to obtain a copy of the report to play at the hearing—the only news report shown at that Congressional event or referenced by any member of Congress.

We stand by our reporting on the FEMA trailers. And we firmly believe that they were characterized appropriately as both new and exclusive.

In the future, please feel free to contact us when you are writing about our work. We are more than happy to discuss our reporting with you.

Sincerely,

Keith Summa

Sr. Producer, CBS News, Investigative Unit

Aug. 10, 2007

My point-by-point reply:
His letter is in boldface;
My reply is in brackets.

Dear Mr. Block:

As a former journalist, we know you are as concerned about accuracy in reporting as we are at CBS News.

[Dear Mr. Summa: I'm reluctant to pounce on any letter-writer, but I can't ignore that dangling modifier: "as a former journalist" refers to me, but it modifies "we," which refers to you and other folks at CBS News.]

So, we would like to address some errors in your blog posting of August 2, 2007 concerning our series of reports on the CBS Evening News with Katie Couric about the formaldehyde problem with FEMA trailers.

You wrote that our stories were neither exclusives, nor news. However, as the following list of details about our reportage makes clear, they were exactly that:

[Let's look at who reported what when. Couric introduced the story on May 16 [2007] by saying, **"We're beginning tonight with a CBS News exclusive, another scandal in the aftermath of Hurricane Katrina. Many survivors of the killer storm are now getting sick, and their government-provided trailers may be to blame. Nearly two years after Katrina, 86,000 families are still living in FEMA trailers, and every day more and more of them are developing health problems. We have two reports tonight, beginning with our chief investigative correspondent, Armen Keteyian."**

[Couric's first sentence presented the *exclusive* as "another scandal": many survivors "are now getting sick."

[*Now getting sick*? In fact, since mid-2006, as we'll see, newspapers, broadcasters and websites have reported on the sicknesses.

[Couric's saying on May 16, 2007, that many survivors of Katrina are "now getting sick" brings to mind a remark often credited to Marie Antoinette (or her hairdresser), "There is nothing new except what's been forgotten."

[Also on May 16, CBS News posted at its website three articles related to the story on the *Evening News*. None of the articles used *exclusive*. Two articles bore the bylines of Keteyian and Michael Rey, a member of the CBS investigative unit. The other CBS article, which quoted Keteyian, was headed with a question: "Are FEMA Trailers Making Residents Sick?"

[One Keteyian-Rey article—"FEMA's Own Documents Tell the Formaldehyde Story"—said, "When the Investigative Unit heard that some of the more than 144,000 trailers used by FEMA for temporary housing across the Gulf could be making people sick, the first thing we did was file a Freedom of Information Act Request with FEMA."

[The CBS article went on to say the two CBS investigators filed the FOIA request on March 30—the day they said they heard about the sicknesses. Yes, they said when they heard of people getting sick, it was the same day, March 30, 2007.

[In his report for the *Evening News* of May 16, Keteyian did not refer to anything as exclusive. If the items were exclusive and significant, why didn't Couric present them at or near the top?

[The first person Keteyian interviewed in his package was Angela Orcutt, then her son, Nicholas. She said her boy's symptom of sickness was coughing. The next person Keteyian interviewed in the package was Dr. Scott Needle.

[But two weeks before the CBS newscast, Dan Rather, in an episode on HDNet titled *Toxic Trailers*, broadcast an interview with Dr. Needle. He said many of his young patients in Bay St. Louis, Mississippi, had ear infections, sinus infections, pneumonia and other ailments. He said they apparently arose from living in FEMA trailers.

[And three months before the CBS newscast, the *Nation* of Feb. 26 carried a long article—"Dying For a Home: Toxic Trailers Are Making Katrina Refugees Sick"—that included Dr. Needle and the Orcutts; Angela Orcutt spoke of her son's "choking and coughing." On May 16, 2007, the Orcutts and Dr. Needle re-told their story to Keteyian on the *CBS Evening News*.

[Going back even further, to July 25, 2006, msnbc.com carried an article quoting Dr. Needle, a pediatrician, and Paul and Melody Stewart. The head on the article read, in part, "Private testing finds high levels of formaldehyde; residents report illnesses." The residents were living in trailers provided by FEMA.

[The Stewarts first appeared on WLOX-TV in Biloxi, Mississippi, on March 17, 2006. They told of living in a trailer and getting headaches, burning eyes and scratchy throats. They said they obtained a testing kit and found the level of formaldehyde in the trailer was twice what the Environmental Protection Agency considered acceptable.

[After that, the media carried many stories about Katrina survivors living in FEMA trailers who reported getting sick.]

The CBS Evening News reported, for the first time, on never-before-seen documents that revealed FEMA itself had testing data showing that formaldehyde fumes in trailers were at dangerous levels.

[Even though those documents—about the testing of 28 trailers—might have never been seen before by an outsider, FEMA had a much larger study, of 96 trailers, a study FEMA had requested. The trailers were tested in the last quarter of 2006. FEMA made this study public 10 days before Keteyian went on Couric's broadcast of May 18. This study also found that many trailers had formaldehyde levels that were unsafe.

[Another federal agency, ATSDR, had conducted the study of the 96 trailers: "Health Consultation: Formaldehyde Sampling at FEMA Temporary Housing Units, February 1, 2007."

[ATSDR's preface to its study said: "During the summer of 2006, the Federal Emergency Management Agency (FEMA) asked the Agency for

Toxic Substances and Disease Registry (ATSDR) to analyze formaldehyde sampling data collected in 96 unoccupied trailers by the Environmental Protection Agency. These unoccupied trailers were similar to those distributed by FEMA to house persons displaced by Hurricane Katrina."

[The preface went on to say: "ATSDR's consultation was intended to answer the question 'Do empty trailers have formaldehyde levels that can adversely effect [*sic*] human health?' The short answer is yes."

[FEMA posted the 10-page study at its website on May 8, ten days before Couric's broadcast of May 18. That's when Keteyian first spoke of the 28 trailers.

[On May 4, four days before FEMA's posting of the ATSDR analysis—and two weeks before Keteyian's presentation about the 28 trailers—FEMA made the ATSDR report the subject of a news release. In a summary and elsewhere in the release, the focus was on preventive and remedial action. The title: "FEMA Study: Ventilating Travel Trailers Can Significantly Reduce Formaldehyde Emission Levels."

[Similar findings of formaldehyde's dangers were reported by the media since at least mid-2006. msnbc.com reported on July 25, 2006: "Air quality tests of 44 FEMA trailers conducted by the Sierra Club since April have found formaldehyde concentrations as high as 0.34 parts per million....And all but four of the trailers have tested higher than the 0.1 parts per million that the EPA considers to be an 'elevated level' capable of causing watery eyes, burning in the eyes and throat, nausea and respiratory distress in some people."

[The msnbc.com article quoted Dr. Needle as saying he noticed some unusual and persistent health problems among patients living in the trailers. The article also reported that Paul and Melody Stewart said formaldehyde had forced them out of their trailer into their truck.

[Two nights after the *Evening News* of May 16, 2007, Couric said: **"We're beginning tonight with a CBS News exclusive, a follow-up on our report exposing an emerging health crisis for thousands of survivors of Hurricane Katrina. As we reported earlier this week, many people living in trailers provided by FEMA are getting sick. Tonight we can tell you FEMA has known for a long time that the trailers are toxic but did little about it. CBS News chief investigative correspondent Armen Keteyian, who first broke this story, has the follow-up tonight."**

[That *tonight we can tell you* sounds as if Couric is about to make a significant disclosure. But one year earlier, on May 16, 2006, the Sierra Club, an environmental organization, issued a widely reported news release that began: "A new study conducted by the Sierra Club shows that the indoor air quality of FEMA trailers contains excessive levels of formaldehyde, a carcinogen that can cause various forms of cancer with repeated exposure."

[The news release said the Sierra Club had tested the air in 31 FEMA trailers in Mississippi and Louisiana to measure formaldehyde levels. The release said only two tests were at or below the maximum safety limit recommended by the EPA and that several trailers were more than three times over the limit.

[Also on May 16, 2006, the same day the Sierra Club issued that release, CNN said it had tested two trailers. One tested "80 percent higher than federal recommendations," according to CNN, and the other "tested 50 percent higher." A CNN anchor said, **"We tagged along with the Stewarts and some local environmentalists as they tested 31 FEMA trailers** (for formaldehyde fumes). **Twenty-nine tested above the federal standard."**

[And on Aug. 4, 2006, msnbc.com reported that a FEMA official said the agency had already determined "there is a problem with elevated formaldehyde levels in 'two or three brands' of the at least 10 brands of travel trailers provided to the government under emergency contracts in the wake of Hurricane Katrina."

[Newspapers, broadcasters and websites told of FEMA's playing down or pooh-poohing the complaints.

[As for Couric's saying CBS *first broke* the story, that's redundant. Whoever is the first to report a story is the one who broke it.]

[Again, on July 23, Couric told of CBS's breaking the story, **"And now an update on a story Armen** (in the previous story, she had used his full name) **broke back in May about the health problems of Katrina refugees living in FEMA trailers...."**]

The CBS Evening News reported, for the first time, that FEMA was warning its own employees that merely inspecting the trailers exposed one to the risk of "cancer" from the formaldehyde.

[How can anyone be sure no newspaper or broadcaster or website reported the item previously? Besides, many news organizations had long been reporting the possible cancer risk for trailer residents.]

The CBS Evening News reported, for the first time, information from a supervisor at a factory that manufactured the trailers that they were made with shoddy materials and often manufactured too quickly.

[None of the *Evening News* scripts that figured in this examination—those of May 16, May 18, July 19 and July 23, all in 2007—used the word *shoddy* or a synonym. CBS quoted a factory supervisor as saying his crew worked at a "breakneck pace," which, he says, "forced the company to use cheaper wood products." But *cheaper* isn't necessarily shoddy. And what the supervisor said was not new. Nor was the word "breakneck," not an everyday word, which had previously been used in the *Nation* article of Feb. 26, 2007.

[The *Nation* said: "Trailer manufacturers set up ad hoc assembly lines, advertised in local newspapers and hired temporary workers to fill FEMA orders at breakneck speed. On some assembly lines, workers say, they were expected to produce a trailer in eight to ten minutes. Twelve-hour shifts and six-day workweeks were common. 'Under the best of conditions, some trailer manufacturers do not really have good quality control,' says Connie Gallant, president of the RV Consumer Group, a nonprofit that rates the quality of mobile housing and trailers. 'In a mass production frenzy, that quality control pretty much goes out the window.'"

[The author of the *Nation* article, Amanda Spake, also quoted an attorney who had sued FEMA. He said that after he filed the suit, several Indiana workers hired by trailer makers told him they had come down with headaches, nosebleeds and flu-like symptoms.]

The CBS Evening News interviewed, for the first time on this topic, FEMA administrator Paulison during which he said he didn't know why the children are getting sick.

[During which *what*?

[Whether Paulison's answer was correct, his remark could be construed as self-serving: if he didn't know why the children were getting sick—and perhaps didn't want to know—he might have figured that he couldn't be blamed for not taking corrective action regarding formaldehyde. Some critics of his call it FEMAldehyde.]

Most news organizations qualify new or never seen or reported before information relating to any news event as exclusive. And in this case, we weren't the only ones with this understanding. After our first broadcast, others in the press, as well as elected officials, pointed to our reporting as new information that required action from FEMA.

[The meaning of *exclusive* is elusive. Does it mean a reporter has scooped the competition with a blockbuster? Or does it mean that the reporter was the only media rep present? Or the only reporter at an interview an hour before the next interviewer showed up? Or an hour after the previous interviewer left? Or is a story *exclusive* because no one else wanted it? Or had already carried it? Or is an *exclusive* a fact or a story that a reporter dug up and has alone and is worth using but hardly anything to get excited about?

[And what do listeners think when they hear that a story is exclusive—that all the other stories on the newscast come from a pool or from the newswires?

[The news outlets that break the most exclusives that might be considered truly worth calling *exclusive* are *The New York Times*, *Washington Post*, *Los Angeles Times* and *Wall Street Journal*. But they don't brag and call their stories exclusive. That word, after all, has less to do with journalism than with hucksterism.]

Senator Landrieu, after viewing us, called for an investigation into the formaldehyde problem. The day after our first story aired, Congressman Jindal, quoting data from it, called for a Congressional hearing. When Congress held hearings on this issue on July 19, Congressman Waxman's staff called CBS News to obtain a copy of the report to play at the hearing—the only news report shown at that Congressional event or referenced by any member of Congress.

We stand by our reporting on the FEMA trailers. And we firmly believe that they were characterized appropriately as both new and exclusive. In the future, please feel free to contact us when you are writing about our work. We are more than happy to discuss our reporting with you.

Sincerely,

Keith Summa

Sr. Producer, CBS News, Investigative Unit

August 10, 2007

[Thank you for writing to me.]

(October 2007)

How CBS's *First* Didn't Last

One of the riskiest words to use in a script is *first*. Using a *first* may make a story seem stronger, but a careful writer doesn't use *first* without being certain, and then only if an event's *firstness* is significant. Let's look at a recent network story and see how *first* fizzled. On Sunday, July 31, the anchor of CBS's *Evening News,* Mika Brzezinski, said:

"On Tuesday, historic Alexandria, Virginia, will be making some modern history, becoming the first local government to offer free outdoor Internet access, but on Capitol Hill, right across the Potomac, not everyone is thrilled, and Joie Chen tells us why."

Two days after the broadcast, on Tuesday, Aug. 2, Alexandria issued a press release saying the city was launching "Wireless Alexandria" that day. The release said the pilot project would offer "the region's first free, outdoor, wireless Internet zone." The *region*'s first, not the country's first local government, as the CBS anchor had said.

But *The Washington Post* said, accurately, that the free service in Alexandria had begun seven weeks earlier. Not until August 2, though, did the service begin "officially." The *Post* article also said Alexandria was "the first local government to offer alfresco Web surfing at no charge." By saying *local government*, the *Post* might have meant it was the first government in the newspaper's circulation area to offer free outdoor Internet access. But when a broadcast network says *first local government,* that covers a lot of ground: every municipality in the United States.

As the anchor said, Alexandria is historic, but no more so than many other places in Virginia. Further, how can the newswriter say any particular place will be *making modern history*? Would anyone hope to make ancient history? In any case, newswriters don't decide who will be "making history"; historians will decide—and not tonight.

The correspondent began by having a college student tell us what Wi-Fi is: a system that provides wireless access to the Internet. Then the correspondent said:

"The city spent 20-thousand dollars on four sets of unobtrusive antennas, following the lead of more than 80 communities around the country, places like Lafayette, Louisiana, and the city of Philadelphia, which are in the process of setting up Wi-Fi networks."

If Alexandria was following the lead of more than 80 communities, it surely wasn't the leader, as the anchor said. Rather than first, Alexandria may be eighty-first. Not all those communities, though, have systems up and running. Delete *in the process of*; the sentence will still mean the same. Also delete *the city of*.

Long before Alexandria began providing outdoor Wi-Fi free, many other places were already doing so. A year ago, Hermosa Beach, Calif., began offering it. Last September, Culver City, Calif., also did so. And on Aug. 7, 2005, the columnist Nicholas Kristof wrote in *The New York Times* about what he said seems to be the largest Wi-Fi hot spot in the world—600 square miles in eastern Oregon and southern Washington. Kristof said the free service has been operating for more than a year and a half.

As a brief search on the Internet showed, Alexandria was not first. Not even close. Which is why a prudent anchor, before writing a lead-in, or delivering one, finds out what the correspondent has said, or is going to say, and resolves any conflicts between the lead-in and the correspondent's copy.

Better yet: when time allows, the correspondent writes the first sentence of a piece so that it can work as the anchor lead-in. Then the correspondent opens the piece with her second sentence. If the CBS anchor and the correspondent had done that, there would have been no conflict—and no phony *first*.

(August 20, 2005)

When A Network Script Should Be Scrapped

The anchor of the *CBS Sunday Evening News* started strong:

"We begin tonight with news of a crisis that leaders say threatens to topple governments and trigger wars around the world. The head of the International Monetary Fund calls the soaring price of food an extremely serious problem and said, 'The planet must tackle it.' According to the I-M-F, 37 countries are in dire need...."

The anchor, Russ Mitchell, had no need to say he was beginning; as soon as he began, we knew he had begun. And he had no need to say it was *tonight*. When he began, at 6 p.m. ET, on Sunday, April 20, we already knew it was *night*.

Mitchell's abrupt shift from the present tense *calls* to the past tense *said* is jarring.

But what Mitchell called news was not news. Two and a half days earlier, on Friday, the AP had reported that story:

"PARIS (AP)—The head of the International Monetary Fund warned Friday that soaring world food prices can have dire consequences, such as toppling governments and even triggering wars."

The first sentence in the CBS script made use of the AP's *toppling* and *triggering*. *Triggering wars*, though, sounds suspiciously like a cliché. Besides, can someone or something *trigger* a war? Why not simply say *causing wars*? The AP article went on:

"Dominique Strauss-Kahn told France's Europe-1 radio that the price hikes that set off rioting in Haiti, Egypt and elsewhere were an 'extremely serious' problem.

"'The planet must tackle it,' he said."

The AP article ran on for 136 more words. Although Russ Mitchell spoke of a warning by *leaders*, he mentioned only one person, the head of the IMF. That's an important position, but is Strauss-Kahn someone we think of as a leader? About an hour after the AP moved that story, the AP sent it out again, this time inserting a paragraph about one other person, France's president. But he didn't do any *warning*. Which means the CBS script's use of the plural *leaders* was wrong—unless a solid source somewhere said *leaders*.

Before Mitchell said he was beginning, he had said, **"We'll show you a village that's ground zero in the crisis."** So after he delivered the lead story, he introduced a CBS correspondent in Uganda.

Ground zero? Not so. Wikipedia says: "The term has often been associated with nuclear explosions and other large bombs but is also used in relation to earthquakes, epidemics and other disasters to mark the point of the most severe damage or destruction. Damage gradually decreases with distance from this point." Uganda is not the center of the food shortage, its situation is not the worst. And the correspondent didn't say it was.

On Friday, April 18, the day the AP transmitted the IMF story, the CBS News website posted an article—"IMF Head: Food Shortages Can Spark War." It read:

"The head of the International Monetary Fund warned Friday that soaring world food prices can have dire consequences, such as toppling governments and even triggering wars.

"Dominique Strauss-Kahn told France's Europe-1 radio that the price rises that set off rioting in Haiti, Egypt and elsewhere were an 'extremely serious' problem.

"'The planet must tackle it,' he said."

Do those three paragraphs seem familiar? They should. The CBS website had picked up the first three paragraphs of the AP article—verbatim. In the AP's 7:07 a.m. version, *price hikes* was changed to *price rises*. The CBS website posting continued:

"The IMF chief said the problem could also threaten democracies, even in countries where governments have done all they could to help the local population. Asked whether the crisis could lead to wars, Strauss-Kahn responded that it was possible.

"'When the tension goes above and beyond putting democracy into question, there are risks of war,' he said. 'History is full of wars that started because of this kind of problem.'"

Those two paragraphs of the CBS posting were also word-for-word transplants from the AP. The long CBS posting also included material not provided in the AP copy. Despite the posting's dependence on the AP for the first 157 words, the article CBS posted was attributed to "CBS/AP"—not "AP/CBS."

It was two days later when the CBS *Sunday Evening News* called the same AP story *news*, even though the AP had moved its first account at 6 a.m. ET, Friday, April 18—60 hours earlier.

No matter what, let's credit the *Sunday Evening News* of April 20 with this: they didn't call it *breaking news*.

(May 28, 2008)

How Two Network Newsmen
Turned Day into Night

If you think only a solar eclipse can turn day into night, lend me your ears.

When you turn on the news at night, you're bound to hear *tonight* embedded in scripts. But unless you're tone-deaf, you can often detect, or suspect, a false note. Even from networks. On the *CBS Evening News* recently, a correspondent in Washington introduced video:

"Saudi investigators say that altogether they've now swept up 11 suspects in the Riyadh bombings earlier this month [could it be later this month? of course not]**...The Saudi interior minister said tonight that the 11 were rounded up without incident over the past two days near the holy city of Medina...."** *Said tonight?* I wondered whether that was true. So I did a little Sam Spadework. When the correspondent spoke, just after 6:30 p.m. ET, May 28, the time in Saudi Arabia was 1:30 a.m.— seven hours ahead of the time in network newsrooms.

That means the Saudi interior minister must have made the announcement after midnight over there. But five hours before the CBS newscast, at 1:31 p.m. ET, the French news agency AFP (Agence France-Presse) quoted the Saudi interior minister as telling a news conference that 11 people had been arrested in the past two days.

When the CBS correspondent said, **"...altogether they've now swept up 11 suspects,"** the *altogether* was also suspect. Reporters in Riyadh for the *Chicago Tribune* and *Los Angeles Times* wrote that the minister said— on May 28—at least 21 suspects had been arrested, 11 in the past two days. The AFP story of 1:31 p.m. ET, also attributed "21" to the minister.

Is it even plausible that the interior minister would hold an additional news conference to repeat or amplify his announcement? And after midnight? In fact, the Trib's man in Riyadh, Cam Simpson, told me (by phone after he returned to the States) that there was no post-midnight conference.

113

On the same night as the CBS newscast, Peter Jennings, anchor of ABC's *World News Tonight*, said:

"Overseas, now, for the latest on terrorism. In Saudi Arabia, authorities say they have arrested 11 people in connection with those bombing attacks [*bombings* alone would do the job] **two weeks ago in the capital, Riyadh."** Then the anchor introduced a correspondent, **"here with the latest."** [*Latest* twice in one lead-in? Yep. Isn't news always the newest?] The correspondent narrated video:

"The 11 Saudi suspects were arrested outside this Internet café in the holy city of Medina. Tonight [the correspondent was in Manhattan, not over there], **the interior minister, Prince Nayef, told reporters the men and three non-Saudi women with them were captured without gunfire...."**

Didn't the anchors know that Saudi Arabia is in a different time zone from Manhattan?

Tonight? Not so. But how about other purported facts?

The correspondent said the suspects were arrested outside the Internet café, but the AP had moved a story at 7:18 a.m. ET, that a Saudi paper said three suspects were arrested inside. And six minutes later, AFP carried the same account. Other wire and newspaper stories also said the three men had been arrested at (inside or outside) the café—and the other suspects arrested elsewhere in or near the city. But I couldn't find a print story saying all 11 suspects had been arrested outside the café. Or that the women were arrested at the café.

Neither the ABC nor CBS scripts identified the source(s) of their information.

As for ABC's mention of **"the men and three non-Saudi women with them,"** the next day the BBC Monitoring Service circulated a partial translation of the interior minister's news conference. The BBC noted its source as an article in Arabic posted at the website of the Saudi Press Agency (SPA) at 1713 GMT, May 28—1:13 p.m. ET.

The BBC said the SPA article reported the minister had told the news conference that a man was arrested **"on his way between Medina and Mecca along with three women who seem to be the wives of some of them."**

On the day of the news conference, SPA also provided an English-language account of the minister's remarks. SPA quoted the minister as saying 11 suspects had been arrested in Medina, which state-run SPA said brought the total to 21 arrested. By early that afternoon, ET, AFP was reporting both figures. At 7:01 a.m. ET, and all day long, the AP was saying that since the bombings, the Saudis had "detained about 100 people." Even so, that evening, CBS said, **"...altogether they've now swept up 11 suspects."**

Makes you wonder about some network newscasts (NBC's *Nightly News* didn't run the story that night): Were the correspondents misinformed? Didn't the anchors know that Saudi Arabia is in a different time zone from Manhattan? Unaware they should present the time element according to the place where they're broadcasting? Sloppy or simply indifferent about taking liberties? Caught up in the pursuit of *night*hood? Or were their inaccuracies inadvertent, a matter of misspeaking—sort of a bad air day? What do you think?

But at the end of the day (yet another cliché), does it really matter whether their *tonight* was factually correct? If you don't know the right answer to that one, you're in the wrong business.

(June 2003)

Hard Look Finds Weak
Script Fading to Blah

I drink tea. A lot of it. Mug after mug. Day after day. Been drinking it since I was a kid. So I've been glad to hear tea may be good for us. But I'm teed off by tea stories that seem to have more holes than a sieve. One of those stories caught my ear recently on a network evening newscast:

"There are several new studies out tonight on the health benefits of tea, especially the green and black varieties that are rich in antioxidants. Researchers found drinking tea can reduce levels of bad cholesterol and help prevent heart disease and cancer." (Dan Rather, *CBS Evening News*, Sept. 24, 2002)

That's it, 41 words. Most arresting is the assertion about what researchers found:

"Researchers found drinking tea can reduce levels of bad cholesterol and help prevent heart disease and cancer."

Although we've been hearing for several years about possible benefits from drinking tea, I wondered who conducted the new studies mentioned in the script's first sentence. And I wondered how much tea it would take to do me any good. How much and how often? What kind of tea: powdered, bottled, bagged or loose leaf? Which variety? Assam? Darjeeling? Oolong? Lapsang Souchong? Made with what kind of water? At what temperature? And brewed for how long? Taken with sugar? Lemon? Milk, cream or straight? Can tea help any viewer? Especially me?

Also, I wondered how the new studies supported, differed from or advanced the stories we've been hearing for several years. So I poked around the Internet and the news world's solar plexus, LexisNexis. And I made some phone calls.

Two hours before the Sept. 24 newscast, Reuters sent out a story at 4:23 p.m. ET. (I found no coverage by the AP.) The story was based on a news conference that day for the previous day's Third International Scientific Symposium on Tea and Human Health, held in Washington, D.C.

The gathering had been sponsored by the U.S. Department of Agriculture, the American Cancer Society, scientific groups and the Tea Council, representing the tea industry.

The Reuters story began, "Solid evidence is mounting that drinking tea can prevent cell damage that leads to cancer, heart disease and perhaps other ills, scientists said on Tuesday."

Reuters went on to say the Department of Agriculture had reported on a study *suggesting* (the word used by Reuters) that tea drinking can reduce the risk of heart disease by lowering cholesterol. And it said the U.S.D.A.'s Human Nutrition Research Center in Beltsville, Maryland, had tested eight men and eight women who agreed to eat and drink for several weeks only what they were given at the lab. As a result, the director of the lab said drinking tea had lowered their low-density lipoprotein ("bad" cholesterol) up to ten percent.

Although the CBS script said researchers found drinking tea can reduce "bad" cholesterol, here's what you and I would find by reading the whole Reuters article:

1. Only 16 people were studied.
2. And for only a few weeks.
3. They ate only a special diet. And they experienced an average lowering of "bad" cholesterol by only up to 10 percent.
4. The study only *suggested* certain benefits. *Possible* benefits.

Hardly the stuff of headlines. And a news item on a network newscast is equivalent to a page-one story across the country.

Speaking of *only* (and please don't use that kind of transition), if only the editor had asked the writer of the script, "Can you give me one good reason we should broadcast this—only one?" Or if only the anchor had asked the producer. If only.

The Reuters article also told of another report at the day-long symposium: a researcher at the University of Arizona and the Arizona Cancer Center said she had tested 140 smokers to see whether drinking tea could affect levels of chemicals associated with DNA damage. The trial looked at a chemical, 8-OhDG, which Reuters said is found in urine and linked to damage of DNA. For four months, the volunteers drank water, black tea or green tea. At the end of the trial, the researcher said, her team found that those drinking only green tea underwent a 25 percent decrease in their 8-OhDG, an apparently favorable outcome.

But the Reuters health and science correspondent, Maggie Fox, ended her article by cautioning, "Much more research would be needed to see if lowering levels of 8-OhDG, or other markers of DNA damage, is actually associated with a lower risk of cancer."

Another account of the symposium was even more cautious. Several hours before Reuters moved its article, the Tea Council—a trade group that promotes tea—wrote a press release distributed on the PR Newswire at 9 a.m. The release said circumspectly:

"The results of a new clinical study *suggest* [emphasis added] that tea consumption *may* [emphasis added] decrease LDL ['bad'] cholesterol by 10 percent when *combined* [emphasis added] with a 'Step 1' type diet, moderately low in fat and cholesterol, as described by the American Heart Association and the National Cholesterol Education Program. The study, conducted at the USDA Beltsville Human Nutrition Research Center in Beltsville, MD, is the first investigation of tea in which the subjects' diets were precisely controlled by having them eat meals prepared at the research facility."

> Is there a lesson to be learned from our trip down the tea trail? Yes: Don't swallow everything you hear.

(The acting director of the U.S.D.A. Center, Dr. Joseph Judd, a research chemist, told me the other day that that paragraph is "pretty accurate.")

Although the Tea Council's press release did mention the special diet followed by the trial's participants, the release didn't bother with other details of the trial, details that would dilute the findings further: only 16 people took part, and for only a few weeks.

Sixteen people might have entered the trial, but the abstract of the study says 15 finished the first two three-week stints. And for the third and final phase of the trial, the number of participants in the three-week stint slipped to 12. The abstract also acknowledges the role of Unilever, which Dr. Judd told me provided "the treatment beverages and partial financial support for the study." He identified the "treatment beverages" as tea and placebos. Unilever packages Lipton tea.

But even when tea is accompanied by a healthful diet, the possible benefits may be limited. The Tea Council's press release did not quote or paraphrase the key judgment in the abstract for the U.S.D.A. study: "Based on this study, we conclude that black tea consumption as part of a[n] NCEP [National Cholesterol Education Program] Step 1 type diet may reduce blood lipid risk factors for CVD [cardiovascular disease] in mildly hypercholesterolemic adults." So they think tea—along with a special diet—may help if your cholesterol is *slightly* high.

The network newswriter had a tough assignment, even with the Reuters article about "solid evidence" that it said was "mounting" (you might call it "making a mounting out of a molehill"): he had to boil down all the information into broadcast copy that ran about 15 seconds.

Not long after I heard that script on the air, I spent some time with Ed Bliss, the grand old man of broadcast newswriting, and I decided to conduct an experiment of my own: I asked him to write a 15-second script based on the Reuters story. Ed had been a newswriter (for Edward R. Murrow), an editor (for Walter Cronkite), author (*Writing News for Broadcast*) and a college teacher (American University). I gave him only the Reuters story. I didn't tell him about the CBS script of Sept. 24, nor did I mention my curiosity about it. Ed probably figured I was up to something or other, but he was too polite to ask.

A few days later, he e-mailed his script and, at my request, gave me permission to use it:

"Drinking tea may be good for your health. Researchers have found evidence—no proof yet—that tea has ingredients that lower the risk of heart disease and cancer. This finding, announced today, is based on tests conducted by the University of Arizona and the Department of Agriculture." (47 words; the network's was 41.)

Ed had realized the story was flimsy: his first verb was *may*. And he stressed: no proof. (In late November, Ed died at age 90.)

But the network's script said in its second sentence that the efficacy of tea was proved:

"There are several new studies out tonight on the health benefits of tea, especially the green and black varieties that are rich in antioxidants. Researchers found drinking tea can reduce levels of bad cholesterol and help prevent heart disease and cancer."

Are...out tonight is weaker than dormitory tea. Because *are* and other forms of *to be* don't convey action or movement, we can't tell whether the new studies came out an hour ago, a week ago, or a month ago. Hundreds of thousands of studies are *out tonight*. In fact, the studies mentioned in that broadcast script did not come out that night. Another problem with that CBS script: no clue as to who conducted the studies or the name of the scientific body or journal that reported them.

Let's credit Ed Bliss with saying *today* instead of straining to insert *tonight*.

Is there a lesson to be learned from our trip down the tea trail? Yes: Don't swallow everything you hear.

Let's not stir up a brewhaha, but our inquiry also raises another critical question about tea: Am I getting enough?

(January 2003)

60 Keeps on Ticking,
But Its Writing Takes a Licking

CBS's *60 Minutes* investigates wrongdoing, but let's try to right—or rewrite—some of their own wrongs. Fortunately, we can benefit from their missteps because each one provides a lesson. So let's look at some of their flawed scripts.

"They say that the only reason they let you go was because of an act of clemency by King Fahd." (Ed Bradley, May 9, 2004) Clemency is an act of leniency, so delete *an act of*. *The New York Times* stylebook says: "*...because* and *why* are built into the meaning of *reason*. So avoid *the reason is because* and *the reason why*." And delete that *that*. And that's that.

Verbal abuse: **"South American shoplifting teams feed a black market for stolen goods that flourish in most big cities."** (Steve Kroft, July 11, 2004) Subject-verb disagreement. *Stolen goods* don't flourish; *a black market* flourishes. The verb should agree with its subject, not with a word that comes between them.

Overkill: **"Saddam tried to have him assassinated eight times."** (Bob Simon, March 30, 2003) Talk about overkill. Correct: "Saddam tried eight times to assassinate him."

Update (Aug. 28, 2004): A reader has rejected my rewrite. He says Saddam didn't personally try to kill the intended victim but sent underlings. So the reader prefers "Saddam tried eight times to have him assassinated." My defense: People say, "Hitler murdered millions," "Stalin murdered millions" and "Mao murdered millions."

Update (Oct. 1, 2004): Don Kirk, a journalist, also objected to my rewrite. So now it's 2-1 against it, and I'm the lonely only 1. Don, writing from Baghdad, says Saddam himself well might have murdered eight people—or eighty. But in the script I dealt with, Saddam had farmed out the job. Inasmuch as he's reputed to have sometimes taken such matters into his own hands, my rewrite should have taken that into account.

So I'm reversing myself and redoing my rewrite: "Saddam tried eight times to have him assassinated."

Double trouble: **"Ricker said in a sworn affidavit that he witnessed that inaction...."** (Bob Simon, May 11, 2003) *Sworn affidavit* is redundant. If it's not sworn to, it's not an affidavit. *Witnessed*? Why not *saw*? And how on earth (or in orbit) can someone witness inaction? Also: the script has one *that* too many.

A grammatical lapse: **"This whole question of those mobile labs roaming around the country making biological weapons was a big factor in us going to war."** (Lesley Stahl, March 7, 2004) *Us* should be *our*. Why? Because a pronoun preceding a gerund should usually be in the possessive form. But even if a correspondent gets it right ("our going to war"), the wording raises questions: Is *60 Minutes* at war? Does *60* have its own militia?

Oops: **"But the plot is ripped from the pages of the Bible, so it all winds up here in Israel, where, according to the Book of Revelations...."** (Bob Simon, June 8, 2003) According to the *New Testament*, it's the *Book of Revelation*—no *s*. (A mistake like that could lead to *Lamentations*.)

Dangler below: **"Born in 1943, his mother was a Boston blue blood and his father was an Army Air Corps pilot who later became a Foreign Service officer, which meant that [John] Kerry, the second of four children, moved from place to place in the United States and Europe."** (Ed Bradley, Jan. 25, 2004)

The subject of that sentence is John Kerry, and he was born in 1943. But the sentence says Kerry's mother was born in 1943. Besides, the sentence is too busy and too long (46 words).

And the correspondent said of Kerry's wife, **"Born in Mozambique, Africa, her father was a Portuguese doctor."** Same problem. Mrs. Kerry was born in Mozambique, but the sentence says her father was born there. (He was not.)

Strunk and White's *Elements of Style* says: "A participial phrase at the beginning of a sentence must refer to the grammatical subject." Sentences violating that rule, the book says, are often ludicrous. And it offers this priceless (or priced less) example: "Being in a dilapidated condition, I was able to buy the house very cheap."

Another correspondent spoke of deadly chemicals:

"The American Chemistry Council did oppose Corzine's bill, which required chemical companies to stockpile less chemicals on

site...." (Steve Kroft, June 13, 2004) *Less?* No, *fewer*. If the correspondent had been talking about a bulk quantity of one chemical, less of the chemical would have put him on safe ground. Maybe he meant fewer chemicals and less of them.

The verbivore Richard Lederer says: "*Less* means 'not so much' and refers to amount or quantity. *Fewer* means 'not so many' and refers to number, things that are countable—'less food' but 'fewer cookies'; 'less nutrition' but...'fewer calories.'"

The grammarian Patricia T. O'Conner advises in her book *Woe is I*, "Use *fewer* to mean a smaller number of individual things; use *less* to mean a smaller quantity of something." *Something* is singular. And *less* takes a singular noun. So for that *60 Minutes* script's "deadly chemicals," *less* is wrong.

Another lapse: **"This fifth installment in the Harry Potter series will doubtless set all sorts of new publishing records."** (Lesley Stahl, June 15, 2003) *New record* is an old redundancy. When someone sets a record, it supersedes the previous record, so it *is* new. And when someone tells me something will occur without a doubt, I begin to doubt.

According to the *New Testament*, it's the *Book of Revelation*—no s. (A mistake like that could lead to *Lamentations*.)

Unconvincing: **"After convincing one of his customers to loan him $500, Cuban launched MicroSolutions...."** (Steve Kroft, Feb. 15, 2004) *Convince* should be followed by *that* or *of*, not *to*. *Persuade* is followed by *to*. As for *loan*, *The Wall Street Journal* stylebook advises: "Avoid as a verb. Use *lend, lent*."

Another slip: **"They run their regions like fiefdoms...."** (Lesley Stahl, May 4, 2003) *The New York Times* stylebook points out: "*fief* means land or domain. So *fiefdom* is redundant." The stylebook of *The Wall Street Journal* and that of the British newsweekly *The Economist* say tersely, "Fief, not fiefdom."

Misplaced modifier: **"It's gotten so bad that today most of the young women only feel safe if they're covered up or if they stay at** [no need for *at*] **home."** (Christiane Amanpour, May 16, 2004) *Only* is in the wrong place. The sentence should read "...young women feel safe only if they're covered up or if they stay home."

Another error: **"Faenza says medical research shows that a past history of serious mental illness is not a predictor of future violence...."**

(Steve Kroft, June 29, 2003) All history is past. And the business of a predictor is to predict the future. So delete *past* and *future*.

Wrong word: **"But fake golf clubs don't begin to suggest the enormity of the problem."** (Bob Simon, Aug. 8, 2004) The problem is *enormity*. The stylebook of Canada's *Globe and Mail* says of *enormity*: "It means heinousness, extreme wickedness or an outrageous or heinous [offense]. It has nothing to do with size, for which we would have to use the word enormousness or, preferably, a less awkward synonym such as immensity...." Willie Weinbaum of ESPN suggests *magnitude*.

Free advice: **"If we want advertising, we'll stay home and watch it for free on television."** (Andy Rooney, Aug. 15, 2004) *Free* can be a verb, an adverb, or an adjective. But, as *The Wall Street Journal* stylebook notes, "It is not a noun, so *for free* is a solecism. Drop the *for*." *Free* means *at no cost* or *for nothing*. (Did anyone ever tell you there's no such thing as a for-free lunch?)

One in the eye: **"You're one of the few theater owners who doesn't run commercials before the feature film starts."** (Andy Rooney, Aug. 15, 2004)

Should be: "You're one of the few theater owners who *don't* run commercials...." An explanation by Bryan A. Garner in his *Modern American Usage*: "...the verb should be plural because who or that is the subject, and it takes its number from the plural noun to which who or that refers...." Garner is one of the experts who explain it best.

A cluster of boo-boos in one *60 Minutes* story:

"He [an economist] says the average French citizen hands over fully 46 percent of all his income to the government in all kinds of taxes. The average American, he says, hands over just 30 percent. That's more than 15 percent less." (Mike Wallace, Dec. 3, 1995)

Whoa! And woe unto those of us who trip over simple numbers. The difference between what Americans pay, 30 percent, and what the French pay, 46 percent, is 16 percentage points. And the American payment is about 33 percent less, not 15 percent.

The last sentence of the boldface excerpt—**"That's more than 15 percent less"**—poses another problem. With *more* and *less* so close, it's hard for a listener to get the point.

But the numbers in that script aren't its only problem. The words also need work. The correspondent says the average American hands the government *just* 30 percent of his income. *Just* 30 percent? Just or unjust, let the number speak for itself: *30 percent* will do. As for "*fully 46 percent*," *fully* is fluffy.

The correspondent also reports that the director of a French orchestra says the government provides "a full 20 percent" of his budget. I don't want to fulminate about *full* and *fully*, but they suggest that the writer was straining to build up the amount.

Another faux pas: the correspondent calls the Champs-Elysees, an elegant boulevard, "noisy and fume-filled." Noisy it may be. But "fume-filled" is not conversational. "Full of fumes" is conversational, but how could the Champs-Elysees—230 feet wide and 6,266 feet long—be full of fumes?

The correspondent goes on to say that a French actress in the 60-percent tax bracket must pay an extra wealth tax that boosts her tax rate to 70 percent. He calls the jump to 70 percent from 60 percent an increase of "10 percent." Wrong. It's an increase of 10 percentage points. Correct: 16.7 percent.

If you're an innumerate, welcome to the club. Many of us need to review a high school textbook that deals with percentages. And we all need to keep in mind some advice in the newsletter *Copy Editor*. It offers five rules from Edward MacNeal, author of *Mathsemantics: Making Numbers Talk Sense*. The rules are worth reviewing:

- Mistrust all percentages over 100. Don't use the word *times* with comparative modifiers, such as *more, larger, better, less, fewer, smaller* and *worse*.
- Double-check comparisons containing words like *tripling* and *three-fold*.
- Avoid mixing fractions, percentages and decimals within [a script], and never mix them within a single comparison.
- Mistrust percentages added to other percentages.
- *Copy Editor* also passes along a passel of other tips on percents. Two of them:
- A tripling is an increase of 200 percent, not 300 percent. A quadrupling is an increase of 300 percent. [Doubling is a 100 percent increase.]
- A phrase like *six times fewer than* is absurd.

To see that your math doesn't do a number on you, make sure someone else in your newsroom checks your math. (No, it isn't called aftermath.)

As for *60 Minutes*' correspondents, they need to take more time.

(August 2004)

CNN

Trying to Keep
Them Honest

Autopsy of an Anderson Cooper Script

When a newscaster says an event is "happening right now," what does that mean?

You guessed it: it depends on the meaning of *now* and *happening*, right? *Happening right now* is a happening phrase at CNN, and a newscast that uses the phrase happens to be *Anderson Cooper 360*. Cooper, the anchor, is quoted in CNN ads saying, "Find the facts, find the truth." So let's.

At 10 p.m., Nov. 16, a Wednesday, Cooper broadcast this extended headline under the umbrella of *happening right now*:

"Tonight, another journalist is coming forward to say he was tipped off about the identity of C-I-A officer Valerie Plame. Bob Woodward says an unnamed Bush administration official told him about Plame a month before she was publicly identified. The Washington Post editor says his source was not Lewis Scooter Libby, the former vice president's chief of staff, now indicted for the leak."

Three defects in that script:

1. Libby was not indicted for the leak. His indictment charges perjury and obstruction of justice in connection with the leak. (CNN calls itself "the most trusted name in news." And Cooper says in full-page ads, "We want to bring you information accurately...." A viewer would be justified in asking, "What's stopping you?")
2. Libby was not the former vice president's chief of staff. Cheney is not a former. Libby is Vice President Cheney's former chief of staff.
3. The AP moved the story about Woodward at 12:11 a.m., Wednesday, 22 hours before Cooper said Woodward is coming forward. Even earlier, that morning's *Washington Post*, usually available before midnight, had run the Woodward story on p. 1. And Woodward himself had released a statement Tuesday night disclosing he had testified the previous day that a high administration official gave him the name of the CIA agent a month before she was publicly identified. At 5

a.m., Wednesday, and throughout the day, CNN reported the story. So Cooper's saying that tonight Woodward is coming forward was misleading.

Next, Cooper said:

"At this hour, the Pentagon is denying accusations that U-S troops deliberately burned Iraqi civilians with a weapon called white phosphorus. That charge is coming from an Italian report [a questionable TV documentary] **saying the incendiary shells targeted civilians** [shells don't target people; people target people] **in Fallujah last year. The Pentagon insists that is simply not true but admits to using** [better: *acknowledges using*] **the weapon on insurgents."**

At this hour? Twenty-nine hours earlier, at 5 p.m., Tuesday, AFP (Agence France-Presse) reported the charge and the Pentagon's denial. Also, at 7:05 p.m., Tuesday, the AP moved a story with the denial. And at 4 p.m., Wednesday, CNN broadcast the story, along with the denial.

Later in his broadcast, Cooper said: **"It would be easy to say that the Pentagon denies doing any such thing. The fact is, the Pentagon does deny the charge, but there's nothing easy about these allegations."** What does that mean?

Cooper might have thought his earlier use of *at this hour* lacked sufficient urgency, so when he introduced the Pentagon story at 11 p.m., in the second hour of his newscast, he said, **"At this moment, the Pentagon pushes back on an allegation that U-S troops used a fire-producing chemical** [white phosphorus] **on civilians in Fallujah last year...."** *At this moment?*

The last headline Cooper delivered near the top of his 10 p.m. newscast: **"And tonight we learned that five more U-S troops died in Iraq today...."** *Tonight we learned?* In fact, CNN reported four of those deaths at 10 a.m. that day, and reported the fifth death at 1 p.m. That was nine hours before Cooper said at 10 p.m., *"We learned...tonight."* Learned tonight?

I learned that Cooper needs to learn a lot more.

Happening right now? Phony baloney.

Keeping them honest? Dishonest.

All in all: too many faults, too much false.

(January, 2006)

Cooper's 'Keeping Them Honest' Raises Questions

Anderson Cooper often says, **"Keeping them honest."** But I don't get it. Honest.

Cooper, anchor of a two-hour nightly newscast on CNN, introduced that phrase, "Keeping them honest," 16 months ago, on Nov. 10, 2005: **"Tonight, we begin a new segment. "Keeping Them Honest," we're calling it. And we start by looking at the levees** [in New Orleans]. **Remember them?"**

After playing his taped interview with a New Orleans newspaper reporter, Cooper said, **"Let's just remember, Washington stops dealing with things when we stop talking about stuff."** What things, what stuff, and who's *we*?

The next night on his *Anderson Cooper 360*, he said, **"Every night we've been keeping the focus on the Gulf in a segment we call 'Keeping Them Honest.'"** After only one night on the air, he said *every night*? Yep.

Ten days later, Cooper said: **"Tonight, in our 'Keeping Them Honest' segment, a look at the allegations out of** [correct: *in*] **Jackson, Mississippi. As the New York Times has reported, you had residents in the area who hadn't suffered any real loss due to the storm, but they were embraced by**

Anderson Cooper

129

cash-rich relief agencies determined to give away millions of dollars in aid." Cooper introduced a CNN reporter who Cooper said had been investigating.

The reporter said the U.S. District Attorney was sifting through about 1,000 complaints and had set up an 800 fraud-complaint hotline. When the reporter signed off, Cooper added, "**'Keeping them honest' tonight.**" Made me wonder: Who had the reporter been keeping honest—the federal prosecutor, the grand jurors, the victims of fraud or the crooks?

The next night, Nov. 22, Cooper made a cameo appearance on the Larry King show to promote his own show. And he plugged the story in Jackson, Mississippi: **"Tonight, we're learning there are indictments for fraud being handed down."** (Indictments are handed *up*.)

"Over the next few days," Cooper said on June 13, 2006, from Los Angeles, **"we're going to be keeping them honest in many places, on many fronts, and bringing you exclusive reports."** But in his four nights on the West Coast, he presented only two reports that he called *exclusive*—a look at tunnels that smugglers used to sneak illegal immigrants into the United States and a look at a vault full of drugs that smugglers had been trying to bring into this country from Mexico. Both those so-called *exclusive*s were broadcast that night. The next night, a CNN announcer said, "This is a special edition of *Anderson Cooper 360*, 'Keeping Them Honest on the West Coast.'" Sounds like a tall order.

That night, June 14, Cooper mentioned only one *exclusive*: **"Angelina Jolie will be with us next Tuesday."** Not exactly. The next night, June 15, in San Francisco, Cooper told his listeners: **"A programming note about my exclusive interview with one of the most talked-about people on the planet, Angelina Jolie. Yesterday, I sat down with the actress and activist, just four days after she and Brad Pitt returned from Namibia with their new baby."** Which suggested she would not be with Cooper the next week in the flesh but on tape. And that's how her broadcast appearance turned out: all on tape. Cooper used *exclusive* that night (June 14) six times, all for his interview with A. Jolie.

The next night, June 16, Cooper's *360* originated in Seattle. "Millions spent to build a jail," the announcer said at the top. "Two years later, it's still not open, and criminals are walking the streets. We're keeping them honest." If CNN is keeping them honest, how? And if they're being kept honest, how can they still be criminals—and still walk the streets?

"We've been here on the West Coast all week keeping them honest," Cooper said. **"We're in Seattle, as I said tonight, right next door to Oregon. We found a story that, well, kind of made our jaws drop.**

A brand-new jail, cost tens of millions to build, but it has never been used. It has been sitting empty now for two years." *We found a story?* In fact, three months earlier, *The Seattle Times* carried an article about the unused jail (in Portland, Oregon) that had run (1,917 words) in the *Los Angeles Times*. Even then, the story had whiskers.

That night, Cooper said *exclusive* five times, again only in connection with the Jolie interview.

When Soledad O'Brien sat in for Cooper on Feb. 27, 2012, she squeezed in **"Keeping them honest"** eight times in an hour. After she identified four CNN anchors who would be delivering news about an election, she said, **"Coming up, 'Keeping them honest,"** then mentioned Syria's government and the fighting in Syria. But she didn't say who was being kept honest. Nor did she say who's keeping them honest—whoever *they* are.

"You said you wanted change in Washington," Cooper said on Jan. 4, 2007. **"You voted for a Democratic Congress. Now they are in power. And we're here in Washington 'Keeping them honest.'"** But he didn't identify anyone being kept honest. Nor did he explain how anyone could be kept honest or would be kept honest after he, Cooper, turned his attention elsewhere. The previous night, Cooper had said of the new Congress, **"We'll be keeping them honest."**

Although Cooper is a full-time employee of CNN, he appears on CBS's *60 Minutes* several times a year. CBS's website says, "His exceptional reporting on big news events of the past five years has earned Cooper a reputation as one of television's pre-eminent newsmen."

Recently, the CNN segment called "Keeping Them Honest" expanded its scope. On Jan 2, Cooper said: **"I want to tell you about a way you can be part of *360*, a way to help us in what we consider one of our missions, keeping them honest. If there is a wrong that needs to be righted in your community, go online and tell us about it."**

CNN's website has reinforced the new approach with this request: "Keeping them honest. It's what we're about at *360*. It includes challenging authority, whistleblowers, corruption. And we want your help. Please send us your tips with enough detail for us to investigate them...."

On Feb. 8, Cooper told his audience: **"We're keeping them honest here in New Orleans. And we want you to help us keep them honest, too. If there's a wrong that needs to be made right in your community in the United States, go online, tell us about it at cnn.com/360."**

Wrongs that need to be righted? How about anchors who promise more than they could ever deliver? And how about keeping *them* honest? (March 2007)

CNN: 'Keeping Them Honest'

When it comes to **"keeping them honest,"** probably no one exceeds Anderson Cooper. Exceeds him, that is, in saying **"keeping them honest."**

On his 10 p.m. newscast of June 25, Cooper said "keeping them honest" eight times. And a correspondent tossed in one more "keeping them honest." So in one hour, they used that phrase nine times, averaging once every 6.7 minutes.

But before people are *kept* honest, they need to be honest already or made honest, but how? And how can Cooper tell whether they're honest? His first use that night of **"keeping them honest"** occurred near the top of the hour:

"And a new twist to the danger we first reported on, sleazeballs peddling prescription drugs over the Internet, no prescription needed. Your age doesn't matter. What are online companies doing to stop it? What about the government? You might not like the answer. [Please don't fret about whether I'll like the answer.] **We're keeping them honest tonight."** Keeping whom honest? The government? Online companies? *Sleazeballs?* If the *sleazeballs* are being kept honest, are they still *sleazeballs*? Besides, how can Cooper, even the whole staff at CNN, keep a sleazeball honest?

As for *the danger we first reported on*, Cooper was not the first, not even the 101st. Nor was CNN the first news organization to report on *sleazeballs peddling prescription drugs over the Internet.* Cooper was not even the first CNN anchor to report on the danger. Every year for at least the past nine years,

> ### Praise for Cooper
>
> When Cooper was hired as a contributor to *60 Minutes*, a CBS press release of May 8, 2006, quoted the executive producer, Jeff Fager, as saying, "Anderson is among the very finest reporters of his generation, and he's got what it takes to be a perfect fit here at '60 Minutes'...."

countless stories—wire service, newspaper and broadcast—have reported the danger of unlicensed pharmacies selling on the Internet prescription drugs with no prescriptions. Long before Cooper's broadcast, other networks reported the danger:

Nine years ago, on July 30, 1999, NBC's *Nightly News* ran a piece that began: **"A government crackdown coming against some of the 300 companies that now sell drugs on the Internet, targeting a growing number operating without license, doctors or legitimate prescriptions. The U-S Food and Drug Administration announcing tougher monitoring as a congressional committee hears horror stories: online drug companies that sent drugs to this seven-year-old girl, to this cat, and to someone who passed away 25 years ago."** *Passed away* should be *died.* And, yes, the correspondent should have said "*is* coming" and "*is* announcing." English-speaking writers not liking that script's *Ing*lish. ABC and CBS also reported the problem of illegal online pharmacies years ago.

> As for other firsts, Cooper may well be the first anchor to make regular use of *keeping them honest* and may also rank first in frequency of its use.

One month before Cooper's broadcast of June 25, he said on May 23's *Anderson Cooper 360*: **"Just ahead, an exclusive CNN investigation: dangerous drugs sold over the internet, prescribed by doctors for people they've never met. It is a big business. It's illegal. It can also be deadly. We're keeping them honest...."** *Exclusive? Keeping them honest?* If they're being kept honest, why is CNN investigating them?

After a commercial, Cooper said: **"A CNN special investigation has uncovered a huge hole in the safety net. With just the click of a mouse, almost anyone who wants to buy prescription drugs can on the Internet. It is so easy it will shock you...."** Then he said, **"CNN's Drew Griffin tonight is keeping them honest."** In the next several minutes, Cooper said **"keeping them honest"** four times. And when Griffin ended his second story that night about Internet prescriptions, Cooper said, **"Drew Griffin, keeping them honest, as always."** Of course.

Three months before Cooper delivered his script of June 25 and spoke of **"the danger we first reported on,"** another CNN anchor, Kiran Chetry, introduced a story about the danger. On March 13, she said: **"The number of websites selling prescription drugs without a doctor's prescription has simply exploded. And many of those buying the potentially lethal medications are actually teens."**

As for other firsts, Cooper may well be the first anchor to make regular use of *keeping them honest* and may also rank first in frequency of its use. If he *is* keeping so many people honest, how come the *sleazeballs*, as he called them, are still operating?

Why raise these questions about Cooper and CNN? I'm just trying to get them to raise their standards a few notches and trying to keep *them* honest.

(July 7, 2008)

CNN: Blitzer Cries Wolf

"Happening now," the anchor Wolf Blitzer exclaimed recently, **"a CNN exclusive—our own Drew Griffin—he catches up with the embattled Illinois governor, Rod Blagojevich, and asks him about the scandal that has state officials now moving to try to force him from office. Stand by. You'll see it for the first time."**

Then Blitzer delivered several other headlines and said dramatically, **"You're in the Situation Room."** Time: 5 p.m., Dec. 12. Immediately, an announcer said, **"This is CNN breaking news."**

Blitzer resumed: **"But first we have some breaking news** [as the announcer just said] **we're working on—exclusive, brand-new video just coming into the Situation Room right now—an exchange between the embattled** [again!] **Illinois governor, Rod Blagojevich, accused of trying to sell Barack Obama's senate seat, and our own Drew Griffin of CNN's Special Investigations Unit. State officials are now moving to oust Blagojevich. Will he step down? I want you to listen to what he said."**

What viewers were about to see was a threefer: not only *exclusive* but also *breaking news* and *happening now*. It sounded as though we were about to hear something big, something important. And Blitzer told viewers to listen. But if they weren't already listening to him, how could they hear him say they should listen? Also, listeners might wonder, How come he didn't tell viewers to watch?

Next, videotape of the CNN reporter in Chicago intercepting Blagojevich as he left his lawyer's office, and the reporter identifying himself: **"Governor, Drew Griffin with CNN. Can you say anything to the people of the state of Illinois, sir?"** No reply. *State* of Illinois? Most of us are already aware that Illinois is a state. Or was Griffin asking about the state of Illinois' well-being? And why did Griffin ask a yes-or-no question? Especially when we all knew that the governor *could* answer a question. But we didn't know whether he *would* answer a question. In any case, don't preface an interview (or would-be interview) by asking whether the subject could or would answer a question; just ask your question.

A few questions a reporter might have asked: What's your response to the allegations against you? How do you plan to defend yourself? How do you explain this to your family—and friends and neighbors? How does it feel to see the contents of your private phone conversations spread around the world? A reporter might have time for only a few of those questions, but at least he'd be steering clear of yes-or-no questions. Don't ask a yes-or-no question unless you want a one-word answer.

Griffin: **"Do you have anything to say?"** [Almost the same as his first question.]

Blagojevich: "I will, at the appropriate time, absolutely." [Suggested response for the reporter: "Why not right now?"]

Now he tells us—after he sells us. The story Blitzer peddled as *exclusive, breaking news* and *happening now* turns out to be no grabber, just a gabber.

Griffin: **"Are you going to resign, sir?"**

Blagojevich: "I'll have a lot to say at the appropriate time." [Suggested response: "I'll give you all the time you want—right now.]

Griffin: **"Governor, are the authorities right in their petition, that criminal complaint? Did you do what they say you did?"** [The governor, who's a lawyer, was highly unlikely to answer those two questions. And indeed he didn't.]

As the governor slid into his car, Griffin asked, **"Governor? Just 30 seconds for anybody? For the state of Illinois?"**

Again, no response. And that's how it ended. Griffin had asked six questions, more or less, all yes-or-no. The governor said next to nothing, only that he'd have something to say at the right time—but nothing now.

When the tape ended, Blitzer chatted with Griffin and told him bluntly: **"At least, he answered one of your questions. At least, he stopped a little bit** [on the way to the car]—**not very much, though."** (CNN re-ran the Griffin-Blagojevich encounter on several newscasts that night. And the next day, CNN re-ran the tape on at least four newscasts.)

When Blitzer had introduced the story, he said it was *happening now*, that it was *breaking news* and *exclusive*. But Griffin's attempted interview was played on tape, so it was definitely not *happening now*. *Breaking news?* Breaking, it was, but hardly news. After all, we assumed Blago would talk when he thought the time was right. As for *exclusive*, that's true: no other reporter was present. Blitzer had promoted the encounter as an *exchange*, but it was small change.

One hour later, Blitzer again promoted the so-called *exchange* as taking place at that very moment. He said on his 6 p.m. newscast: **"Happening now: the embattled Illinois governor talks exclusively to CNN....Listen to what he said in this exclusive exchange."**

Two days later, on Sunday, Dec. 14, at 11 a.m., on *Late Edition*, Blitzer re-played the Griffin-Blago encounter. When the piece ended, Blitzer told Griffin briskly that Blago **"obviously didn't answer...."**

Now he tells us—after he sells us. The story Blitzer peddled as *exclusive, breaking news* and *happening now* turns out to be no grabber, just a gabber. CNN does have a huge news hole to fill, so running the Griffin-Blago exchange was justifiable. But from start to finish, CNN's handling of the story was bad news.

Two CNN anchors who tamper with the time, Blitzer and Cooper, are still at it. At 10 p.m. ET, May 6, 2011, Cooper said on his one-hour program, *Anderson Cooper 360*, **"In other breaking news, there's also, already, been a U-S strike against at least one of the key al-Qaida figures who could make a bid for that leadership. Tonight, we learned, a United States military drone fired a missile some time within the past 48 hours in Yemen aimed at the U-S-born radical cleric Anwar al-Awlaki."** But more than four and a half hours before Cooper delivered that *breaking news*, Blitzer reported the story. The Huffington Post reprinted a Reuters story at 6:01 p.m. reporting the drone attack on al-Awlaki.

Blitzer had begun his "Situation Room" at 5 p.m. ET, by saying, **"Happening now: details of a reported safe house used by the C-I-A to spy on Osama bin Laden...."** *Happening now?* The *National Journal* posted a *Washington Post* story about the CIA safe house the day before, May 5, at 9:08 p.m.—20 hours before Blitzer called it *breaking news*.

At 11 p.m., when Cooper's one-hour program is replayed, any story that he has already called *breaking* becomes an hour older. No problem.

(January 19, 2009)

When Hype Turns to Tripe

The CNN anchor Don Lemon began his 10 p.m. newscast on April 17 grandiosely:

"It is big. It is historic. And it has even grounded the president of the United States. Tonight, the latest on a volcano interruption [whatever that is] **for millions of air travelers worldwide. It's a CNN exclusive."**

Shortly after his own eruption, Lemon crowed:

"This exclusive CNN video from earlier today, a view of the volcano you won't see anywhere else." *Earlier* today? All news happens earlier than any newscast reporting it.

And then Lemon said:

"CNN's Gary Tuchman did something extraordinary today. As you know, he has been reporting from the base of the Iceland volcano. [No, I didn't know.] **Today, he was able to fly around and next to the volcano in a helicopter—the only network TV reporter to get airborne. Tonight, here is his exclusive report."** The *only* network TV reporter to go aloft? We'll see about that. Up to this point, Lemon's complete script (excerpted here) includes three *today*s, three *tonight*s and three *exclusive*s.

Tuchman said his copter had flown **"a few hundred feet"** from the volcano.

Despite Lemon's flamboyant hard sell, Tuchman's coverage was not *exclusive*.

More than 14 hours before Lemon's newscast, on April 17, Neal Karlinsky, on ABC's *Good Morning America*, began his report from a 'copter, **"You can see some exclusive footage looking down into the eruption."**

Three-and-a-half hours before Lemon's broadcast, at 6:30 p.m. ET, ABC's *World News* ran another piece by Karlinsky showing him flying in

138

a chopper. He said he was 600 yards from the volcano. Then he apparently flew closer.

And on NBC's *Nightly News* that evening, Chris Jansing reported on her helicopter flight **"very close"** to the volcano.

This isn't the first time CNN boasted of an exclusive that's not exclusive. And probably not the last.

(April 22, 2010)

When *Breaking News* Needs a Brake

How long is it OK for newscasters to keep calling a story "breaking news"? After the news breaks, when does it cease to be *breaking news*? After two hours? Four hours? Let's look at a recent case that points up the problem:

Last Friday at 6 a.m., on CNN, Alina Cho told her audience, **"Boy, a lot of news overnight. If you went to bed early, it's a very busy news day."** If it's *a very busy news day*, it makes no difference when anyone went to bed.

Then Cho's co-anchor on *American Morning*, John Roberts, said: **"We've got it all for you this morning. We start with breaking news in Missouri."** The story was that of the man who barged into a city council meeting the previous evening and shot five people dead. Then police killed him. But the next morning, was it still *breaking news?*

"A senseless and horrific crime scene at city hall," Roberts said. I've heard of senseless crimes but never senseless crime *scenes*. Anyway, have you ever heard of a crime that was sensible? I don't want to carp, but Roberts said, **"We've got it all."** If anyone could ever have it all, he wouldn't have time to tell it all. A CNN correspondent in Kirkwood, Missouri, said the shooting had begun about 7 p.m. CT.

At the top of CNN's 7 a.m. newscast, Roberts said, **"We begin with breaking news this morning in Kirkwood, Missouri....Five people are dead."** But the killer was also killed, making six dead.

An hour later, near the top of the 8 a.m. newscast, Roberts said, **"Breaking news in Kirkwood, Missouri...."** That was 12 hours after the shootings. Was it still *breaking news?* I had heard that story on the late local news the night before. Yes, the next morning, the story was still news—and there were new details. But *breaking news?*

Another anchor team took over for CNN's 9 a.m. newscast. This time, CNN didn't call the Kirkwood story *breaking news*. After the Kirkwood story was told, an announcer broadcast one sentence, **"Live breaking** news, unfolding developments, see for yourself in the CNN Newsroom."

That sounds like a pitch from a circus barker trying to lure rubes into the tent. At least, it wasn't as tasteless as a line on New York City's "all-news" WINS. An anchor reported the shooting deaths of eight people in a Nebraska mall before Christmas: **"There was more red than green at a mall in Omaha yesterday."**

On CNN's 9 a.m. 'cast, the co-anchor Heidi Collins said five people had been "gunned down" in Kirkwood. "Gunned down" is ambiguous. It can mean "shot dead" or "shot down." So *gunned down* is a good phrase not to use—unless the script first established that the victim was dead. After a CNN correspondent reported from Kirkwood, Collins said, **"What a terrible story."** Without her appraisal, I might not have realized how bad the massacre was. Does she make that same pronouncement after stories about multiple deaths in Darfur, Kenya, Iraq and elsewhere?

The first to report the Kirkwood shootings on the air nationally was MSNBC. Dan Abrams presented the story shortly before 10 p.m. ET, Wednesday, the previous day.

Right after that, at 10:13 p.m., Greta Van Susteren reported what she called a "Fox News alert": the six deaths in Kirkwood.

About 10:30 p.m., CNN carried news of the rampage. The anchor, John King, said, **"Some breaking news now out of the Saint Louis suburb of Kirkwood, Missouri, a shooting, a bad one...."** Better: "from [or *in*] the Saint Louis suburb," not *out of*. King said a gunman shot and killed five people, then was shot dead by police.

The next morning, though, was it still acceptable to call that news *breaking*? It's hard to pin down how long news can rightly be called *breaking*. But 12 hours is far beyond my breaking point.

(February 12, 2008)

CNN Anchor Fobs Off
Old News As New

CNN began its newscast at 10 p.m., June 8, with a jolt:

"Tonight, an attack on Iran, quote, "Unavoidable." Words from an Israeli cabinet official that are setting off a firestorm of concern, reaction, and this: Tonight, gas has hit the four-dollar mark. That is the new national average."

When listeners heard the first five words, they might well have thought an attack was under way. That's because the opening sentence fragment violated a basic rule of broadcast newswriting: attribution precedes assertion. As for the *firestorm*, keep it away from gasoline. As for the cost, this would be better: "The new national average for a gallon of gas has hit four dollars."

After the anchor presented video clips of the program's top stories, he resumed:

"And hello again, everybody. I'm Rick Sanchez. Tonight, politics, energy and the threat of war. An Israeli cabinet minister is saying tonight that an attack on Iran [by whom?] **is, quote, 'Unavoidable.' "**

The cabinet minister *is saying tonight*? No, he wasn't. And it wasn't news; it was olds. Two and a half days earlier (almost 60 hours), about 10:30 a.m. ET, Friday, June 6, CNN itself carried the story of the threatened attack. A CNN reporter said then:

"An Israeli official is quoted as saying an attack on Iran's nuclear site [*sic*] **looks, quote, 'unavoidable.'"** The reporter didn't say who might do the attacking.

Reuters had already said. Five hours earlier, in a story from Jerusalem moved at 5:08 a.m. ET, Reuters wrote, "An Israeli attack on Iranian nuclear sites looks 'unavoidable' given the apparent failure of sanctions to deny Tehran technology with bomb-making potential, one of Prime Minister Ehud Olmert's deputies said on Friday."

That day, June 6, shortly after 3 p.m., a CNN correspondent reported that an Israeli official had said **"a conflict with Iran is unavoidable."**

The threat of a *conflict*, as CNN put it, doesn't pack the punch of the threatened *attack* on Iran. And *conflict* doesn't necessarily mean *armed* conflict. *Webster's New World College Dictionary* says *conflict* "refers to a sharp disagreement or collision."

That night, on CNN's 10 o'clock newscast, a CNN senior political analyst remarked that Israel said war with Iran was inevitable. Again, no mention of the threatened attack. The threat was made by a deputy prime minister; should his threat be attributed to the government? I don't think so.

Two nights later, people listening to CNN's 10 o'clock newscast of Sunday, June 8, were subjected to the time-twisting, either deliberate time-twisting or unintentional time-twisting—if there is such a thing.

Ten minutes after Rick Sanchez's dramatic opening, he acknowledged, perhaps inadvertently, that the threat about an attack on Iran wasn't made that night. He said: **"It's an ominous threat by an Israeli official about attacking Iran.... [He] sent shockwaves through world markets the other day."** *The other day.*

Time-twisters, wherever they work, should know that the facts may eventually come to light. Truth will win out—sometimes.

(June 23, 2008)

CNN: When Bad Things Happen to a Sad Story

A baseball story with a sack of errors: a CNN anchor, T. J. Holmes, recently told viewers:

"A Texas Rangers fan fell 20 feet, head first, to his death at a game last night. The man was at this game with his son when he [the father or the son?] **reached over the railing for a ball that was thrown into the stands by star outfielder Josh Hamilton.** [Where was the game?] **The fan was not immediately identified."** *Not immediately identified?* The fan had been identified at various websites for many hours before Holmes delivered that snippet last Friday, July 8, about 2:20 p.m. ET. Maybe he meant the fan was not immediately identified after the accident. But why say he hadn't been immediately identified 18 hours after the accident—and long after the fan had been identified?

More than seven hours before Holmes told us about the accident, the AP had moved a story identifying the fan as Shannon Stone, 39, a fireman, of Brownwood, Texas.

About 20 minutes after Holmes mentioned the accident on his Friday afternoon newscast, he told viewers:

"We are just getting [better: *we've just received*] **a statement in** [delete *in*] **from Major League Baseball we want to share with you.** [Anchors and reporters everywhere: Don't *share* with us; *tell* us.] **You have seen probably by now the story.** [Sounds like Pennsylvania Dutch: "Throw mama from the train a kiss"; and why tell viewers they've probably seen the story?] **Unfortunately** [no need to tell us it was unfortunate; it's obvious; in fact, it was far worse than *unfortunate*], **a man, a fan at a Texas Rangers game** [where was the game? And what's the name of the other team?] **last night died when he fell from the stands. He went down** [better: *fell*] **head first some 20 feet as he was trying to reach for** [*trying to reach for = reaching for*] **a baseball that one of the players just tossed into the crowd so the fans could have.** [Yes, the

144

last word in that sentence should be *it*. But I'm adhering to the wording of the CNN transcript. CNN calls it a "rush transcript...that may not be in its final form"; Holmes should proceed chronologically in describing the fan's reaching for the ball and then falling.]

"It was one of these foul balls. [*These?***] It was out of play** [Most non-fans probably don't know what *out of play* means.] **and oftentimes** [*often!*] **they'll just toss them up and let the fans have them. He** [who *he?*] **was reaching for it and fell over. He went down 20 feet** [repetitious].

"He was actually [needless] **conscious, the players say, as he was leaving on the stretcher** [better: The players say he was conscious as he was leaving....], **but then died later as he was being rushed to the hospital.** [better: He died in an ambulance taking him to a hospital.] **Major League Baseball putting out** [correct: *put out*] **this statement, and I'm just going to quote here for you** [delete *and I'm just going to quote here for you*.]. **It says** [delete *it says*], **'All of us here at Major League Baseball are shocked and saddened over the tragic death of Mr. Stone, the evening, last evening. Our thoughts and prayers are with his son and his entire family. Major League Baseball has the utmost sensitivity** [self-serving; anchor should remind audience of source.] **to the safety of all the fans that come to our ballparks. Our players are encouraged to be fan-friendly, and we will carefully review this incident with our clubs to continue to ensure a safe environment for our fans.'**

"Now [*now?*], **they mentioned the son in the statement there** [*there?*]. **The son was right there with him and watched his dad go over the railing there.** [*There* three times in one breath.] **Some of the ball players** [note to transcriber: *ballplayers* is one word] **report** [better: *say*] **that even** [*even?*] **the man was asking about his son, saying, "Someone check on my son" as he was being taken out.** [better: "Some players say that after the man fell, he was still alert—and asked about his son"; the son's age should be included; he's 6.]

"But an unfortunate [again, unfortunately] **incident last night, Major League Baseball alluding to possibly looking at changing not necessarily a policy, but of having the players toss the balls up into the stands, because oftentimes when foul balls, any time the balls go into the stands, fans oftentimes** [*oftentimes* twice in one sentence? And used for the third time? Wouldn't *often* do the job? Further, the MLB statement didn't say or imply what Holmes said.] **go after them pretty aggressively.**

We have seen incidents and accidents [why both?] **before, people be-ing injured, but a death here** [*here*? In the CNN studio? The fatal fall was the second such fall in a major league ballpark this season], **and it's certainly** [*an*] **unfortunate one. But the latest there** [*there* again?] **from Major League Baseball."** Still missing is Shannon Stone's first name. I'm old school: I like first and last names. I'd also like to know Stone's age, oc-cupation and where he lived.

Also missing: a coherent account.

I don't have the time or patience to point out all the broadcast's short-comings, but I'd like to know, Where was the editor? Where was the producer? Where was Holmes himself?

That CNN presentation deserves a K; baseball fans who keep score-cards know that's the symbol for a strikeout.

(July 14, 2011)

CNN Anchor Likes Astrologer, Astrology and Astrologizing

Of all the *ism*s and *ology*s in the world, one of the flakiest is astrology. It has been denounced, discredited and declared dead by scientists for centuries—but not by CNN. Or, at least, not by everyone at CNN.

Network newscasters rarely mention astrology, so when I saw a CNN anchor take an astrologer seriously, I was taken aback.

Despite the widespread debunking of astrology, many Americans believe in the pseudoscience; one in four, according to the Pew Research Center. And many Americans believe in ghosts, extraterrestrials and other nonsense. But a journalist?

On CNN's 3 p.m. newscast, Jan. 14—according to a CNN transcript—the anchor, Brooke Baldwin, said:

"Coming up next, a story everybody is talking about today. [*Everyone?*] **You perhaps always considered yourself a Gemini, perhaps a Cancer. Now I'm a Gemini. I don't know what is going on. Maxine Taylor hopefully knows.** [Let us hope anchors learn how to use *hopefully* correctly—and then not use it at all.] **She is our** [*our?*] **astrologer, and we'll talk to her and get to the bottom of this, next."**

Then the so-called interview:

Baldwin: **Now this—is this the dawning of the age of—this is so tough to pronounce, Maxine Taylor, Ophiuchus, the third sign? We'll go there in a minute. I knew I'd botch that. The Internet is buzzing over the realignment of the stars, and it supposedly adds this 13th sign to the zodiac. Suddenly 'what is your sign' is taking on a whole new meaning. Thought you were Libra, you may be Virgo, perhaps this new sign I can't pronounce altogether. Maxine Taylor is an astrologer and here to walk me through what all of this means. The whole thing started because of this newspaper interview with**

147

an astrology [*astronomy!*] professor who says the wobble of the earth and the orbit just changed everything a little bit. People are so upset about this. Are you buying this?"

Maxine Taylor, astrologer: Not at all.

Baldwin: **Why?**

Taylor: First of all, he is an astronomer, and that explains everything to me, thank you very much. [Astronomers deal with facts; they don't promote superstition.]

Baldwin: **Oh, burned.**

Taylor: What it is, bottom line, every few years somebody says, oh, there's a 13th sign. Well, you've met him at the cocktail lounge.

Baldwin: **Maxine.**

Taylor: Seriously, there are 12 signs. There have always been 12 signs. Let's talk about the fact that some people are worried they're being bumped back a sign.

Baldwin: **People are worried they've got like their Sagittarius tattoos or Cancer posters and it's your self-identity for people into this kind of thing, and they're perturbed.** [*got like*? I no like].

Taylor: Very perturbed. Here's what it is. Years and years ago, thousands of years ago, the zodiac was discovered. We use that zodiac. It's called the tropical zodiac. This is what astrologers use. There is another zodiac that some astrologers use as well. It's called the sidereal zodiac, and that deals with the constellations rather than the signs. Because of the precession of the equinox, you'll have to Google that one.

Baldwin: **Oh, goodness.**

Taylor: What this means is, there are two. Bottom line, they both work for the people who use them. Most of the world uses the tropical. And what that means is that you will be, if you are born a Cancerian, you will be a Cancerian until you leave.

Baldwin: **This is your line of work. You have people coming to your home. You have a website. Have you been, you know, is your phone ringing off the hook from people worried?**

Taylor: I've been inundated with e-mails, particularly on Facebook, and yes, people are concerned, because, as I said, every five, ten years somebody rediscovers the fact that there are two zodiacs. Hello. They've been around.

Baldwin: **Are you surprised so many people are so bothered? I mean, the people that are shaking their heads at those of us who are so bothered by it.**

Taylor: No, not at all.

Baldwin: **Horoscopes. Who knew they mattered?**

Taylor: Nobody would change their sign. Would you change yours?

Baldwin: **I'm a Cancer. I've taken Cancer on as my sign. I can't imagine being a Gemini.**

Taylor: I am a Gemini. That's why I'm able to talk like this. I wouldn't want to be a Taurus. Nothing against Taurus. If you're a Leo, you like being a Leo. If you're a Sag [Sagittarius], you like that. You don't want to bounce back.

Baldwin: **So bottom line, people shouldn't buy the hoopla about the 13th sign I can't even pronounce.**

Taylor: Not at all. And I can't pronounce it either. This, too, will move along. Tomorrow there will be more news.

Almost two years ago, Brooke Baldwin "interviewed" the same Atlanta astrologer. On CNN's 11 a.m. newscast, Feb. 6, 2009, the anchor Tony Harris introduced the segment by saying (according to a CNN transcript):

"These financial tough times prompting people to seek advice in unusual places. Some even looking to some celestial bodies. Our Brooke Baldwin explains."

Excerpts from the "interview":

Baldwin (on camera): **Have you ever been wrong?**

Taylor: Yes.

Baldwin (voice-over): **Only once, according to Maxine, and that was an accident. She says she tells it like it is. And in her 42-year career, so far, so good.** [How did Brooke Baldwin know Taylor has been wrong only once?]

Taylor: We are going to be having help with the economy this summer. [What kind of help? From whom?]

Baldwin: **That's one prediction that might convince even the nonbelievers to watch for the planets and the stars to align. Brooke Baldwin, CNN, Atlanta.**

The day after that "interview" ran, CNN's noon newscast ran it again. Might make you wonder whether CNN stands for Celestial News Network. Unfortunately, astrology is still alive and sick.

(January 19, 2011)

CNN: *Out in the Open*

Yes, Paula Zahn is perky, but some of her scripts are quirky.

Maybe quirky isn't the right word, but it does rhyme. Maybe the word I'm looking for is *strange*. At least, strange for a network anchor.

"Out in the open tonight," she said, **"America's newest guilty pleasure. See why everyone is fascinated by the death of Anna Nicole Smith."** (CNN, *Paula Zahn Now*, 8 p.m. ET, Feb. 16)

Out in the open? Had it been secret? *Everyone*? As newscasters say, More on that later. Zahn went on:

"We start with the country's favorite story. Don't bother denying it. We have seen the ratings. We have watched the magazines fly off the racks. We know millions of you are out there." *Millions of you*? Her viewers were recently estimated at 400,000.

"So tonight, why everyone seems to be [*to be* need not be] **fascinated with the Anna Nicole Smith story. We are bringing the reasons out in the open tonight...."** Bringing them out in the open? The reasons were hardly hush-hush: sexpot goes to pot. And sex sells. Smith herself had never been one for concealment. Even before *Playboy* uncovered her in 1992, she had been a stripper, all out in the open.

Zahn told viewers that the previous night she had asked viewers to go to her website and vote on this question: "Are you interested in the Anna Nicole Smith story?" She added, **"Tomorrow we're going to have the results and bring out in the open reasons why people are so fascinated with this dirty laundry."** *Reason why* is redundant. And *dirty laundry* is misused: dirty laundry, also called dirty linen, applies to private matters that could cause embarrassment if made public. Smith is—and was—beyond embarrassment.

On the next night, Feb. 16, Zahn reported 29 percent of the voters said yes, they're interested in the Smith story; even though 71 percent said no, they were not interested, Zahn said **"everyone seems to be fascinated...."** Her one-hour program gave the Smith saga about 20 minutes.

The same night, Zahn also described four other stories as **"out in the open,"** but they, too, were widely known. Her program features what she calls an "Out in the Open Panel." Panels have three members, not always the same three, and they express their views, but not every night. And not about every story.

A month later, Zahn said:

"Tonight, I want to bring one of the unforeseen consequences of the war out in the open. For all the talk we hear about supporting the troops, here is a shameful truth: hundreds of U-S veterans have come home from the war only to find themselves homeless." (March 19)

Stories about homeless Iraq veterans have been reported in the media for several years. Three weeks before her broadcast, msnbc.com posted a *Newsweek* story about homeless Iraq vets (Feb. 24); the first two words in the article were "Kevin Felty." In Zahn's coverage on March 19, the first person seen and heard on the videotape: Kevin Felty.

CNN's website says, "'Paula Zahn NOW' takes you inside the news and behind the headlines from around the country and across the globe." Shouldn't that be "*across* the country and *around* the globe"?

A few more of Zahn's *out in the open*ings:

"And who actually is fit to adopt? China says, if you're fat or gay or single, you aren't. Should China get away with it?" (Jan. 5) Say, it's their bat and ball.

"Just about eight minutes from now, we will shine a light on America's hidden secrets, bringing intolerance out in the open." (Jan. 29) Zounds! Intolerance? Who ever would have suspected that in some places it's still tolerated? And secret?

"Out in the open: the quiet crisis, mortgage meltdowns that could cost you your house and affecting just about everyone else, potentially destroying the economy." (March 23) Cost me my house? I don't have one. Destroying the economy? She might have meant *damaging*.

"And we are bringing a shocking fact out in the open tonight. We were just stunned when we heard this: one-third of the people who live in Washington, D-C, the nation's capital, are functionally illiterate." (March 20) *Out in the open*? The AP had moved the story about illiteracy 31 hours earlier.

"Well, tonight, with the Iraq war now going into its fifth year, we're bringing the search for an endgame out in the open." (March 20) Had the search been on the QT?

"Out in the open tomorrow night," she said on March 21, **"you're not going to believe this one. A Florida preacher launching a series of sermons on sex...."** Please don't tell me what my reaction is going to be. Besides, if someone tells me I'm not going to believe it, why should I? OK, OK, I know it's intended as a lure, but it's so trite, it lacks allure. That week, Zahn used *you aren't going to believe this* three times. Believe it.

Sex sermons out in the open? Two months earlier, on Jan. 27, a newspaper in Fort Myers, Florida, ran a story about those local sermons advertised on a highway billboard. That huge ad was certainly out in the open. And now so is Zahn's *out in the open*.

(April 2007)

TWO-TIMING, INCORRECT, UNHEALTHY NEWS

Wanted: Network News People Who Can Spell

If *60 Minutes* had taken one more minute to check the spelling in a graphic, CBS News would not have wound up recently with ugh on its face.

A full-screen illustration on *60* had the title "Fairwell to a Queen."

"Fairwell"? No such word. The word is "farewell." A spell-checker should have flagged it, because "fairwell" is a non-word. No matter what, a human who knows how to spell should have double checked.

Was the person who misspelled "farewell" a golfer, with his mind on a fairway—or a gofer? (The Queen in that graphic on Jan. 25 refers to the passenger ship QE2.)

CBS also had a spelling problem with the prospective auction of what the would-be seller had said was a vial of blood from President Reagan. But on the *Evening News* of May 22, 2012, while a correspondent was speaking, CBS displayed the words "BLOOD VILE." Below those words was a shot of the vial. The blunder prompted the ESPN producer Willie Weinbaum to quip in an e-mail, "That was a vile-ation of good spelling practice."

More and more, networks seem to care less and less about spelling. Not just Aaron Spelling, but also errin' spelling. Yes, "err" is pronounced "ûr" as in urn, not like "air." But I made use of my unexpired poetic license.

ABC News has also had trouble with its ABCs. *World News Tonight* ran a graphic Feb. 20 on prisoners but spelled it "prisioners." Whoever let that get past may be guilty of what the law calls misprision—observing an offense and failing to stop or report it. If he were found guilty, I suppose he'd be a misprisioner.

And NBC's *Today* misspelled the name of one of NBC's most famous stars, a pioneer host of the *Tonight Show*, Jack Paar. The morning after his death, in a tribute on *Today,* Jan. 28, at 8 a.m. ET, a graphic spelled it "Parr." That's sub-par.

CNN *Headline News* ran "Whistler Blower's Allegations." *Whistler?* Yep. That's what the graphic said. It ran at 11:30 p.m., Feb. 13. Apparently, no one at CNN blew the whistle, because it ran again. (And maybe again. And again.) Further, whistle-blower is not two words. Either hyphenate it or spell it as one word.

The Fox News Channel, at 8:30 p.m., Feb. 28, ran a story about Mormons with a graphic about "Mormans." How did that happen? Maybe the person responsible wrote it after reading about the Normans. (No, I don't mean Mailer, Rockwell or Greg Norman.)

And it's only sporting to include ESPN. At noon, Feb. 3, it ran a graphic for Duluth, Minnesota, spelled "Diluth." Makes you wonder: was the culprit an intern who's a collidge athalete?

And at the BBC News website, a correspondent in Columbia, South Carolina, wrote, in an item updated at 1:39 p.m. ET, Feb. 3, "I'm at a school in Colombia."

Misspellings can have unhappy consequences on both screens and scripts. A misspelling in a script can cause an anchor to mispronounce a word. Or cause a production assistant who's looking for the correct spelling to walk away from you misinformed. And a misspelling can cause a copy editor to wonder whether she needs to keep a close eye on a writer who's careless and couldn't care less.

Getting it right is more than a matter of pride and professionalism. If a newsroom misspells a simple word that goes on-screen, viewers might wonder whether it's also careless in its reporting. Although misspellings detract from a station's or a network's credibility and authority, and call into question the quality of the newscast itself, many broadcasters don't seem overly concerned. That's apparent to anyone who watches the news crawls.

Good spellers don't rely on spell-checkers, and poor spellers shouldn't. A spell-checker can't determine from the context whether the word being checked is the right one. If you write that a Congressional committee *overseas* an agency, your spell-checker wouldn't object because *overseas* is a word, and it's spelled correctly. Spell-checkers also accept *martial* when you mean *marshal*. And accept *alter* when you mean *altar*. That confusion inspired this doggerel:

I have a spelling checker
It came with my PC;
It plainly marks four my revue
Mistakes I cannot sea.
I've run this poem threw it,
I'm sure your pleased too no,
Its letter perfect in it's weigh,
My checker tolled me sew.
—*Janet Minor*

Connoisseurs of misspellings might savor a few choice morsels from my collection of scripts from stations around the country:

"Meanwhile, ____'s parents say thier son was in a car accident 8 years ago that left him unconscience for 27 days." (Their son wasn't the only one unconscious.)

"... families are in temporary homes this morning after loosing their apartments to fire. Still, their are stories of hope." (But little hope for a script that's a loser.)

"Dallas police say a man who's body was found in the trunk of a car was murdered." (Whose responsibility was it to police that script?)

"The town through a party instead." (A thorough editor would have thrown that back to the writer.)

"80 pigs parish in a farm fire." (Trapped in their pew?)

" ...testifying before a Congressional committee about last week's trajick fire." Even when *tragic* is spelled correctly, it's one of the most abused, misused and overused words in news scripts.

"High school students in Durham region set to write exams in the morning may not half to." (But editors have to be examiners.)

People who know how to spell may think that networks, at the peak of the industry's pyramid, would certainly see to it that words appearing on screen in a newscast were spelled correctly. Wrong. But the networks and the locals need only buy a hand tool invented in the 18th century: the English dictionary. Not an online dictionary but an on-paper dictionary. (I recommend the *American Heritage*.) Then make sure people use it. When they do, they'll fare well—at least spellingwise, if not otherwise.

(April 2004)

Network News Often
Gives Us a Bad Time

We're being two-timed, and I'm not going to take it any more. At least, not until I complete this complaint. Here's my problem, really *our* problem:

The most elastic words in our language are *taffy* and *Slinky®*. No problem there. But in some broadcast newsrooms, the most elastic words are *today* and *tonight*. And they're twisted daily. For some listeners, it's irritating. Makes us wonder whether fresh scripts are fed into a time machine that rejiggers the time elements, digitally advancing the time: *yesterday* news is *today*ed. And *today* news is *tonight*ed—at the speed of dark.

Let's look at a story where time was stood on its head—and listeners were misled:

On Monday, Jan. 20, at 2:30 a.m. GMT, the AP moved a story from London about a police raid on a mosque there. The British news agency Press Association reported that the raid had started at 2 a.m., GMT, which is five hours ahead of ET in the United States. That means the AP story reached newsrooms in this country at 9:30 p.m. ET, Sunday. In New York City, I heard it on the late news, Sunday, Jan. 19.

The next day, Jan. 20, I did a double take when I heard a newscaster speak of *today*'s raid. And I wanted to find out whether other newscasters were tinkering with the time. They were.

About 4:30 a.m. ET, Monday, Jan. 20, an anchor of *ABC World News This Morning* said the raid took place **"this morning"** and introduced a correspondent in London. He reported, **"It was 2 a.m. this morning when British anti-terrorist police...."** (Yes, *2 a.m. this morning* is redundant, but he was right about the time where he was.)

Wherever we are, we operate by the time in that place. If I board a plane in Chicago for an 8 p.m. London flight, in London it's already tomorrow there. Once I'm settled in my seat at 7:45 p.m., would I use a

phone to tell someone, "I'm leaving for London tomorrow"? Not unless
I've gone haywire.

How did other national newscasts present—or misrepresent—the time
of the raid? Here are snippets from several 'casts:

NBC's *Today* said, **"Police in London raided a mosque this morning...."**

CBS's *Early Show* reported an **"early morning raid,"** but didn't say
today.

CNN said, about 10 a.m., **"Police in Britain have raided a mosque
this morning."** With the present perfect tense—*have raided*—we don't
use a time element. And certainly not one that's false. If any newscaster
in the States had consulted a clock, a calendar and his conscience, he'd
have acknowledged that the raid was made the previous night. Sure, *last
night* and *yesterday* are dirty words in a lead, but that's why God created
the present perfect tense. The day after the raid, Jan. 20, cnn.com posted
an article datelined London, saying, correctly, the raid had taken place
Monday around 2 a.m., GMT—9 p.m., ET, Sunday, Jan. 19.

About 3 p.m., Monday, Jan. 20, NPR said, **"Police raided a London
mosque today."**

Claire Shipman*, ABC World News Tonight,* said, **"Before dawn in
London today, police raided a mosque...."** Then she said to a Washington correspondent, **"I take it the discovery** [*discovery?*] **of the raid of
this temple** [*temple?*] **was no surprise."** The correspondent's first words
were **"It was really no surprise."**

Dan Rather, *CBS Evening News*, said, **"Also in London today, police
raided a mosque and arrested seven men.**

Tom Brokaw, *NBC Nightly News*, said: **"Now to London, where a
controversial mosque was the target today of the war on terror. British police have arrested seven men, and they say the mosque has
connections to terrorist cases in this country, including the so-called
shoe bomber."**

Also at 6:30 p.m., the Fox News Channel said, **"Police in London
used battering rams and ladders to raid a mosque this morning...."**

A half hour later, MSNBC said, **"Police in London making seven arrests in a raid at a mosque...."** But anchor not speaking English. Sounding as if police making arrests at that very moment even as newscaster
misspeaking. Who talking that way?

At 10 p.m., in Toronto, CBC-TV's *The National* said, **"In London today, officers from Scotland Yard used battering rams to raid a mosque...."**

Just as easily as some scripts convert *yesterday* into *today*, some scripts turn *today* into *tonight*. On Jan. 8, a Turkish Airlines plane crashed in Turkey about 2 p.m. ET. Yet Dan Rather of the *CBS Evening News* said, **"The British-made Turkish Airlines jet went down as it tried to land tonight...."**

Shifting time ahead may make the news sound more newsy. But for smart listeners, it can make the whole newscast sound shifty. As the legal maxim puts it, *Falsus in uno, falsus in omnibus*: False in one thing, false in everything. So when a witness in court is caught lying, all his testimony becomes suspect. And that's the way it is, in courtrooms and in newsrooms.

(February 2003)

How Newscasts Fiddle
with the Time and Day

For Einstein, not everything was relative: "The separation between past, present and future is only an illusion...."

Physicists may accept that, but journalists? And how! In many broadcast newsrooms, *yesterday*, *today* and *tonight* have melded into a single, seamless span.

True, *yesterday* is a dirty word in broadcast leads, but for reporting an event that happened yesterday, many newscasters say, "No problem." As long as they think it's fine with Einstein, they apparently figure it's all right to say it happened *today* or *tonight*. Doesn't that make the news newsier?

The earthquake off Sumatra (an island in Indonesia) struck Sunday, Dec. 26, at 7:59 a.m., local time. But in this country, the quake struck Saturday, Dec. 25, at 7:59 p.m. ET. At 9:31 p.m. ET, the AP moved 160 words on the earthquake. A reporter in Indonesia could have correctly said the quake occurred *today* or *this morning*.

Anchors are expected to tell the time according to where they sit (or stand). They could have avoided the dreaded *yesterday* or *last night* by using the present perfect tense: "An earthquake has struck...."

But an anchor on NBC's Sunday *Today*, Tom Costello, turned it into a *today* story: **"A series of tidal waves has crashed into Southeast Asia and India today...."** CBS News also *today*ed it: at 9 a.m., the anchor of *Sunday Morning*, Charles Osgood, said, **"One of the worst earthquakes since 1900 struck Southern Asia today."** In fact, on Saturday night in Manhattan, by 11 o'clock, ET, the westbound tsunami had already swept past Sri Lanka and the southern tip of India.

Also at 9 a.m. ET, Sunday, a CNN anchor, too, said the quake and tsunami occurred *today*. (But at 7 a.m., another CNN anchor had referred accurately to **"last night's"** quake.)

At noon, Sunday, an anchor for NPR said, **"The most powerful earth-quake in 40 years occurred in Southeast Asia today...."** And at 4 p.m. ET, a CNN anchor said, **"The fifth largest earthquake ever recorded and the massive tsunamis it triggered today...."**

Prosecutors sometimes accuse defense attorneys of trying to confuse jurors by throwing sand in their eyes. Similarly, when it comes to stories from the Middle East, some newscasters throw sand in the eyes of viewers.

On Dec. 24, a fuel truck exploded in Baghdad. Reuters moved five sentences at 2:23 p.m. ET. Three hours later, a CNN anchor said, **"Happening now in Baghdad** [an explosion in slo-mo?], **an apparent suicide bomber explodes a fuel tanker in a residential neighborhood."** And at 6 p.m., another CNN anchor said, **"Tonight a suicide bomber kills eight people in Baghdad."** More than four hours after the explosion, John Roberts said on the *CBS Evening News*, **"A bomb planted in a butane tanker truck exploded in a huge fireball tonight in an affluent west Baghdad neighborhood."**

Another network newscast also fast-forwarded the time:

"Israeli security forces confirm tonight that they were behind the assassination of a Hamas leader in Syria." (John Seigenthaler, *NBC Nightly News*, 6:30 p.m. ET, Sept. 26, 2004.) *Tonight?* Israelis had confirmed their role long before that newscast. At 10:05, a.m. CT, that day, KXAN-TV, the NBC affiliate in Austin, Texas, posted an AP story on its website: "Israeli security sources acknowledge that the country is responsible for the killing of a top Hamas leader...."

The farther away from us the story takes place, the greater the likelihood that a newscaster will make time fly, as when police prevented a terrorist attack outside the U.S. consulate in Karachi—about 7:15 a.m., Monday, March 15, 2004, local time. Pakistan is 10 hours ahead of New York City, where it was about 9:15 p.m., the previous day, Sunday.

Yet, on Monday, at 6:30 p.m. ET, March 15, Dan Rather, the anchor of the *CBS Evening News*, said, **"A terror attack against a U.S. target in Pakistan came oh, so close today."**

And Peter Jennings, the anchor of ABC's *World News Tonight*, said, **"Tonight, a large bomb was found outside the U-S consulate in the Pakistani city of Karachi...."** Jennings broadcast that from Iraq, where it was already the next day, Tuesday.

Two nights later, on March 17, 2004, John Roberts spoke of another story on the *CBS Evening News*: **"As the anniversary of the U-S invasion of Iraq approaches, terrorists there are stepping up their attacks.**

They struck hard tonight in the very heart of Baghdad. A huge bomb blew up a hotel...."

Tonight? Reuters reported the explosion at 12:16 p.m. ET. CNN quoted Reuters at 12:20 p.m., and ABC News broke into regular television programming with a bulletin at 12:44 p.m.—about six hours before the CBS newscast said the explosion happened *tonight.*

In broadcast obituaries, time-twisting can keep a death from being untimely:

"Actor Peter Ustinov died today at a clinic in Switzerland," Dan Rather said on the *CBS Evening News*, 6:30 p.m., Monday, March 29, 2004. Twelve hours earlier, CBS's *Morning News* said correctly that Ustinov had died the night before.

Another man who died after his time:

"Oscar-winning composer Elmer Bernstein, who wrote the music for some 200 movies, has died today at the age of 82." (Scott Pelley, *CBS Evening News*, Thursday, Aug. 19, 2004). But at 7 a.m. that day, CBS's own *Early Show* reported Bernstein had died the day before.

There may be no evidence that those newscasters were trying to deceive audiences. But there is proof that some serial offenders are, at the very least, careless with the truth.

Newscasters who shift time don't do it all the time, only from time to time. No matter what the frequency, fogies, fussbudgets and fuddy-duddies fixated on factuality object. After all, really before all, time-shifting fails the first test of journalism: is it true?

(January 9, 2005)

Network Mistakes Leave Big Tips

We may smile when someone says, "Doctors bury their mistakes, lawyers appeal theirs, and architects plant vines." But don't smirk; many of our mistakes get broadcast.

Even so, some good can come from our mistakes, as long as a newsroom post-mortem points them out, corrects them and sends us home with a few lessons. Let's look at several network mistakes and see what lessons we can carry away:

"She is the wife of one president, the mother of another. Barbara Bush occupies a unique place in political history ...." (Stone Phillips, NBC, *Dateline*, Oct. 19, 2003) *Unique* means "one of a kind." But someone else was there first: Abigail Adams, wife of President John Adams and mother of President John Quincy Adams.

"There was another suicide bomb [*sic*] in Baghdad tonight, this time at the Turkish embassy." (Peter Jennings, ABC, *World News Tonight*, Oct. 14, 2003) Not *tonight* there wasn't. In fact, the AP reported the bombing occurred about 2:45 p.m., Baghdad time. That was nine hours ahead of ET. Thus, the explosion occurred about 5:45 a.m. ET—13 hours before the anchor said it happened *tonight*. On CNN's *American Morning*, 7 a.m. ET, a correspondent reported from the bombing scene. Almost 12 hours after that broadcast, when ABC said *tonight*, was that a mistake? Or a misrepresentation? What do *you* think?

That script's use of *another* detracts from the newsiness of the story. Suicide bombings take place in Iraq almost every day, so *another* seems to shrug off the gravity of the bombing, making it just another item. The script would have been much stronger if it had skipped *there was* and gone straight to the core of the story: "A suicide bomber in Baghdad blew up his car today at the Turkish embassy...."

"As the casualties mounted, Americans grew skeptical and the President's approval sunk to pre-September eleventh lows." (John Roberts, *CBS Evening News,* Dec. 31, 2003) *Sunk* should be the past tense *sank*.

"The conjoined twins are laying on a special 360-degree table built just for this operation." (Jim Cummins, *NBC Nightly News,* Oct. 11, 2003) The twins are *lying* on the table. The table was built just for this operation, so there's no need to say it was special.

"If you take away the accountants and the C-E-O's, you're left with a small, insular world filled with renegades and outcasts who like to flaunt society's rules." (Steve Kroft, CBS, *60 Minutes*, Nov. 23, 2003) *Flout*, not *flaunt*. Flaunt means "exhibit ostentatiously." Flout means "show contempt for."

"So it's a very large area that they are walking by foot, trying to find anything under trees, under old fences, in the wrecks of old cars, houses that have been destroyed." (CNN, 4 p.m., Dec. 27, 2003) *Walking by foot*? Well, at least, he didn't say "walking by pedal extremities."

"So far, 15 former HealthSouth employees have pled guilty." (Mike Wallace, *60 Minutes*, Oct. 12, 2003) Stylebooks—those of the AP, *Washington Post*, *New York Times*, *Los Angeles Times* and *Wall Street Journal*—say the past tense is *pleaded*. And they plead: don't use *pled*.

"This is an amazing story. Some are even calling it a miracle. [I'm not. I was taught that *miracle* is a religious term.] The family of a toddler being treated for a deadly form of cancer gets an unexpected surprise." (CNN, 5 p.m., Nov. 14, 2003) *Unexpected surprise* is redundant. A surprise *is* unexpected. If something is expected, it's not a surprise. On the same newscast, the anchor said in another story: "A very bizarre twist in this very sad story. Sheriff Furlong, thanks very much for joining us." *Very*, *very*, *very*: self-defeating.

"Judge Patricia Wald formerly sat on the International Criminal Tribunal for the former Yugoslavia." (NPR, 8 p.m., Dec. 14, 2003) Formerly means "at a time in the past." But the newscaster used the past tense *sat*, so *formerly* is unnecessary. Even if *formerly* were needed, *formerly* and *former* shouldn't show up in the same short sentence.

"In close proximity was a spider hole with a three-foot-deep entranceway." (Thalia Assuras *CBS Evening News,* Dec. 15, 2004) *Proximity* is closeness. *Close proximity* is redundant.

"And here is a mug shot for the ages, the picture that says it all: the reign of terror of Saddam Hussein in power, and more recently in hiding, is finally over." (Fox News, 9 a.m., Dec. 14, 2003.) Whatever Saddam was doing in hiding, he was no longer imposing a reign of terror. *Says it all* says nothing at all; it's a meaningless cliché. A photo says something, but no photo says it all, especially that photo. It only raises questions: How was Saddam caught? Why didn't he resist? Or did he resist? How did the troops find him? How long had he been in that hole? How had he avoided capture for so long? Who, if anyone, had been helping him? What was his life like on the run? What was it like to live underground? How's his health? Where's his wealth? Will he cooperate? Does he know the whereabouts of any of the missing cards in the deck? Will he turn them in? What about WMD? Where's his wife? What will his capture mean to the insurgency? What's going to happen to him now? What will his status be? Will he try to make a deal? Even if we get answers to those and countless other questions, all the answers won't *say it all.*

"Less than 20-thousand people have set foot here since it was discovered in 1911." (CNN, 8 p.m., Feb. 9, 2003) Should be *fewer*, not *less*. When talking about countable things, we use *fewer*; when talking about the uncountable, we use *less*. A Dictionary of Modern American Usage by Bryan A. Garner says: "Strictly, *less* applies to singular nouns (less tonic water, please) or units of measure (less than six ounces of epoxy). *Fewer* applies to plural nouns...or numbers of things." And *The American Heritage Book of English Usage* says you can use *less than* before a plural noun that denotes a measure of time, amount or distance.

"When the U-S invasion came last spring, with promises of democracy and self-rule, people in Karbala were among the first to try and take charge of their own affairs." (Steve Kroft, *CBS 60 Minutes*, Dec. 7, 2003) *Try and take* should be *try to take*.

"Self-confessed cannibal Armin Meiwes tells his trial in Kassel of a lifelong obsession that led to him eating a fellow human." (BBC News website, Dec. 3, 2003) *Self-confessed?* Delete *self*. Only he himself could confess his crime. So *self-confessed* is redundant. Also: *him eating* should be *his eating*, a pronoun that modifies a gerund usually requires the possessive.

"The Cole was attacked by terrorists while it was docked in Yemen in October of the year 2000, leaving 17 sailors dead." (NPR, 11 a.m., Feb. 3, 2003) The U.S. Navy destroyer was not docked. The author of *All About the U.S. Navy*, Capt. Edmund Castillo, USN (Ret.), told me the Cole had been in the process of mooring to a barge anchored in the harbor. *In the process of* is usually superfluous, but there, I hope, it helps to clarify the scene. (No, I don't think that NPR newsman should be docked.)

"It isn't hard to see where Hurricane Isabel collided with the Chesapeake Bay...." (Bob Orr, *CBS Morning News*, Oct. 6, 2003) Only moving objects collide. The storm hit the bay. Or struck it, or pounded it, or hammered it or swept across it.

"This is the town of Devore, where today two of the big fires joined and where winds whipped up flames and smoke so badly that at times you couldn't even see across the street." (James Hattori, *NBC Nightly News,* Oct. 26, 2003) The winds did bad things, but the winds didn't do anything *badly*. Better: "Two of the big fires joined here in Devore today. The winds blew the flames and smoke into a haze so dense that at times you couldn't see across the street."

"It's a program that helps troops on leave from Iraq fly home for free." (Fox News, 4 p.m., Dec. 5, 2003) *Free* can be a verb, an adverb, and an adjective. But *The Wall Street Journal* stylebook notes: "It is not a noun, so *for free* is a solecism. Drop the *for*." A grammatical violation like a solecism isn't permissible even if you're a free agent.

"Lots of interesting things coming across the transit." (Forrest Sawyer, CNBC, 10 p.m., March 19, 2003) Across the transit? Publishers say unsolicited manuscripts come in *over* the transom—a small window above doors in older buildings. By extension, people say an unsought offer comes in over the transom. (If you stop to think about it, nothing can come in over the transom because over the transom is a wall.) As for that newscaster, he used *across the transit* twice that night.

Doctors can hide some of their mistakes, but not broadcasters. Yes, mistakes happen. But as the old saying has it, Better one mistake avoided than two corrected.

(Feb., 2003)

Network Scripts That Need Work

An ancient sage said, "From the errors of others, a wise man corrects his own." He wasn't ancient when he said it, but he lived in ancient times. Even so, his advice is timely—and timeless. A wise man—OK, a wise person—does learn to correct his errors. But in newsrooms, errors should also be corrected by copy editors. Yet, when you run across errors like those that follow, you may wonder whether copy editors have been deleted:

"Good evening tonight from the French Quarter in New Orleans...." (Campbell Brown, *NBC Nightly News*, Feb. 28, 2006) *Good evening tonight?* Was *tonight* inserted in the belief some listener didn't understand *evening?* Or is it merely the newscast's practice of using *tonight* as often as possible? (I was told of that night's odd coupling by Rohan Bridge, a TV news producer in Australia—a Bridge too far.) In fact, the newscast had used a variation of that strange duplication previously:

"In this country this evening, the flow of commerce along the vital Eastern Scaboard has been disrupted tonight by a tanker-truck accident." (Brian Wiliams, *NBC Nightly News*, Jan. 10, 2005) As Prof. Michael Daniels of the University of Southern California reminds us, the use of the present perfect tense—*has been disrupted*—precludes the use of a time element. Besides, the script distorted the time element: the accident had happened more than eight hours before the newscast. No wonder someone (named Block) suggested renaming the program *Tonightly News*.

"Myself and other journalists were allowed back into the court just in time to see the case adjourned...." (Lara Logan, *CBS Evening News*, March 15, 2006) *Myself* should never be used in place of *I* or *me*. Correct use: "I will do it myself." (Intensive.) "I hurt myself." (Reflexive.)

That report was delivered live, so no one could have caught the misused *myself* in time. But I wonder whether a producer or anchor later told the correspondent of the mistake. Better: "The reporters were let back into the court just in time...." No need for the self-reference; as the adage has it, "No newsman is bigger than the news."

"In World War II," Logan said on *60 Minutes* (Jan. 8, 2012), **"there were five brothers serving on a battleship in the Pacific that was attacked by the Japanese."** They were serving on a warship, not a battleship. Battleship was the class of the largest Navy ships. The Sullivan brothers served on a cruiser, and it was more than *attacked*. It was sunk.

"An escaped convicted killer is still on the loose. Write this name down: Charles Victor Thompson. He was able to walk out of a Texas jail...." (CNN, noon, Nov. 5, 2005) Please don't tell me what to do. Anyway, what good would it do for me to write down his name?

"The number of attacks against Americans are still stable or falling, and it's the Iraqi security forces that are paying the highest price." (Kimberly Dozier, *CBS Evening News*, April 16, 2006) Another live report, but still subject to the rules: because *number* was preceded by *the*, it should be followed by *is*, not *are*. If *number* is preceded by *a,* it would be followed by *are*.

"The storm bore down on a 20-mile stretch along the Mississippi River from Illinois to Missouri to Kansas." (Don Lemon, *NBC Nightly News*, March 12, 2006) Also live. Not even a storm could have moved Kansas to the Mississippi.

"It's just one more thing to angst about in a season that already stresses out millions." (Bob Orr, *CBS Evening News*, March 23, 2006) *Angst* is not in too many listeners' vocabulary. And the reporter's verbification of *angst*, which is a noun, made its use even riskier. If a word isn't widely known and commonly used, then it's not a "broadcast word." So using *angst* like that gives me agita.

"I'm Trish Regan on the Paraguay-Brazil border, and you'll never believe what you can buy here." (*CBS Evening News*, March 6, 2006) Why wouldn't I believe it? For years, I've been reading in *The New York Times, The New Yorker* and elsewhere about smuggling, counterfeiting and other illegal activities in Ciudad del Este. What I do find hard to believe is that a network newscast would treat a thrice-told tale like big news. The lead-in to the two-parter called the place the new "Crossroads of Crime." *New*? More than three years ago, a *New York Times* reporter wrote, in a 1,600-word article, March 15, 2002, "The Triple Frontier where Argentina, Brazil and Paraguay meet has long been South America's busiest contraband and smuggling center, a corrupt, chaotic place where just about anything from drugs and arms to pirated software and bootleg whisky are available to anyone who can pay the price."

"Iran today lashed out against a resolution by the U-N nuclear monitoring agency that could lead to Security Council sanctions against Iran." (NPR, *Morning Edition*, Sept. 26, 2005) The problem is *today*—on two counts. The Iranian "lashing out" occurred about 24 hours earlier. *Today*—really *yesterday*—almost always should follow the verb, not precede it.

"Does he have to nominate a conservative to satisfy the base of his party or a moderate who would be acceptable enough to Democrats to avoid a long and prolonged fight." (Bob Woodruff, ABC *World News Tonight*, Oct. 27, 2005.) *Long* and *prolonged*? Way too much longitude.

"Up next, the man still in the eye of a political hurricane, Michael Brown, the former director of FEMA. Our exclusive interview with him in a moment." (*Fox News Sunday*, 9 a.m., March 5, 2006) *Exclusive?* NBC's *Nightly News* also had an "exclusive interview" with Brown Feb. 28. Eleven days before that, Feb. 17, CNN carried what it called an exclusive look at a filmmaker's interview with Brown. Almost six months earlier, on Sept. 1, 2005, Ted Koppel interviewed Brown on ABC's *Nightline*—but did not label the interview as exclusive. Nor did Martin Smith call his interview, broadcast Nov. 22 on PBS's *Frontline*, exclusive. Months later, though, Fox and NBC did call their interviews of Brown exclusive. No wonder *exclusive* is almost meaningless.

"Obviously, you must be very elated at this news." (NPR, *Morning Edition*, March 23, 2006) Please don't tell an interviewee how she feels. *Ask* her how she feels.

"The fires in Texas, Oklahoma, now spreading to New Mexico, are being fueled by the worst drought in decades." (Bob Schieffer, *CBS Evening News*, Jan. 2, 2006) I don't want to add fuel to the fire, but how can a drought *fuel* a fire?

"Inch after inch, the rain fuels these rivers through towns with strong currents." (Michelle Kosinski, *NBC Nightly News*, Oct. 13, 2005) Can rain *fuel* a river? Come on, let's stop fueling around.

One of the most unusual fuelings took place on NBC's *Nightly News* on Jan. 29, 2012 when the anchor, Lester Holt, said (in part):

"With less than two days to go, the language, the characterizations and accusations being traded back and forth between Mitt Romney and Newt Gingrich have reached a new level of harshness, and it's fueling plenty of volatility entering the final stretch." Trade *is* back and forth, so delete *back and forth*—forthwith. *Fueling...volatility?* The most common definition of volatility is "the property of changing readily from a solid or liquid to a vapor." How could *volatility* be *fueled?* Where was a copy editor?

(May, 2006)

Health News That's Not Healthful

Television commercials for heartburn, back pain and stomach distress aren't the worst ailments afflicting network newscasts. Most of us probably take the commercials with a grain of salt. But if you examine some of the evening newscasts' medical stories, you may want to start taking *them* with a gram of salt.

Why the skepticism? Because some of the medical stories we'll look at are inaccurate, some are misleading, and some suffer from other disorders. Here is how they were delivered by the networks—in their entirety (except as noted):

"The surprising results are out tonight from one of this country's longest-running medical studies. The study finds 90 percent of older Americans already have or can expect to develop high blood pressure. Researchers note that millions of people with high blood pressure are not getting treated for it or do not have it under control." (Dan Rather, *CBS Evening News*, Feb. 26, 2002)

Surprising? For whom? Careful writers don't characterize news as surprising, or disturbing, or amazing, or shocking, or good, or bad. Or label news in any way.

Most important, though, the script is wrong. One goal of that long-range study was to see how many of the subjects would develop high blood pressure. Contrary to what the script said about 90 percent of older Americans, that the study found some have high blood pressure, the study's co-author, Dr. Ramachandran S. Vasan of the Boston University School of Medicine, told me the study didn't accept anyone who already had high blood pressure. The figure of 90 percent applied only to an estimate of the risk of *developing* high blood pressure.

Older Americans? The AP account called them "middle-age Americans." If an age (55) had been used in the script, many viewers and the anchor himself might have considered the subjects of the study not older

Americans but younger Americans. On top of all that, the first sentence in the script is blah.

Results are out tonight is weak because *are* doesn't express action. *Are* and *is* are linking verbs; all they do is link, not move. Example: "Grass is green." But you get movement when you say, "The grass is growing." There, *is* doesn't link; it serves as an auxiliary or helping verb. Linking verbs merely say the subject of the sentence *is* something. That's true of any form of *to be.* (But don't touch Hamlet's soliloquy.)

As a result of saying results *are out* in the script, the first sentence is not newsy. Better: "A new study says...." Not outstanding, but better. If you say something is out, you raise questions: But is it new? Did it come out today? How long has it been out?

Air time is precious. If a story is important enough to use on a network newscast, listeners should be told exactly who conducted the study. Or, if it was published, the name of the journal. Would you accept medical advice—or information—from someone who's unidentified?

On the night that script was broadcast, another network evening newscast carried the same story, the only instance in this random review when more than one network evening newscast ran the same medical story:

"The Journal of the American Medical Association reports this week that Americans 55 years and older face a staggering 90 percent chance of developing high blood pressure in their lifetime. High blood pressure, or hypertension, is a major risk factor for heart disease and for stroke, which together account for more than a third of all deaths in the country." (Peter Jennings, ABC, Feb. 26, 2002) As in the first script, there's no hint that the 90 percent chance is an estimate; Americans *may* face those odds. And *may* doesn't mean *will*. The AP account, which probably served as the basis for the broadcast scripts, used *estimates* in its first sentence. But neither of those scripts used *estimates* or an equivalent.

Why *this week*? And why did the script call the odds *staggering*? Perhaps because the AP had quoted the Secretary of Health and Human Services as using that word. In their lifetime? When else? Better: "...chance of eventually developing high blood pressure." Neither script bothered with the AP story's second sentence: "But experts say many can still beat the odds with diet and exercise."

Next case: **"Research into the common cold has yielded an uncommon finding. It appears a glass of wine a day—especially red wine— may help prevent colds. Authors of the study say they have no idea**

why. But they have found stress raises risk for catching colds." (Dan Rather, *CBS Evening News*, May 1, 2002)

Who conducted the study? A little research on the Internet shows that the study was conducted in Spain by a professor at the University of Santiago de Compostela. The study said people who drank 8 to 14 glasses of red a week had a 40-percent-less chance of catching a cold than people who drank no wine. Red wine? Spain? Hmm. I wonder who sponsored the study. A winemaker? The study found stress raises risk for catching colds? That's not new. (My search on the Internet found an item in the *Journal of the Florida Medical Association* that said almost 10 years ago (June 1993), "Human subjects with a high stress index were shown to be more susceptible to infection with common cold viruses.")

The wine/common-cold study surveyed 4,272 faculty and staff members at five Spanish universities; for one year, they filled out questionnaires about their health and their activities, including alcohol intake. *Wine Spectator* said (May 15, 2002) participants also rated any symptoms they had, such as chills, headaches and sneezing. Every 10 weeks, the participants sent their questionnaires to the researchers, who decided which participants had had colds.

The Spanish study fell "far short of proving that wine wards off infections," according to *Science News Online* (May 18, 2002). And a virologist for New Zealand's Ministry of Health was quoted in Wellington's *Evening Post* as saying (May 20, 2002) that before any link could be established between the drinking of red wine and the prevention of colds, much more research would be needed. He said only a scientific trial could establish a link, a trial in which two groups of people were exposed to the common-cold virus, one group regularly drinking water, one drinking wine.

Three weeks after that CBS script was broadcast, researchers at the University of Buffalo reported that white wine improves lung functioning more than red, inspiring a letter printed in the *Times* of London:

"Sir, If red wine is beneficial for the cardiovascular system...and white wine is of benefit to the lungs...should we not all be drinking rosé?"

In recent years, research has suggested that attributing apparent health benefits to wine drinking is mistaken, that people who drink wine are healthier because they lead more sensible lives. The latest study, published in *The American Journal of Clinical Nutrition* (August 2002), relied on questionnaires filled out by 4,435 alumni of the University of North Carolina who've been subjects of a long-running survey.

The researchers reported: "Subjects who preferred wine had healthier diets than those who preferred beer or spirits or had no preference. Wine drinkers reported eating more servings of fruit and vegetables and fewer servings of red or fried meats. The diets of wine drinkers contained less cholesterol, saturated fat, and alcohol, and more fiber. Wine drinkers were less likely to smoke...."

Another broadcast story: **"There is health news for people at high risk for diabetes because of obesity or high blood pressure. A study in tomorrow's New England Journal of Medicine finds moderate exercise and better diet can delay the onset of diabetes, even help prevent it."** (Dan Rather, *CBS Evening News*, May 2, 2001)

There is and *there are* are dead phrases. Starting a script either way is stepping off on the wrong foot. (There are exceptions.) The use of *there is* delays the appearance of a verb with muscle. Instead of writing, "There's a disagreement between the mayor and the governor," make it, "The mayor and governor disagree." Or "The mayor disagrees with the governor."

If you have news, tell it. Don't waste time by saying there is news. Of course there's news on a newscast. Isn't there? Hold on. If you look up that study in the medical journal, you'll see that it doesn't mention blood pressure, high or low, as a risk factor for diabetes. The study does talk about elevated "plasma glucose concentrations," which the AP translated correctly as "high blood sugar"—not the same as high blood pressure. Except, perhaps, to someone writing under high pressure.

Still another script with a limp lead: **"A study out tonight finds drinking black or green tea may increase survival rates among people who've had heart attacks. This research indicates both kinds of tea contain the same beneficial antioxidants as some fruits and vegetables."** (Dan Rather, *Evening News*, May 6, 2002)

But the AP article said, "Heavy tea drinking could reduce the risk of dying after a heart attack, a study suggests." The AP writer had proceeded cautiously, with *could* and *suggests*; the CBS script made it solid with *finds*. But *suggests* or *indicates* does not mean *finds* or *proves*. And one study, taken alone, seldom proves anything. Once more, a script provided no source for a story. Another gap in the script: how many cups of tea a day would heart attack survivors need to drink? The AP story cites "heavy tea drinking." The television script doesn't offer a clue.

The news release from Boston's Beth Israel Deaconess Medical Center quoted the study's lead author (May 6, 2002) as saying that though the findings strongly suggest that tea consumption reduces the risk of death after a heart attack, controlled clinical studies would be needed to firmly establish the link. The release defined heavy tea drinkers as those who drank at least two cups a day. The heavy drinkers were 44 percent less likely to die than non-tea drinkers over the next 3.8 years. According to the study, the key to this protection, if that's what it is, is the tea's antioxidants.

So where did all that leave listeners who heard the item about tea on the evening newscast? How could they act on the information? They didn't even get the name of an institution or a publication they could call or write to learn more. (They were left holding the tea bag.)

Another script: **"There's a study out tonight about personal hygiene with important public health implications. Ninety-five percent of people surveyed say they wash their hands when leaving the rest room. But observation indicates only about 67 percent do wash their hands. Hand washing is the single best way to prevent the spread of infections."** (Dan Rather, *Evening News*, Sept. 18, 2000)

There's that *there is* again. But that's the least of the script's problems. What's the source of that study with such *important public health implications*? And if the implications were so important, why did the other two network evening newscasts ignore the story? One possibility is that the other newscasts didn't recognize the importance of the study.

On the Internet, I learned that the study was done by a research company for the American Society for Microbiology. The company says it conducted a national phone survey of 1,021 adults and that 95 percent said they wash their hands after using the restroom. But we know that many interviewees tell interviewers what they think the interviewers want to hear, or tell them what they think will make themselves look good. When interviewees are asked about washing their hands, how many do you think are quick to say no?

Even so, the people interviewed by phone were not the same people who were observed by researchers. The researchers said they watched people in restrooms in New York City's Pennsylvania Station and Grand Central Terminal, Chicago's Navy Pier, the Atlanta Braves' ballpark, a New Orleans casino (the Treasure Chest) and San Francisco's Golden Gate Park.

Of the 7,836 adults said to have been observed in those six places, 67 percent were reported to have washed their hands. Because they were not the same people questioned by phone, the story is not about hypocrisy—

people saying one thing, doing another. And if those observed were not a scientifically representative sample—and they weren't—the story is pointless. Also, four years earlier, the same research company conducted the same kind of study—one part by phone, nationally, and one part observational in the same six places. The outcome was almost identical: 68 percent of those observed washed their hands.

The last sentence in the television script, about the importance of hand washing, is true. And has long been true. And has long been reported. But news is what's new, right? The only thing new in that script is that the percentage of those who washed their hands—or reportedly washed their hands—was an insignificant one percentage point less than in the previous survey. And the script didn't mention the previous survey. What about the margin of error? Did those observed washing their hands use soap? Or did they merely rinse their hands? And who cares? You could call it much ado about a handful of nothing.

A footnote; rather, a handnote: The researchers said they observed 2,283 people in the restrooms of New York City's two big train stations, and that 51 percent of them didn't wash their hands. So in a city of 8 million people, 1,164 reportedly didn't wash their hands. One sixty-eighth of one percent does not a city make. And how many people in the train stations' restrooms were arriving or departing out-of-towners, not New Yorkers? Yet an AP reporter wrote, "Apparently the city that never sleeps is also too busy to wash up."

So many medical studies conflict with one another that a Net wit (not at all a nitwit) wrote this parody now ricocheting around the Net:

"The Japanese eat very little fat and suffer fewer heart attacks than Britons or Americans.

"The French eat a lot of fat and also suffer fewer heart attacks than Britons or Americans.

"The Japanese drink very little red wine and suffer fewer heart attacks than Britons or Americans.

"The Italians drink plenty of red wine and also suffer fewer heart attacks than Britons or Americans.

"Conclusion: Eat and drink what you like. Apparently what kills people is speaking English."

Next: **"A study in the journal Neuroscience shows that a diet rich in folic acid may help prevent the damage caused by Alzheimer's disease. Laboratory mice that do not get enough of the vitamin in**

their food suffer a more rapid loss of brain cells." (Elizabeth Vargas, ABC, March 1, 2002)

I'm a man, not a mouse. How does that item affect me? Or does it affect me? The National Institutes of Health said in a news release (March 1, 2002) reporting the study in *The Journal of Neuroscience*, "People who have Alzheimer's disease often have low levels of folic acid in their blood, but it is not clear whether this is a result of the disease or if they are simply malnourished due to their disease." The NIH said a human clinical trial is being planned.

The first sentence of the script should have said it was referring to an animal trial. And even if scientists had conducted human trials, we'd need to know how much folic acid we should take. Or are we already getting enough in our diet? For several years, research has shown that folic acid can be beneficial. In fact, since 1998, the Food and Drug Administration has required the addition of folic acid to flours, cereals, enriched breads, cornmeals, pastas, rice and other grain products.

> Close-ups of a showerhead spraying water had conveyed a sense of menace reminiscent of Hitchcock's *Psycho*. The CBS package seemed to imply: don't dare take a shower.

Even if I were a mouse, I wouldn't know how to react to that script. Should I eat more cheese? More grains? (And risk migraines?)

At the top of another network evening newscast, the anchor delivered this headline: **"And the deadly lung disease that could be lurking in your shower."** Lurking? Later, the anchor teased: **"Next up..., a health hazard lurking in the mist inside your shower stall."** (John Roberts, CBS, June 28, 2002) Still lurking? In my shower? The anchor told about the disease in his lead-in to the reporter:

"It's called N-T-M for short, and the long and short of it is, N-T-M is an illness that can cause serious lung damage, is hard to diagnose and often hard to cure. The question is: why are so many women in the South coming down with it, and where is it coming from? Bobbi Harley is hot on the trail." Hot on the trail? Five days earlier, *Time* had run a full-page article about NTM (nontuberculous mycobacteria). One week before that, *The Miami Herald* (June 19, 2002) printed a two-column article about NTM. And two years before that, *The Johns Hopkins News-Letter* headed an article (April 6, 2000): "New lung disease lurks in hot tubs and/indoor pools that create an infectious mist." Even then, it wasn't new.

The CBS package (quoted here only in part) featured four people, two who had been mentioned in *Time*, two in *The Miami Herald*. Three of the four in the newscast's package had appeared 18 months earlier in the story on NTM carried by WTVJ-TV, Miami, on Nov. 20, 2000. The WTVJ medical reporter also did a follow-up about NTM on May 3, 2002, eight weeks before the network's story.

Still hot on the trail, the network reporter said from Miami: **"The bacteria have always been in water and soil.** [Always?] **Recently, they've been showing up in people, primarily in the southeast United States and most often striking thin white women...."** Recently? That adverb is elastic, but it can't stretch back a decade. A few fast facts: the Centers for Disease Control and Prevention says 19,339 cases of NTM were reported nationally in 1993. The most southeasterly state, Florida, ranked first with 3,970 cases, more than twice as many as second-place Texas.

Most often striking thin white women? True, but that's not the half of it. The *Herald* provided a far clearer picture of those apparently most susceptible. It quoted Dr. Michael Iseman of National Jewish Medical and Research Center, a leading institution in treating NTM, as saying 85 percent of his NTM patients are women who tend to share one or more characteristics: slight curvature of the spine, a sternum that bows slightly inward, mitral-valve prolapse (a heart abnormality), and a family history of lung disease. None of that was mentioned in the network story.

Another doctor from National Jewish said on-screen in the network's package, "When we take our morning shower, we're creating a mist that is just the right particle-size for us to breathe into our lungs." But neither she nor Dr. Iseman advises NTM patients not to take showers. As for showers' role in spreading NTM, Dr. Iseman, Chief of Mycobacterial Service of National Jewish, in Denver, told me, "The hypothesis has not been substantiated."

The CBS package ended with a former NTM patient who said she still took showers but didn't stay in long. The reporter wrapped it all up by saying that another patient, seen and heard earlier, had stopped taking showers. On that note, the curtain came down on the piece. From the headline to the finish line, the network story turned the heat on showers. Close-ups of a showerhead spraying water had conveyed a sense of menace reminiscent of Hitchcock's *Psycho*. The CBS package seemed to imply: don't dare take a shower. Dr. Iseman's icy observation: "I don't think it was a particularly responsible approach."

What was left lurking in my mind was the thought that whoever approved the scary headline, the tease and the script should have been sent to the showers.

In our last medical case (not reprinted in its entirety), an anchor teased, **"Up next... The disturbing news on asthma, the surprising information in new research."** (Tom Brokaw, *NBC Nightly News*, March 1, 2002) Next came video of a doctor saying, "Children in day-care settings who have illnesses early on seem to be more resistant to asthma as they get older."

Then Brokaw said, **"A growing epidemic of asthma among children. Are scientists getting closer to finding out why?"** An epidemic? If it is an epidemic, it seems to be a perennial event. Soon he introduced a correspondent by saying: **"A growing problem all over the world... Tonight, leading experts are meeting to share the results of some surprising new research...."** *Surprising? New?*

Three weeks after that broadcast, the Public Health Policy Advisory Board said in a news release: "Despite decades of data, researchers are no closer now to understanding the roots of the asthma epidemic than they were when it first began 20 years ago." And in advance of this year's World Asthma Day (May 7), the sponsors provided a sample news release for local groups to send out in their own name. The release referred to a "continuing asthma epidemic." Two years earlier, in May 2000, the Secretary of Health and Human Services told of confronting an "epidemic of asthma." And a year before that, the Secretary also spoke of an "epidemic of asthma."

The Secretary wasn't alone. In November 1999, *Scientific American* referred to "the asthma epidemic." And in May 2000, a news release from the Johns Hopkins School of Public Health said, "The nation is in the grip of a rapidly growing asthma epidemic...." So, almost two years later, it hardly seems worthy of such excitement on a network evening newscast.

Despite this epidemic of *epidemics*, asthma *is* a major public health problem. But it's not new. Although the anchor called the "news" about day care and asthma disturbing and surprising, a little reportorial research shows that it was neither: 19 months earlier, *The New England Journal of Medicine* (Aug. 24, 2000) published a study that said, "The incidence of asthma among children who had two or more older siblings or who attended day care during the first six months of life was significantly lower than among children who had one sibling or no siblings and who did not attend day care." In other words, as the head on the story in the AP archives puts it: "Exposure to other kids' germs can be a good thing."

The study apparently lent weight to the "hygiene hypothesis," which has held—for more than a decade—that a focus on cleanliness has kept infants from developing an immunity to infection. Immunity would presumably reduce the risk of developing asthma and allergies. So the doctor's remark on camera about day care and asthma was not new. (The AP coverage of the *NEJM* study said its main conclusion, quoted above, "echoes the hot new 'hygiene theory.'")

Shortly after the *NEJM* published that study, *The Washington Post* reported (Oct. 1, 2000) that the Statistical Assessment Service (STATS), described as a media watchdog organization, said the news about day-care attendance wasn't so promising as it seemed. A STATS news release had raised several questions about the validity of the findings and said that in the previous year two studies (in *Pediatrics* and *The Journal of the American Medical Association*) reported—contrary to the *NEJM* study – day-care attendance posed a risk to infants.

Back to that NBC newscast: after the anchor's intro, the correspondent said the number of asthma cases had risen 154 percent in 20 years—and that a second doctor thought he knew why. Then this doctor spoke: "Our clean living ways perhaps might be leading to this global rise in asthma and allergies." *Perhaps? Might?* We know that *might* indicates a possibility less likely than *may*, so *might* is hardly the keystone of confidence.

The correspondent resumed: **"Did he say clean living? Most people assume asthma comes from air pollution or other dirt in the environment, but the opposite is true. The latest research shows the cleaner the environment, the more asthma....What does this mean for Americans? For one thing, day care might have a positive effect."** Yes, it might. And the debate about day care and asthma still goes on.

All in all, no wonder *The Journal of the American Medical Association* published a study (June 5, 2002) concluding: "The current press coverage of scientific meetings may be characterized as 'too much, too soon.' Results are frequently presented to the public as scientifically sound evidence rather than as preliminary findings with still uncertain validity."

The *JAMA* study suggested that news organizations "apply the same level of skepticism in covering these stories as they do in reporting on political matters." In this way, the study said, "the press might help readers to develop a healthy skepticism about the breakthroughs they repeatedly encounter in the news."

A week later, an editor of *JAMA* was quoted by *The New York Times* (June 11, 2002) as saying that medical and scientific journals publish "a massive amount of rubbish."

As you've seen, several scripts in this review were also rubbish. A few were shoddy, a few were shady, and some were both shoddy and shady. The medical response to those problems? Diagnosis: tabloidosis. Recommended therapy for the offenders: stick to the facts, and clean up your acts.

Advice for broadcasters reporting medical news:

1. Never use the word *miracle*. Leave that to ministers, mayonnaise-makers and sportswriters.

2. Don't use *breakthrough*. I'm not saying, never ever use it under any circumstances whatsoever. But breakthroughs are infrequent, and the word *breakthrough*, like *controversy*, is so overused that it has lost much of its impact. (Remember: *impact* is a noun, not a verb. And *major breakthrough* is redundant. As wiseacres say, Help stamp out and eradicate superfluous redundancy.)

3. Avoid *cure*. Announcements of cures are rare, and they must be handled with utmost care. But there's one cure that's simple, one you can help bring about: the cure of hype.

4. *May* doesn't mean *will*.

5. *Suggests* or *indicates* doesn't mean *finds* or *proves*.

6. *Contributes to*, *is associated with*, or *is linked to* does not mean *causes*. (Thank you, University of California, Berkeley Wellness Letter. But, dear reader, please don't use *wellness* in a script or a conversation unless you're in Berkeley.)

7. If you have time, download the study you're writing about (if available) or the original news release and see what's what for yourself.

8. One study by itself seldom proves anything. So don't treat the results of a study as the last word. In many (most?) cases, it's the first word.

9. Identify the source of the story. Apply a basic rule of broadcast newswriting: Attribution precedes assertion. So before telling what was said, tell who said it. If you start like this, "A new study says," then in your next sentence, identify the publication or institution: "The Institute of Cranial Exploration says its study looked into...." And proceed cautiously.

10. Don't be an alarmist. Don't exaggerate. Don't speculate. Cogitate.

11. You can't believe everything you read, but you should believe everything you write.

(August 23, 2002)

Networks Mangle and Strangle Language

Writing in plain English requires the writer to know plain English. But English has been taking a pasting, even on network newscasts. Some recent assaults:

"More than anything, he cared about the men he led, and they all got home safely, all but he." (John Roberts, *CBS Evening News*, July 5, 2005) *But* in that sentence means *except*, making it a preposition. So *he* must be in the objective case: "all but him."

"Now, this special ops team member was on the ground last week when the helicopter carrying 16 other special ops team members were [should be *was*] **looking for he or she and their team members there on the ground during this."** (Fredricka Whitfield, CNN, 4 p.m., July 3, 2005) *For he or she?* *For* is a preposition, so that phrase should be *for him or her*. As for the last *this*, this what? Specify. *Their* and *there* so close are confusing to the ear. Searching on the ground? Where else would they be searching, in the sky?

"And that determination also extends to finding whomever is responsible for the massacre here...." (John Roberts, *CBS Evening News*, July 8, 2005) *Whoever*, not *whomever*. Deciding which to use is determined by its being the subject of the following verb, not by its being the object of a preceding verb or preposition.

"It is laying there on the ground." (Anderson Cooper, CNN, 4 p.m., July 10, 2005) It was *lying* on the ground. *Lie* means "to repose" or "to occupy a place"; *lay* means "put down" or "place." The correspondent should lay a grammar book on his desk and read it, not just let it lie there.

"Lacking the proper steel plating to protect soldiers from enemy mines and rocket-propelled grenades, they had been jerry-rigged with plywood and sandbags." (Steve Kroft, *60 Minutes,* July 17, 2005) *Jerry-rigged?* No such word. *Jury-rig* means "to rig or assemble for temporary emergency use." (But rigging a jury is criminal.) *Jerry-build* is "to build shoddily, flimsily and cheaply." So the correspondent was guilty of mixing and mashing.

"Inside the medical hospitals of Iraq." (Lisa Sylvester, CNN, 4 p.m., July 24, 2005) *Medical hospitals?* Fortunately, that tease made clear that the story wouldn't be about archaeological, geological or mythological hospitals.

"Killen [convicted in Mississippi that day] **could face charges of up to 20 years in prison for each count of manslaughter."** (Mike Von Fremd, ABC's *World News Tonight*, June 21, 2005) *Charges?* Charges are accusations, and after Killen was convicted, the charges were no longer pending. Better: "Killen faces a sentence of up to 20 years in prison for each count of manslaughter."

"Late tonight we learned of the latest price tag for continuing the war effort in Iraq and Afghanistan...." (Brian Williams, *Nightly News*, Jan. 24, 2005) Since when is 6:30 p.m. *late tonight?* As for *price tag*, tear it up. Instead, use *cost*, *price* or something other than the cliché *price tag*— unless you're talking about goods that carry price tags.

"According to the Brookings Institute, in the month of the handover last year there were 18 suicide bombings...." (NPR, 10 a.m., June 28, 2005) The name is Brookings Institution. And in that excerpt, *during* would be better than *in*. *During* means "throughout the duration of." *In* could apply to a single day.

"Dennis was no menace, it was a monster..." (Jim Acosta, *CBS Evening News*, July 10, 2005) A monster is a huge menace.

"No let-up in Iraq's increasingly bloody insurgency." (Mika Brzezinski. *CBS Evening News*, July 17, 2005) Now that's a shocker. Strunk and White's *Elements of Style* tells us to put statements in a positive form: "Make definite assertions. Avoid tame, colorless, hesitating, noncommittal language." The anchor's next sentence provides material for a strong, positive lead: **"At least 22 people died today in a wave of suicide attacks in and around Baghdad."** But they didn't just die of heart attacks or boredom. Better: "Suicide attacks in and around Baghdad have killed 22 people." That way, there's no need for *today*. The anchor's next sentence: **"This came as the Iraqi government formally filed its first criminal charges against Saddam Hussein."** That news, too, could provide the lead. *Formally?* Had those charges ever been filed informally?

"She's on an emotional roller coaster, but somehow, in the midst of it all, she is also managing to reach out to...." (Deborah Roberts,

ABC's *Good Morning America*, June 10, 2005) *Emotional roller coaster* is so old, so rickety, so hackneyed, it's unsafe.

"Whatever your taste in art, you'll probably agree this is pretty amazing." (Dan Rather, CBS's *Evening News*, Feb. 16, 2005) I tend to disagree with people who tell me I'll probably agree.

"It's hard to know just where to start in summing up the remarkable life of Peter Ustinov." (NPR, evening, March 29, 2004) Yes, writing a lead can be hard. But listeners have problems of their own; they don't tune in to hear yours.

Newsrooms' problems are another matter. As those excerpts point up, newsrooms need stronger editing. Sharper editing. Educated editing. And that's the remedy—in plain English.

(August 22, 2005)

TIPS, TESTS
AND QUIZZES

The Eyes Have It:
a Broadcast Writing Cliché

One minute, newscasters report all eyes are looking somewhere, the next minute they have all eyes looking elsewhere.

CNN, 7 a.m. ET, May 4: **"All eyes are focused on tonight's block-buster exposé** [of *American Idol*]." But two hours before the sexposé was broadcast, an anchor on CNN's *Headline News* said: **"Now all eyes on the Jackson defense team."**

A few days earlier, eyes were on the impending arrival in Atlanta of the runaway bride: **"We have got all eyes on that..."** (Fox News Channel, 9 p.m. ET, April 30).

CNN saw eye-to-eye with Fox: **"All eyes have been on the eyes of the runaway bride."** (CNN, 7 a.m., May 6) Eye-catching eyes?

The latest outbreak of *all eyes* started late last year: **"All eyes will be on the president as he enters his second term in office."** (CBS News, 7 a.m. ET, Dec. 28). The eyes of Texas were already upon him, as the song goes, all the livelong day. But at night, at least on Inaugural night, **"All of the eyes were on First Lady Laura Bush..."** (ABC News, 7 a.m., Jan. 21)

A week later, **"While all eyes are on Iraq, elsewhere in this region there is..."** (NBC News, 6:30 p.m. ET, Jan. 29)

A month later, **"All eyes on Rome this morning."** (CNN, 7 a.m. ET, Feb. 25)

Soon, **"Tonight in Washington state, all eyes are on the skies above a landmark after a rather wild show last night, courtesy of Mount Saint Helens."** (NBC News, 6:30 p.m. ET, March 9)

Then eyes shifted: **"All eyes now are on the U-S Supreme Court."** (MSNBC, 10 p.m. ET, March 23)

Three weeks later: **"All eyes are on the Charleston, South Carolina, courthouse..."** (CBS News, 7 a.m. ET, April 15)

185

But the eyes didn't linger. Three days later, they took the long view: **"All eyes around the world are focused on Saint Peter's Square."** (ABC News, 11:50 a.m. ET, April 19)

Then the eyes started roving: **"All eyes are on the biggest oil producer in the world, Saudi Arabia."** (CNBC, 8 p.m. ET, April 21)

Again, the eyes started wandering: **"On Wall Street, all eyes are on the New York Stock Exchange."** (NPR, various times, April 26)

And that evening: **"Now all eyes are on my guest."** (CNBC, 5 p.m. ET, April 26) Isn't that akin to exaggerated self-reference?

Last week, eyes took a new turn: **"Polls in Great Britain closing at this moment, and all eyes on two-term Prime Minister Tony Blair."** (Fox News Channel, 5 p.m. ET, May 5) Where verbs? Gone missing. Wouldn't people interested in the election results have their eyes on the vote count, not on a candidate?

By the end of the week, another swiveling of eyeballs: **"As the defense gets under way in the Michael Jackson child molestation trial, all eyes are on child star Macaulay Culkin."** (Fox News Channel, 9:30 p.m. ET, May 7) If all eyes are on *him*, who's keeping an eye out for the runaway bride?

All eyes that have read this far see that *all eyes* is a threadbare cliché. Worse, it's nonsense.

Writers rely on *all eyes* when they don't have the time or can't take the time to write a solid, sensible script. Or don't know how. But now that writers have been put on notice, let's see whether the culprits reform. I'll be all ears.

(April 12, 2005)

Overnight Needs Oversight

How do you define *overnight*?

When a newscaster says a train derailed *overnight*, do you assume it happened after midnight? Or do you think it might have happened before midnight? Or maybe any time since the previous evening?

But what's *evening*? Dictionaries disagree, even as to when evening begins. Generally, and vaguely, *evening* is described as the last part of the day and the early part of the night. But no dictionary defines *overnight* as extending all the way back to noon the previous day. And certainly not to the evening before that. So imagine my surprise when I found out that a network broadcaster had extended *overnight* to an event that took place about 40 hours earlier.

The event was the capture of Khalid Shaikh Mohammed. Various accounts of the raid that collared him place the time between 2:30 a.m. and 4 a.m., Saturday, March 1, 2003—Pakistan Standard Time. That's 10 hours ahead of our ET. So apparently the raid occurred—as determined on the U.S. East Coast—between 4:30 p.m. and 6 p.m., Friday, Feb. 28. For people on the West Coast, the raid occurred between 1:30 p.m. and 3 p.m. We all set our clocks and tell the time according to the zone we're in. And that's how we should report the time.

At noon ET, Saturday, March 1, CNN broadcast a story of the arrest made **"just a few hours ago."** (People who regard 18 hours as *few* are few.) Later, the networks' evening newscasts played the story big.

And it was still big news even the day after that, Sunday. An NBC anchor, David Bloom, told NBC's Washington bureau chief, Tim Russert, on *Sunday Today*, in present-tense-speak, **"Khalid Shaikh Mohammed is arrested. The president gets a phone call yesterday morning from his national security adviser. He says, 'Fantastic news.' What does it mean for the White House?"**

"Well," Russert replied, **"it's very significant, as you might expect, David, because there had been criticism that the president was not focusing enough resources and time on the war on terrorism...."**

An hour or so later—about 40 hours after the capture, Russert, moderating *Meet the Press*, said:

"But first, overnight, a key Al Qaeda operative and alleged mastermind of the September 11 attacks, Khalid Shaikh Mohammed, has been arrested...."

Overnight? That's what the man said. But even Tim, with all his charm, smarts, influence and authority can't outdo King Canute and make time stop. Or even slow down.

An overnight letter is too slow, so here's my instant insight: Listeners should be able to count on accuracy. Not only in a story's *who*, *what* and *where* but also in the *when*. It's about time.

(March 2003)

Test Your Newswriting I.Q. Against Networkers' I.Q.

If you write for TV, radio, print or the web, you need to write right—to choose the right words and put them in the right order.

And you need to acquire broad general knowledge. One way to see whether you're on the right path is to take a quiz more comprehensive than *20 Questions*: it's *21 Questions*.

Here's how you can take this test: spot the flaw or problem in each of these network excerpts before reading my comment:

"Now he, like I, is fascinated with massive construction projects." (Charles Gibson, *ABC World News*, Sept. 8, 2008) That's a lapse in the anchor's *like*-ability. That *like,* a preposition, should be followed by *me*.

"You've all been on the air and on the phones all day, and we appreciate you coming over to help explain it to all of us tonight." (Brian Williams, *NBC Nightly News*, Sept. 17, 2008) A noun or pronoun before that gerund (*coming*) should be in the possessive. So *you* should be *your*.

"Out in the Atlantic, more trouble—a trifecta of storms headed toward the U-S coast." (Randall Pinkston, *CBS Evening News*, Sept. 3, 2008) A trifecta, according to *Webster's New World Dictionary*, is "a bet or betting procedure in which one wins if one correctly picks the first, second, and third place finishers in a race." Trifecta does not mean three of something. So the script's use of *trifecta* was wrong, even if the storms were in the horse latitudes.

"Nearly nine in ten Americans is a Christian." (Anderson Cooper, CNN's *Anderson Cooper 360*, Dec. 31, 2006) Is they? The script should have said, "Almost nine in ten Americans *are*...."

"He also lauded the city's efforts in rebuilding homes, churches and schools." (Jim Lehrer, *PBS NewsHour,* Aug. 20, 2008) Newspapers use *laud* in headlines because it's shorter than *praise*. But you don't hear people say *laud*—except when Elvis sings, "Lawdy, Miss Clawdy."

"So a lot of numbers still to come tonight, Brian, but that's a first beginning." (Ann Curry, *NBC Nightly News*, Feb. 5, 2008) Delete *first* to rid the script of a redundancy.

"There once was a day when Democrats held their convention that the Republicans would lay low, and vice versa." (Charles Gibson, *ABC World News*, Aug. 26, 2008) The GOP would *lie* low. Better: "In the old days, when the Democrats or Republicans held their convention, the other party would *lie low*."

"The problem is, they may not be going home for some time soon." (Kevin Tibbles, *NBC Nightly News*, July 1, 2007) *For some time soon*? He probably meant *anytime soon*.

"At 16, with bad grades and a self-professed bad attitude, his father allowed him to drop out on one occasion." (John Berman, *ABC World News Sunday*, June 15, 2008) Strike *self*; only the person you're writing about can profess or confess. Unfortunately, the writer uncorked a dangler and unwittingly made the father 16 years old. Better: "His father let him drop out at age 16 when his grades were bad and his attitude, admittedly, was bad."

"Having said that, if General Petreaus or the Chairman of the Joint Chiefs, Admiral Mullen, say to you, "Hey, President Obama...."" (Katie Couric, *CBS Evening News*, July 22, 2008) Should be *says*, not *say*, because *or* means one or the other.

"Drivers save money with an added bonus." (Peter Alexander, *NBC Nightly News*, July 5, 2007) *Added bonus* is redundant: a bonus *is* something extra.

"His final [better: *last*] stop, New York's famed Yankee stadium." (Byron Pitts, *CBS Evening News*, April 20, 2008) Have you ever heard anyone say *famed*? I haven't—except for broadcast newspeople. In any case, if you think you need to call a place famous, how famous can that place be?

"It was the first time he had ever sang with a band." (Gigi Stone, *ABC World News Sunday*, June 1, 2008) *Sang* should be *sung*.

"Also tonight, more than 22,000 people. That's the latest death toll from that cyclone...." (Katie Couric, *CBS Evening News*, May 6, 2008) Don't back into a story. Start by telling us who or what did what to whom. Would you ever tell a friend, "Three people. They were killed in a crash last night near my place"?

"In Iraq tonight, the U-S military fired guided missiles into the Baghdad slum of Sadr City today...." (David Muir, *ABC World News*,

May 3, 2008) *Tonight...today?* Bizarro. That abrupt turnabout could cause whiplash.

"But meantime, good morning to you, and Happy Memorial Day." (Lester Holt, NBC's *Today*, May 29, 2006) A grotesque greeting. Memorial Day is a solemn occasion when we honor the memory of the war dead. There's nothing happy about it. *Meantime* is always a good word to ditch. Although we say *Good morning* to someone, some newscasters add the superfluous *to you.* No matter how many *you*'s or yahoos are out there, there's no need for *you.*

"Her monthly premium is 100 dollars a month." (Priya David, *CBS Evening News*, May 31, 2008) I heardya the first time.

"News was made on a front that is, of course, a major factor in this campaign, a vivid reminder tonight that Iraq remains a very dangerous place...." (Brian Williams, *NBC Nightly News*, Jan. 9, 2008) *News was made?* Clumsy. Whenever a story breaks, *news is made.* Would you ever write, "News was made today in Washington: Senator Jim George of Georgia abruptly resigned"? If *news was made*, go ahead and report it. And who needs a reminder that Iraq continues to be a dangerous place?

"Since being raised in late April, the crane had been inspected multiple times." (Michelle Miller, *CBS Evening News*, May 31, 2008) *Multiple times* sounds like something a bureaucrat would say; it's not conversational. Instead, most of us would say *many times*, or *several times* or *more than once.* Best would be the number of times. And *had* should be *has. Had been* is past perfect, the tense before the past.

"A 17-mile stretch of California beaches are now closed to swimming until Monday." (Miguel Marquez, *ABC World News*, April 25, 2008) The stretch *is.*

"Another developing story happening." (Don Lemon, *CNN Newsroom*, Feb. 28, 2007) *Developing + happening* = overkill and absurdity. Most stories are developing: the bailout, the election, oil, Iraq, taxes, the weather and, as they say, a whole lot more. As for *happening now*, it's almost always untrue.

Time's up. Even if you got them all wrong, don't despair; you still might be as good as the network writers, reporters and anchors who wrote those scripts. If you got 0 to 8 right, you do need help; if you got 9 to 16 right, you could have done worse but you should have done better; if you got 17 to 21 right, you should fill a critical need: copy editor.

(September 30, 2008)

Write This Way, Please

"After all is said and done," they say, "more is said than done." And I say, more can be said about *after*. After I say it, I'll pass along a few other tips to improve your newswriting. For the first tip, let's look at a make-believe lead that uses *after*, a lead constructed like so many we hear on the air:

"Police are searching for a gunman after he robbed a downtown bank and got away with 100-thousand dollars."

The big news is the bank robbery, not the search. Of course, the police are going to search for a bank robber. The search should be reported, but that's not the big story. If the police refuse to search for him, you have news.

When you find *after* in a lead, what comes after *after* should usually go before *after*. The reason is, the more important element has been put in a secondary position. Some writers take that wrong route because they've been told by a superior that at least their first verb should be in the present tense. Your revision of that lead should concentrate on what's most important—and omit *after*. Let's write it right:

"A gunman robbed a downtown bank and got away with 100-thousand dollars."

For a later broadcast, you may need to focus on a new development or find a new angle, even the search. Whatever you do, don't fall back on that old second-day newspaper lead: "Police intensified their search today for...." Remember, police aren't looking for a *suspect*; they're looking for the man who did it, the robber. If he's arrested, though, we call him a suspect.

One more *after*thought: The next lead was written by a broadcaster probably told to write in the present tense:

"A man and a woman are dead after an early morning solo vehicle collision in the East County."

Dull. Flat. Not a newsy start: billions of people are dead. And in that context, *solo* is not conversational. Who ever talks about a *solo accident*?

192

Further, there was no collision; a collision requires at least two moving objects.

With a few facts from the rest of that real-life script, you can write a stronger lead: "A car ran off the road in the East County and overturned, killing two people."

Another way to spark up your copy is to read—and put to use—Strunk and White's *Elements of Style*, particularly Section II's Rule 22: "Place the emphatic words of a sentence at the end."

When the key words wind up in the middle of a sentence, they're less emphatic, as in this excerpt from a network script:

"This from a company that made a 36-billion-dollar profit last year alone." (Byron Pitts, *CBS Evening News*, March 23, 2006)

I'd want to make that profit stand out. When the key words are put at the end of a sentence, they do stand out; they reverberate in a listener's mind. They have the last word: "Last year alone, the company made 36-billion dollars."

Another network script compounds its key-word problem with an *after* problem:

"Three peace activists held for four months by Iraqi kidnappers are alive tonight after being rescued during a daring raid by U-S and British soldiers." (Bob Schieffer, *CBS Evening News*, March 23, 2006)

The key word in that script isn't *soldiers*. What is? *Rescued*. If you say the activists have been rescued, they're alive. If they were already dead when the soldiers arrived, they couldn't have been rescued. Better: "Three peace activists kidnapped in Iraq have been rescued."

One way to improve copy: Don't start a story with "There is" or "It is." They're both dead phrases. There are exceptions; example: "It's raining."

Here's how some network newscasters did use those dead phrases in broadcast scripts:

"There is another hurricane out there, the next storm of this season...." (Brian Williams, *Nightly News*, Sept. 13, 2005) The only verb in that sentence, *is*, expresses no action. Better: "The next hurricane is approaching North Carolina." In that revision, *is* has a different function: it serves as a helping verb. *Is approaching* expresses action. Avoid two *there's* so close to each other—unless you're trying to comfort someone, especially a child: "There, there."

"There's news today that one of the men convicted in the Oklahoma City bombing is about to be released from prison." (Bob Woodruff, *ABC World News*, Jan. 18, 2006) A newscast reports news, so taking the time to label a story as news is pointless. Better: "One of the men convicted in the Oklahoma City bombing is expected to be freed from prison in two days."

"There is a lot of news today from the Gulf Coast. We learned that it could be weeks...." (Brian Williams, *NBC Nightly News*, Oct. 3, 2005) If you have news, report it, not eat up time telling us you have news. I tuned in expecting news, not a williwaw of words. And what does the anchor mean by *we learned*? Everything carried on a newscast is something the staff has learned—either by covering a story or by reading the wires.

That anchor wound up his intro to a correspondent by saying, **"And there is this: many people...."** (Brian Williams, *NBC Nightly News*, Oct. 3, 2005) There's that empty *there*—again. The correspondent said, **"There are trailers available."** Better: "Trailers are available." Strunk and White's battle cry: "Omit needless words." And the minimalist architect Ludwig Mies van der Rohe said, "Less is more."

Another example that's far from exemplary:

"And as we mentioned, there is health news to report tonight." (Brian Williams, *NBC Nightly News*, Sept. 16, 2005) Skip the hollow *there is* and report the news. And why tell us that you already mentioned something?

Still another writing tip can be derived from this network lead-in: **"In Germantown, Maryland, there was a shooting today involving two children at a daycare center. A boy playing with a gun shot a younger child in the arm...."** (Elizabeth Vargas, *ABC World News*, Jan. 24, 2006) It's undesirable to start a script with *In* and the dateline (the place where the story occurred). What captures a listener's interest is *what* happened, not *where* it happened.

Besides using the past tense of *there is*, the writer of that lead buried a verb (*shot*) in a noun (*shooting*). The only verb in that sentence is *was*, a linking verb, not an action verb. Better: "An eight-year-old boy in Maryland has shot a seven-year-old girl. She was shot in the arm—accidentally—and is said to be in good condition. The shooting occurred at a daycare center in Germantown...."

What's wrong with this next script?

"Nicknamed the Cajun Riviera, we saw the first emergency teams arrive here today...." (Kerry Sanders, *NBC Nightly News*, Sept, 25, 2005) Problem: dangling modifier. *Nicknamed the Cajun Riviera* modifies the subject of the sentence, *we*. But Cajun Riviera is not the reporter's nickname. The reporter was referring to the Gulf Coast, not himself.

If you recognize what's wrong with the next—and last (whew!)—script, you're excused from the rest of this article:

"And it's a movement of historic proportions, say the experts." (Byron Pitts, *CBS Evening News*, June 16, 2006)

Say the experts at the end of the sentence is not conversational—and not broadcast style. We don't hang attribution on the end of a sentence. That's print style, and it violates a basic rule of broadcast newswriting: Attribution precedes assertion.

"Writing is easy," Mark Twain said. "All you have to do is cross out the wrong words."

Easy for him to say; he never wrote for radio. Or TV. Or me.

(Oct., 2006)

Are You Ready for the Big Time, Say, *60 Minutes*?

Want to try out for *60 Minutes*? CBS News may not be holding try-outs, but I am. Although CBS hasn't authorized my tryout, it has been authorized by me: I'm in charge of this keyboard. Instead of a writing test, though, this tryout tests your ability to spot mistakes in the spoken word.

Here's how you take my tryout: Note what's wrong with each of these 24 excerpts from *60 Minutes*. For your answers to count, please speak up before I do. Even if you're not in the mood for a tryout, you may still be able to pick up a few tips.

"And the enormity of Obama's grassroots field operation began to overwhelm the opposition." (Steve Kroft, Nov. 9, 2008) *Enormity* refers not to size but to great evil: "The enormity of the Darfur massacres is distressing." The *60* correspondent might have meant *immensity*.

"And soon, he'd convinced the police chief to formally request his help from the Department of Justice." (Katie Couric, Nov. 2, 2008) Instead of *convinced*, the script should have said *persuaded*. The rule: *convince* is followed by *that* or *of*; *persuade* is followed by *to*. I don't make the rules, but I do try to follow them.

"We were with a unit when shots suddenly rang out...." (Lara Logan, Oct. 19, 2008) *Shots rang out* is a cliché. *Suddenly*? How else? Certainly not *gradually*.

"The gunman was dead, his body slumped in the nook where he'd been laying in wait." (Lara Logan, Oct. 19, 2008) The gunman had been *lying* in wait. If a correspondent lies down on the job, the boss should lay down the law.

"And there was Sam Houston, who beat an opposing politician, literally throttled him with his cane." (Morley Safer, June 18, 2006) *Throttle* means *strangle*; you don't strangle someone by beating him.

196

Maybe the correspondent meant *thrash*. *Literally* adds nothing to the sentence except length. Using *literally* in that script—or in almost any script—is littering.

"With the military struggling to fight two wars, there are growing calls to repeal the policy and growing evidence that some commanders could care less about sexual orientation." (Lesley Stahl, Dec. 16, 2007) The expression is "couldn't care less." If the commanders could care less, that would mean they still care.

"But the policy says openly gay soldiers are to be discharged, which is why Darren's case and many more like it will surprise you." (Lesley Stahl, Dec. 16, 2007) Don't tell me what'll surprise me or disturb me or alarm me or shock me; just tell me the story—without a cliché, without delay.

"He barely eked by until those so-called drip paintings started to sell in the early 1950s." (Anderson Cooper, May 6, 2007) Eek! In old-time cartoon strips, when a woman spotted a mouse, the artist would have her shriek "eek." *Eke* means to supplement with great effort or to get with great effort. When *eke* is followed by a preposition, it's *out*. You can eke out a living, but you can't *eke by*. With luck, you can squeak by.

"After years in Jordan, we found Hayder preparing his paperwork for his ninth interview with the officials...." (Scott Pelley, May 18, 2008) The correspondent didn't spend years in Jordan; Hayder did. But the correspondent said *we* spent years there. That grammatical mistake is akin to a dangling participle. The stylebook editor of *The Wall Street Journal*, Paul R. Martin, calls that kind of mistake a disjointed appositive. As a bartender might tell a troublemaker, "Stay away from disjoint."

"He adopted rules for the safety of the fighters and got 21 states to sanction the fights." (Scott Pelley, Dec. 10, 2006) *Sanction* is a word that broadcasters should banish from their vocabulary. The problem is, the verb has contradictory meanings. *Sanction* means *permit* and also means *punish*.

"Sallie Mae disputes this, but studies by three different government agencies say it costs taxpayers about five times less per student loan." (Lesley Stahl, May 7, 2006) *Times* means *multiplied by*: two *times* three is six. So *five times less* doesn't make sense. It is correct to say "five times more." Also: no need for *different*; all agencies are different.

"The burdens of his command weigh heavy." (Lesley Stahl, Sept. 28, 2008) Should be *heavily*, not *heavy*.

"They live on the edge of Adamiya, a violent neighborhood overtaken by hard-core insurgents and under constant attack by Shiite militias." (Lara Logan, April 22, 2007) Should be *taken over*, not *overtaken*. A copy editor should have undertaken to fix it.

"So those bugs were susceptible to many antibiotics, but this petri dish contains M-R-S-A." (Lesley Stahl, Nov. 11, 2007) *Susceptible*? Should be *vulnerable*.

"If it's credible, you run afoul with the government...." (Scott Pelley, June 22, 2008) Should be *afoul of*.

"But we've learned that he remained on the government payroll for 18 months and was only fired after we inquired about him." (Scott Pelley, June 22, 2008) That says he was *only* fired; he wasn't hanged. So *only* in that sentence is a misplaced modifier. Script should say, "was fired only after we inquired."

"The exact whereabouts of that money and the whereabouts of Mister Jumaili are presently unknown." (Steve Kroft, Oct. 22, 2006) When the correspondent said *presently* he probably meant *currently*. *Presently* means soon. There's no need for *now* or *currently* as long as you say the suspect's whereabouts is unknown. Yes, *is* is the way to go. The stylebooks of the *AP, Los Angeles Times, New York Times, Wall Street Journal* and *Washington Post* all say *whereabouts* is used with a singular verb.

"For almost a century it was emblematic of American industrial dominance, with a car for every customer and a brand for every strata of society." (Steve Kroft, April 2, 2006) The word needed is the singular of *strata*: *stratum*. But why not use the simple English word *level*?

"It's the favorite subject at the Eagle Inn, just down the street from the union hall, where we shared a cup of coffee with retirees Steve Flood and Claude Eakins and current U-A-W workers Ron Splan and Matt Symons...." (Steve Kroft, April 2, 2006) *Shared*? Five men sharing one cup?

"It's become a huge subculture comprised mostly of young men that [make that *who*] spend more money on video games than they do on music or going to the movies." (Steve Kroft, Jan. 22, 2006) Careful writers say *comprised of* is unacceptable. The whole comprises the parts; the parts compose the whole. Bryan A. Garner says in his *Modern American Usage*, "The phrase *comprised of* is increasingly common but has always been considered poor usage."

"**Factories, distribution centers and office parks sprung up....**" (Steve Kroft, Nov. 19, 2006) The past tense of *spring* is *sprang*.

"**But mostly, as we reported last March, a self-confessed dog nut.**" (Morley Safer, July 15, 2007) Only a person making a confession can confess. No one can confess for someone else. So *self-confessed* is redundant.

"**Country music singer Kenny Chesney grew up in a Tennessee town of less than a thousand.**" (Anderson Cooper, Feb. 18, 2007) *Less* should be *fewer*. *Less* should be used with something that can't be counted; *fewer* should be used with anything that can be counted (except time and money). For example: Nowadays, you may use your car *fewer* days and buy less gas. (*Less* can also be used for speed and distance, says Prof. Michael Daniels of the Annenberg School of Journalism at the University of Southern California: "I got a speeding ticket even though I was going less than 60 miles an hour" and "It's less than 100 miles to Santa Barbara.")

"**Why is it so unique?**" (Lesley Stahl, April 6, 2008) *Unique* means one of a kind. Something is either unique or not unique. So nothing can be *so* unique, *more* unique, *almost* unique, *very* unique or *most* unique. The correspondent would have been safe in saying *so unusual*.

If you identified all the problems in those excerpts, you're more than ready for *60 Minutes*. Maybe not as a million-dollar correspondent, but at least as a copy editor.

If you didn't spot at least 15 problems, you fell short in the tryout. So you had better hit the books (particularly grammars)—and for more than 60 minutes. If at first you didn't succeed, try out, try out again.

(November 17, 2008)

60 *Minutes* Quiz

How do you stack up against the staff of *60 Minutes*"?

Your challenge: spot what's wrong or undesirable in these excerpts from the CBS newsmagazine. This is an open-book exam, so feel free to consult a grammar (or grampa), a stylebook, even the Internet. Take your time, but no more than 60 minutes.

"Ed Hayes says neither Casso nor Kaplan have any credibility." (Ed Bradley, Jan. 8, 2006)

Have should be *has;* two singular subjects joined by *nor* require a singular verb. Likewise for two singular subjects joined by *or*.

"The third man at the scene, whom prosecutors alleged held a rope around her neck, took the stand in his own defense, and was acquitted." (Dan Rather, Dec. 4, 2005) Treat *alleged* like *said*. So *whom* should be *who*. Prosecutors alleged he held a rope; you wouldn't say, "Prosecutors alleged him held a rope." Nope.

"She was big box-office, made a total of 50 movies." (Lesley Stahl, April 3, 2005) Delete *a total of*. Without it, the sentence means the same, except that now it's leaner. Strunk and White tell us in their *Elements of Style*: "Omit needless words. Vigorous writing is concise. A sentence should contain no unnecessary words ... for the same reason a drawing should have no unnecessary lines and a machine no unnecessary parts."

"He got a group of wealthy investors to cough up at least 5 million dollars each, and sunk the money, about 450 million, in the market." (Dan Rather, Nov. 13, 2005) *Sink* is an irregular verb. Its past tense is *sank*, not *sunk*.

"The Brooklyn Bridge was built in 1869. It's still one of the best-looking things on Earth." (Andy Rooney, Oct. 9, 2005) Work on the bridge began in 1869. It was completed in 1883. *Thing* is a word I was taught to avoid; my teacher had a thing about it.

"Now, with a pension of $124,000 a year, we're not going to hold a tag sale for Fritz Hollings." (Mike Wallace, Dec. 12, 2004) Whose pension is it, the correspondent's or Hollings'? But the correspondent made it his own. Also: *tag sale*, according to my dictionary, is a sale of "used household belongings, with prices typically marked on labels affixed to the items." *Tag day* is what the correspondent meant: "A day on which collectors for a charitable fund solicit contributions, giving each contributor a tag" to wear. Suggested revision of the script: "No one need hold a tag day for Fritz Hollings. He gets a yearly pension of 124-thousand dollars."

"One reason Bollywood films have such universal appeal is because they're squeaky clean, no sex scenes, not even kissing." (Bob Simon, Jan. 2, 2005)

Because means "for the reason that." So *reason is because* is redundant. And so is *reason why*. Better: "Bollywood films have wide appeal because they're squeaky-clean...."

"It was only in 2002, Golan says, that an eminent scholar happened to see the ossuary at his home and told him what the writing could mean. Golan sprung into action." (Bob Simon, Dec. 19, 2004) On reading that, a copy editor or a producer should have sprung into action. The reason: the preferred past tense of spring is *sprang*, not *sprung*.

"Chicago, sure Chicago, hog butcher to the world." (Andy Rooney, Jan. 2, 2005) Carl Sandburg is often misquoted, as he is there. In his poem "Chicago," Sandburg said, "Hog butcher for the world." *For.*

And he pointed out that in the week since he resigned his job, as the A-O-L Time Warner stock dove yet again, he lost another quarter-billion dollars." (Mike Wallace, Feb. 5, 2003) Lost money? Until a shareholder sells, he hasn't lost one cent. Delete *the* before AOL. No matter how many broadcasters say *dove*, the past tense of *dive* is *dived*. *The Associated Press Broadcast News Handbook* says no to *dove*, as do stylebooks of the *Los Angeles Times, New York Times, Wall Street Journal* and *Canada's Globe and Mail.* As Paul R. Martin of *The Wall Street Journal* told the staff (about a different misuse), "The anything-is-right-if-you-do-it-wrong-often-enough attitude is a disservice to everyone."

"He knew enough to design a weapon that today is used by the armed forces of 35 different countries." (Ed Bradley, Jan 9, 2005) Delete *different*. All countries are different. No two countries are the same country.

"There's one-point-five million gallons of water on that stage." (Lesley Stahl, Feb. 20, 2005) *Point* is not conversational. Basic rule for broadcast newswriting: write the way you talk. People talking about that water would most likely say, "There are a million and a half gallons...."

"And whether you call them echo boomers, generation Y or millennials, they already make up nearly a third of the U-S population and spend 170 billion dollars a year of theirs and their parents' money..." (Steve Kroft, Oct. 3, 2004) *Theirs* should be *their*. Or *their own*.

"It's the latest movie by professional provocateur Michael Moore, and it's a take-no-prisoners indictment of the Bush administration." (Bob Simon, June 27, 2004) *Take no prisoners*? That cliché should be imprisoned—for life.

"He's written five full-length symphonies and—listen to this—he's 12 years old." (Scott Pelley, Nov. 28, 2004) I *am* listening. And please don't speak to me in the imperative. I'm not a dog.

"At first, he [not that 12-year-old] was arrested for espionage, aiding the enemy, mutiny and sedition, but the charges were reduced to—get this—adultery and downloading pornography on a government computer." (Lesley Stahl, Nov. 28, 2004) Get this! Sounds like Tony Soprano as he thumps one of his thugs in the chest to stress a point. And Tony's one crude dude.

If you got 14 to 16 right, you're a champ; 11 to 13 right, you're a contender; 7 to 10, you're a comer. But if you got none right, you're not a goner; you matched the *60 Minutemen*.

(February 17, 2006)

For Want of a Nail—and an Editor

Many broadcast newsrooms have essential info taped to a pillar, pinned on a corkboard or scrawled on a wall: phone numbers of pizza joints, doughnut dens and Chinese takeouts. But too many newsrooms lack another essential, one needed to ensure a first-rate newscast: a sharp copy editor. A good one delivers—not like those eateries but by fixing faulty scripts. Every writer needs an editor, but in recent years editing in many newsrooms has been slipping. And in some places, sliding.

Now news directors have to contend with big budget blues. If a bare-bones budget won't allow the addition or retention of a copy editor, an ND can assign someone as the copy editor, someone who takes on the assignment as an additional duty. The ND should choose someone who's a strong writer, knows English well and is confident enough to edit even anchors.

The practice of having copy edited by any staff member who happens to be free may be tolerable *in extremis*. But there's no substitute for the real thing: a qualified copy editor who knows her (or his) business.

If only a pro had edited these scripts before they were broadcast:

"'I heard a loud boom.' Those are the words of the vice president describing the suicide attack...." (Brian Williams, *NBC Nightly News*, Feb. 27, 2007) That first sentence comes across as though Williams were the person who heard the boom. So Williams should have told us at the outset whom he was going to quote. Listeners can't see quotation marks. They need—and deserve—to know at the outset who said what. Remember, we write for the ear, not the eye. Also, writers need to keep in mind a basic rule in broadcast newswriting: attribution precedes assertion.

"And back in this country today, National Guard crews and ranchers stepped up the huge effort on the ground and in the air to save thousands of stranded, starving cattle snowbound by a pair of blizzards." (Charles Gibson, *ABC World News*, Jan. 3, 2007) Buzzards come in pairs but not blizzards. Better: *two* blizzards. Also: Delete *back* *in this country* and, whenever it pops up, *closer to home*. They're clichés and time-wasters. Better: "Colorado ranchers and National Guard crews have stepped up efforts to save thousands of cattle stranded by blizzards." Listeners don't need to be told that Colorado is in this country. Have you noticed that stories preceded by *closer to home* usually turn out to be far from your home?

"It then continued to the Northeast, where some places got 18 inches of the white stuff." (Chuck Gaidica, *NBC Nightly News*, Dec. 17, 2007) *White stuff?* Is that flour or dandruff? If you mean snow, say *snow*.

"Others trained in Pakistan are likely responsible for the attacks in London a year and a half ago, according to U-S and British intelligence." (Andrea Mitchell, *NBC Nightly News*, Feb. 20, 2007) Broadcast writers shouldn't hang attribution at the end of a sentence. That's not broadcast style.

"Tonight, once again, weather is making news." (Brian Williams, *NBC Nightly News*, Aug. 29, 2006) Every subject in a newscast is *making news*. So go ahead and report that news. Also, the anchor's use of *tonight* is unnecessary: viewers already know it's night.

"And another follow-up tonight to another story that's constantly in the news." (Brian Williams, *NBC Nightly News*, Feb. 24, 2005) Start with what's new. *Another* usually detracts from the newsiness of a story. Using *another* twice in that sentence is another problem.

"Now to our other news. Overseas tonight, a story a lot of Americans woke up to today, the rocket attack in Jordan where the hunt is on for the suspected terrorists who tried to hit two U-S Navy ships earlier today." (Brian Williams, *NBC Nightly News*, Aug. 19, 2005) Every story on a newscast is *other* news. Further, that wording—*woke up to*—makes the news seem old. And it's contradictory to talk about overseas *tonight* and then say people woke up to a story. And the unfriendlies who fired those rockets are not suspected terrorists; they *are* terrorists. Of course, the attempt to hit two U.S. warships took place *earlier today*. Everything reported on a newscast occurred *earlier*. It had to, or newscasters couldn't report it—unless they're seers.

"There is a response tonight officially from the Bush administration to Iran's proposal for ending the standoff over its nuclear program." (Brian Williams, *NBC Nightly News*, Aug. 23, 2006) *There is* is a dead phrase. Better: "The Bush administration has responded to Iran's proposal...." The response might have come eight hours earlier, but that *tonight* is almost mandatory in many newsrooms. Also, let's get rid of *officially*; could the administration respond unofficially?

"It first began in early summer." (John Larson, *NBC Nightly News*, July 26, 2006) *First began*? Redundant.

"He said America is at war, adding that the U-S government has an obligation to protect the American people." (Wolf Blitzer, CNN, Nov. 7, 2005) Then came video of President Bush echoing Blitzer: "Our country is at war. And our government has the obligation to protect the American people." The problem is called the echo-chamber effect. Not only did the anchor steal Mr. Bush's thunder, but he also used some of his language, such as *is at war* and *obligation to protect the American people*. Once is enough.

"At the L-A auto show today, Ford unveiled a glimpse of its future." (Barbara Pinto, *ABC World News*, Nov. 29, 2006) A glimpse is a brief look; Ford didn't unveil the car and then quickly re-veil it.

"The next item may spark some outrage, especially after all the news of late about identity theft." (Brian Williams, *Nightly News*, Feb. 25, 2005) That item probably wouldn't spark outrage by anyone. But it would disappoint anyone who knows better than to suggest what listeners' reaction might be. *News of late* sounds stilted. And wilted.

Yes, news executives have a lot to tend to. But their main job is to present a professional product. And to do that, they need copy editors worthy of being called professional.

(March 2, 2009)

The Unexamined Script
is Not Worth Using

Newsrooms should realize: Every writer needs an editor. And every writer needs to be his own editor.

Those adages may seem contradictory, but they're really supplementary. Every writer must examine his script rigorously before turning it in. Duh. And every writer also needs an editor so a second set of eyes can make sure that a script is grammatical and reads right. Also to make sure it's factual and written in broadcast style—for the ear, not the eye. Double duh.

Although those adages are commonsensical, many newsrooms sidestep them—and stumble:

"This is a story about how a bunch of gangsters went to one of the most maximum security prisons in the country and turned it into their criminal headquarters." (Lesley Stahl, *60 Minutes,* Sunday, May 15, 2005) *Most maximum? Maximum* means the greatest possible quantity or degree. So *most maximum* is a howler (to say the minimum). It was certainly not *60*'s finest minute. Also: *This is a story about* is a weak, clichéd, unimaginative way to start a story about anything. As for *bunch of gangsters*, I was taught that only bananas came in bunches. But maybe those inmates are members of the Bonnano gang. Joe was the top Bonanno.

"First up, an unannounced trip to Baghdad for the Secretary of State. C-N-N has learned Donald Rumsfeld arrived in Baghdad less than an hour ago." (Erica Hill, CNN, 10 p.m., April 11, 2005) Now that is a surprise; when did Rumsfeld become Secretary of State? *First up?* Give it up. The first thing someone says is obviously first and needn't be called *first.*

"Those elections produced an unexpected surprise..." (Dan Rather, *Evening News,* Feb. 22, 2005) *Unexpected surprise?* A surprise is something that *is* unexpected. So *unexpected surprise* is redundant. Scripts pass through several hands before they're broadcast, but where were the eyes? Where was an editor? And where was the person who administers the final exam—the anchor?

"End of story? Not hardly." (Edie Magnus, *NBC Dateline*, 7 p.m., Feb. 6, 2005) *Not hardly* is a double negative.

"President Bush has just arrived in Europe..." (Elizabeth Vargas, ABC's *World News Tonight*, 6:30 p.m. ET, May 6, 2005) Mr. Bush had already been in Europe for several hours. The next day's *New York Times* said he had landed in Riga, Latvia, "shortly after 10 p.m."—3 p.m. ET. That's three and a half hours before *World News Tonight* said he had just landed. *Just*, my foot.

"While [tropical storm] **Arlene may not come close to that fearsome foursome that battered Florida last year, the state's hard-hit west coast remains a target."** (Jim Acosta, *CBS Evening News,* June 9, 2005) A storm does not have a brain. It may be on a path toward a particular place, but no storm can target anything.

"Breaking news this morning. Someone sneaked photographs of Saddam Hussein inside his prison cell. How did that happen and what do they show?" (Diane Sawyer, *Good Morning America*, 7 a.m. ET, May 20, 2005) Britain's *Sun* broke the story (and the photos) when the paper rolled off the presses before midnight in London—about 7 p.m. ET, May 19. That means the story and the photos were made public about 12 hours before *GMA* ballyhooed *breaking news*.

"This flight, Flight 847, started shuttling back and forth between Beirut and Algiers." (NPR, 8 a.m. ET, Feb. 24, 2005) Delete *back and forth*. That's what shuttling means.

"So Graff manages her life from her car ... and says her hands-free headset ... is her saving grace." (Sharyn Alfonsi, *CBS Evening News,* 6 p.m. ET, Aug. 8, 2004) She misused *saving grace*. The *Random House Unabridged Dictionary* defines a saving grace as "a quality that makes up for other generally negative characteristics."

"There are predictions here tonight that the event unfolding behind us [in the Vatican] **could be one of the largest in human history before it is over. It is safe to say there is no way the city of Rome expected this, but they are keeping up and keeping it moving. The massive volume of mourners passing by the body of Pope John Paul the Second at the rate of 15-thousand to 18-thousand people every hour. There was simply no way to predict how many people would feel the need to say goodbye. While some are already looking to the**

future, and while news events keep on churning far from here, we begin tonight with what is the largest gathering of its kind on earth." (Brian Williams, *NBC Nightly News,* 6:30 p.m. ET, April 5, 2005) What's particularly worth noting in the script is the anchor's saying at the top that the event *could be* one of the largest in history before it is over, but 90 words later, he says the event is already the largest gathering in history. Mr. Last Sentence, meet Mr. First Sentence.

"As the Vatican prepares for the funeral, Cardinal Szoka showed us the Vatican City you don't often see, including a new innovation for the papal election." (Scott Pelley, *CBS 60 Minutes,* Sunday, April 3, 2005) An innovation—from the Latin *novum* (new)—is something newly introduced. So a *new new* is a no-no.

"Simon Property C-E-O David Simon is our guest, and his company owns, develops, manages regional malls in 40 different states." (CNBC, June 8, 2005) Delete *different*; all states differ from one another.

"For whether Catholic or not, Pope John Paul the Second impacted the lives of every one of us." (Fox News Channel, 10 p.m., April 2, 2005) Impact is a noun, not a verb. And no *whether or not*; the pope was definitely Catholic. The script probably meant those whose lives were affected by the pope were Catholics and non-Catholics.

Rx for all those scripts' stumbles and fumbles: copy editors who scrutinize scripts and anchors who make scripts shipshape.

(July 18, 2005)